The Invincible Family

The Invincible Family

WHY THE GLOBAL CAMPAIGN TO CRUSH MOTHERHOOD AND FATHERHOOD CAN'T WIN

Kimberly Ells

REGNERY GATEWAY
Washington, D.C.

Regnery Gateway™ is a trademark of Salem Communications Holding Corporation
Regnery® is a registered trademark and its colophon is a trademark of Salem Communications Holding Corporation

ISBN: 978-1-68451-426-7
First trade paperback edition published 2023

Published in the United States by
Regnery Gateway, an Imprint of
Regnery Publishing
A Division of Salem Media Group
Washington, D.C.
www.RegneryGateway.com

Manufactured in the United States of America

10 9 8 7 6 5 4 3 2 1

Books are available in quantity for promotional or premium use. For information on discounts and terms, please visit our website: www.Regnery.com.

For my parents

The Invincible Family

PART I
THE WOMAN AND THE MAN xiii

PART II
THE FAMILY 35

PART III
MOUNTING THREATS 85

PART IV
GLOBAL ONSLAUGHT 135

PART V
THE SOLUTION 225

Contents

INTRODUCTION   xi

Chapter One
BELONGING   1

Chapter Two
TRUE POWER   5

Chapter Three
FREEING WOMEN AND SOCIALISM   13

Chapter Four
FREEING WOMEN AND FEMINISM   23

Chapter Five
INSANITY   37

Chapter Six
THE SANITY OF ANATOMY   49

Chapter Seven
PERFECTION, FREEDOM, AND PARENTHOOD   57

Chapter Eight
LOVE OR MONEY   67

Chapter Nine
THE GOODNESS OF MEN   77

Chapter Ten
SEXUAL EQUALITY AND A NEW RIGHT   87

Chapter Eleven
COMMERCIALIZING PARENTHOOD   97

Chapter Twelve
TRANS-FORMING THE ARGUMENT   109

Chapter Thirteen
SOCIALIST FEMINISM AND SAME-SEX MARRIAGE   121

Chapter Fourteen
THE SANITY OF FAMILY 127

Chapter Fifteen
TAKING IT TO THE TOP 137

Chapter Sixteen
SEXUAL RIGHTS AND GENDER EQUALITY 143

Chapter Seventeen
CHILDREN'S SEXUAL RIGHTS 157

Chapter Eighteen
COMPREHENSIVE SEXUALITY EDUCATION 171

Chapter Nineteen
THE GLOBAL HIJACKING OF EDUCATION 187

Chapter Twenty
THE ARTIFICIAL MOTHER 209

Chapter Twenty-One
POTENT WEAPON 215

Chapter Twenty-Two
IN THE CELLAR 227

Chapter Twenty-Three
STAND 235

Epilogue
WHAT YOU CAN DO 239

ACKNOWLEDGMENTS 241
BIBLIOGRAPHY 243
NOTES 279
INDEX 317

INTRODUCTION

In 2013, I joined an international organization working to protect the interests of children and families at the United Nations. During my first exposure to UN proceedings in New York City, I didn't expect to see proposals for the construction of "national care systems" to house all the children of the world. But I did. I didn't expect to hear pregnancy called a "career interruption" or abortion called a "therapeutic interruption of pregnancy." But I did. I didn't expect to hear the director of UN Women rally the General Assembly to "dismantle patriarchy," or to hear educated professionals call prostitution an "informal economy," or to hear people passionately campaign for legalizing "sex work." But I did. Most of all, I didn't expect to sit nose-to-nose with people unabashedly promoting "sexual rights" for children.

But I did.

There is power churning at the United Nations and in legislatures, parliaments, courtrooms, boardrooms, and businesses across the world. But there is greater power elsewhere. This book is about the power that sways the world: where it comes from, who has it, who wants it, and the battle to command the globe.

It is a fact that babies belong to their mothers and fathers. At first blush, this fact may seem unrelated to the United Nations and the global fight to commandeer the world. But it is, in fact, the crux of the issue. The quest to unseat mothers and fathers—to disband the family—and place the reins of life in less noble hands is what the battle at the United Nations and beyond is all about. The armaments currently arrayed against the family are daunting, but not invincible. This book will show you why.

The Invincible Family is organized into five parts. **Part I** makes the case for the family and, in particular, the woman, by exposing rarely articulated facts about the genesis of power and belonging. It shows how modern socialism and feminism aim to oust the woman from her prime place in society and remove men from the circle of the family. **Part II** unearths connections between anatomy, freedom, power, sex, abortion, and civilization, and shows how the family unit bestows resounding sanity on the world. **Part III** is an in-depth exploration of sexual radicalism and how it cleverly unseats the woman, and with her the family, in the name of equality. **Part IV** is a crucial look at how the malignant movements of socialism, modern feminism, and sexual radicalism are exploding on the international stage at the peril of the world's children and families. The final offering in **Part V** is a tenacious shred of hope amid the perils that now surround the family and the civilization that rests upon its shoulders.

PART I
THE WOMAN AND THE MAN

CHAPTER ONE

BELONGING

When I bore my first child, I knew she was mine because she was connected to me by a cord. No one in the delivery room questioned that this baby belonged to me and I belonged to her. Our connection was physically obvious. When the umbilical cord was cut and I clutched this baby's head to my chest, we were no longer tethered to one another, but our connection was inseverable.

The story of every person's life begins at this same place: mother, baby, and a cord connecting the two. And somewhere—often right there looking on—is a father. The father is the second person to whom the baby belongs and on whom the child has an unquestionable claim. Unless the eggs of one woman have been transferred to the womb of another, the child who emerges from a woman's womb is her biological child, bearing her genetic material and formed from her own body. This tethering of child to mother and mother to child ensures that every baby ever born is known and, usually, claimed by at least one person: its mother. No one is born without being tethered to a specific person, and that person is always a woman.

The relationship of belonging between mothers and children has been recognized in virtually every culture in every age. Taking a mother's child from her is a crime. It is considered a crime because we honor the belonging of children to their mothers and fathers. This applies to adoptive mothers and fathers as well as biological parents. Laws that enable adoption are modeled after the inherent belonging of children to their physical parents.

A mother's claim on her child is singular in its origin and endless in its duration. The birth of a baby establishes an irrevocable relationship between parents and children. This biological belonging initiated by conception and birth is unique in the universe. It can be legally signed away, but it cannot be undone. Therefore, the act that leads to conception and birth—sex—has consistently been treated as a big deal.

Two Crucial Points

There are two points that must be made before going further. First, to say that a woman holds a preeminent claim on her children does not mean she cannot or should not hold a claim on other things. Women often excel at owning and managing land, homes, equipment, physical assets, and million-dollar businesses. But a woman's claim on her child by virtue of having borne it is achievable by no one else. Men contribute to the generation of life, but they cannot bring it forth. Only women do this.

Second, I am by no means suggesting that women "own" their babies. A child is not its mother's property, and yet it unequivocally *belongs* to her. We do not purchase or procure children; they are bestowed on us, usually as a consequence of our sexual choices. "Ownership" implies the right not only to possess but to sell, and there is no such right when it comes to people. No one, not even a parent, has the right to sell another human being.

A child—like every human person—has an inherent, independent, and incalculable value. The limitless, non-monetary value of any person is not calculable, purchasable, erasable, or disposable. People ultimately "belong" to themselves, of course, and each person is responsible for his or her own destiny. As the Universal Declaration of Human Rights puts it, every person is "born free" with "equal" value. But since all babies are born helpless, they must be helped by others. The two entities who generate the child—the child's parents—are biologically selected to assist the child until it can take up the job of managing itself independently.

How Children Belong to Their Fathers

Since men do not have umbilical cords physically connecting them to their children at birth, *marriage* has historically been the mechanism by which fathers claim their children. Through most of recorded history, marriage has entailed a commitment by the man and the woman to engage in baby-making behavior—sex—only with each other.

The commitment of sexual exclusivity in marriage makes visible the man's otherwise invisible parenthood. Today, if a vow of sexual exclusivity has not been made or kept, genetic testing can establish a man's biological connection to a child. But throughout history, a man's fatherhood of his children was made manifest through his marriage to his wife.

Two People

The umbilical tethering of babies to mothers is a reasonably reliable mechanism for ensuring that every child who appears on earth is claimed by at least one person: its mother. Marriage takes things a step further. Marriage seeks to ensure that a child is claimed by *two* people: its mother *and* father, the two people who gave it life. Marriage has historically entailed a lifelong commitment, because the parent-child relationship is lifelong.

Other familial relationships—such as aunt, uncle, cousin, grandfather, grandmother, niece, and nephew—also hinge on biological connections that cannot be dissolved. In cases of adoption, the biological mother and father of a child remain its biological parents, but responsibility for the child is legally assumed by adoptive parents. Since marriage is not a biological relationship, it is potentially the most brittle relationship in families. A marriage can be legally dissolved, but children do not become "ex-children" to their parents. A marriage may disintegrate, but biological relationships forged through sex, conception, and birth do not. Because they cannot.

The belonging of babies to their mothers has been and remains key to the ordered functioning of society. The preexisting and preeminent biological connection of mother and child undergirds the political, economic, and social structure of the world. If we alter or challenge the anatomical sovereignty of mothers and fathers, the consequences may prove politically, economically, and socially catastrophic.

CHAPTER TWO

TRUE POWER

Feminists and others have long been hacking away at the bonds between women and their children. Shulamith Firestone (1945–2012), a leader of the second-wave feminists of the 1970s, wrote, "The heart of a woman's oppression is her child-bearing and child-rearing role."[1] The conviction that a woman is inescapably shackled by her own body has become deeply engrained in the feminist mind.

According to feminist theory, since men are not physiologically bound to their children, they enjoy a position of greater freedom, eminence, and power, and women are doomed to eternal inequality with men. In this paradigm, a woman is a second-rate human being with reduced power by inescapable biological design.

Another strain of mid-twentieth-century feminism, articulated by Simone de Beauvoir (1908–1986), rejects the idea that the woman's body is responsible for her unfortunate situation in life. Women are impaired, in Beauvoir's view, not by their bodies but by the gendered culture in which they live. According to Beauvoir, a woman's body (or a man's, for that matter) dictates absolutely nothing. She argued that if we changed society's views on anatomy and gender, the woman would be freed from the dictates of culture and could imagine herself to be anything she wished. We will return to this idea later.

Anatomical Shackles

Feminist writings are peppered with statements bemoaning the disparities between male and female bodies and the resulting "disadvantages" to women:

- Shulamith Firestone wrote, "It was woman's reproductive biology that accounted for her original and continued oppression."[2]
- Kate Millett (1934–2017) wrote, "So long as every female, simply by virtue of her anatomy, is obliged, even forced, to be the sole or primary caretaker of childhood, she is prevented from being a free human being."[3]
- Linda Gordon has called a woman's ability to reproduce her "only significant biological disadvantage."[4]

Margaret McCarthy sums up this strain of feminism: "It is the woman's body that opposes her existence as a person. It is therefore ultimately her own body that the woman must resist."[5] This view could be called the "Tragedy of the Female Body."

To be sure, being pregnant and nursing a baby are physiological realities that tend to keep a woman near her children when they are young, in turn keeping her farther from the boardroom, the courtroom, the field, the operating room, the laboratory, the cubicle, the construction site, the factory, the assembly line, the driver's seat of a semi, or the checkout counter for a portion of her life.

Since by edict of biology men are not required to bear or nurse young children and can therefore more readily plow fields, attend meetings, argue cases, perform surgery, fit pipes, work on assembly lines, drive trucks, sit in offices, and stand behind checkout counters, the woman is said to be at a great disadvantage. "Freeing" the woman from this disadvantageous biological position has become the goal of feminists and social engineers the world over.

Advantageous or Disadvantageous?

But much hinges on what is considered *advantageous* and what is considered *disadvantageous*. Not everyone agrees that bearing and nurturing children puts women at a disadvantage. Many world leaders, ancient and modern, have held a different view of what position is most advantageous. Political leaders, philosophers, and other public figures—including some generally considered "good" and some generally considered "bad"—have maintained a surprisingly consistent perspective on where power lies and what drives the destiny of the world:

- Aristotle: "All who have meditated on the art of governing mankind are convinced that the fate of empires depends on the education of youth."[6]
- Mahatma Gandhi: "If we are to reach real peace in this world . . . we shall have to begin with children."[7]
- Mao Zedong: "The young people are the most . . . vital force in society."[8]
- Nelson Mandela: "Children are our greatest treasure. They are our future."[9]
- Confucius: "If your plan is for one year, plant rice; if your plan is for ten years, plant trees; if your plan is for one hundred years, educate children."[10]
- John F. Kennedy: "Children are the world's most valuable resource and its best hope for the future."[11]
- Sir Herbert Read: "Great changes in the destiny of mankind can be effected only in the minds of little children."[12]

- Vladimir Lenin: "Give me four years to teach the children and the seed I have sown will never be uprooted."[13]
- Adolf Hitler: "He alone, who owns the youth, gains the future."[14]

These statements expose the great "secret" shrewd leaders and philosophers have figured out: Gaining the allegiance of the young is the key to directing the destiny of the world. If a political or social philosophy is going to take hold and persist in a society, the children in that society must embrace it in their youth. And so the race to "own" the young, as Hitler put it, is always on. Nurturing the young in their very first life lessons is the goal of every savvy social reformer, politician, activist, and revolutionary.

She Alone

With this secret in mind, power-hungry leaders have battled to control the minds and hearts of the young and thus to control the future of the world. The Nazis' Hitler Youth program was intended to secure the minds of the youth, and similar efforts have been launched by other eager leaders hoping to educate the young in their respective philosophies. The great battle is to own the young, and he who wins this battle wins the world.

For all the clamoring of competitors through the centuries, women have in large part remained the first possessors of the young. For millennia, women—mothers—have gained and maintained the allegiance of the very young. Mothers have taught children their first life lessons and secured in their minds the philosophies they chose to put there. Thus, it could be argued that women have been and remain primary masters of the destiny of the world. Perhaps the saying should go, "*She* alone who owns the youth gains the future."

But what has put woman in this most sought-after seat and kept her there?

Her body.

The woman's body gives her the young. Her body delivers the young right to her. The young land in her lap, literally. The young begin as *part* of her lap. The woman does not have to conquer anyone, launch any initiatives, raise anyone's taxes, implement any programs, or start a revolution to commandeer the young. They already belong to her.

Profound Power

Shulamith Firestone called pregnancy "clumsy," "inefficient," and an ugly "deformation of the body."[15] But are a mother's physical connection to a new person and her claim on it at birth to be lamented or envied? Is being trusted by small, pliable people something to seek after? Is molding the foundational beliefs, ideals, and destinies of the persons who make up the world really a big deal? It is such a big deal that rulers and governments have been pursuing it for millennia. They're still doing so today, but with limited success. Why? Because mothers remain stubbornly in the way. Mothers keep thinking their babies belong to them and keep teaching them whatever they want.

Great men and women often come from great mothers. But some stray from the good teachings of their mothers and become crooks, while others, raised by horrible mothers, are good anyway. A mother does not necessarily make or break a person, but her influence is profound. No less a figure than George Washington credited his mother for his successes: "All I am I owe to my mother. I attribute my success in life to the moral, intellectual and physical education I received from her."[16] And Abraham Lincoln famously said, "All that I am, or hope to be, I owe to my angel mother."[17]

Research confirms what most people already know: Mothers have a powerful influence in the lives of their children. One long-term study found that the quality of a child's relationship with his or her mother is "the strongest, most consistent predictor" of "cognitive, social, and emotional development" later in life.[18] In other words, a mother's relationship with her child has a profound effect on that child in nearly every measurable way for the bulk of the child's life, surpassing the influence of virtually all other factors.

The Moral Atmosphere We Breathe

German novelist Jean Paul observed, "The conscience of children is formed by the influences that surround them; their notions of good and evil are the result of the moral atmosphere they breathe."[19] For new human beings, the moral atmosphere they breathe has historically been supplied by their families—and principally by their mothers. A mother powerfully impresses on her child what is right and wrong, what is true and untrue, what is noble and detestable, and thus establishes the foundational beliefs of societies, nations, and the world one child at a time.

Whether or not a woman's life-giving capacity is ever activated, women inherently possess unique capabilities that—when recognized and esteemed—deepen, enrich, balance, animate and energize the whole of human experience. A woman's value and usefulness are by no means limited to motherhood. That is simply where her unique proficiencies often find their most dynamic and enduring application.

Mothers are entrusted with virtually unlimited power over their helpless children. Remarkably, they almost always wield this power nobly, frequently at great sacrifice to themselves. There are horrible mothers in the world, of course, but they are the exception, not the rule. The vast majority of mothers, imperfect as they are, love their children, do their best to raise them, and would give up anything for them. There's a reason that "a mother's love" is universally recognized as the gold standard of devotion.

By virtue of their anatomy, women have been put in a position of momentous influence. All men are carried inside of women, born of women, nursed by women, taught first by women, and it is to a woman that a man must return to exercise the power of procreation. The natural sovereignty of women is significant.

Undoing the Mother

Like Confucius, Hitler, Mao, and Gandhi, social reformers of today know that to have the greatest influence over the young—in other words, to sit in the inherently assigned position of the woman—is to sit in the most influential seat in the world. These reformers eagerly seek her seat, but either the evolutionary guts of the universe or God himself made motherhood exceedingly hard to sidestep and almost impossible to break.

So, if the motherhood of women over the population of the world is both supremely influential and virtually indestructible, how do you usurp it or destroy it? If you want to seize the position of key influence in the world but a woman is in your way, what do you do? You must unseat the woman. You must either throw her out of her seat or get her to step down voluntarily.

There are four major tactics afoot for unseating the woman. Variations on these tactics have gone by different names at different times, and all of them are alive and thriving today. They are: 1) "freeing" the woman from family-based living, 2) enforcing state management of childbearing and rearing, 3) commercializing parenthood and making children purchasable commodities, and 4) convincing women to give up their children voluntarily.

Using these tactics, three interlocking movements are currently working to unseat the woman and crush the family: socialism, feminism, and sexual radicalism. This dangerous alliance has converged at the United Nations and elsewhere and is pushing forward ferociously.

The next two chapters offer a crash course in the origins and tenets of socialism and radical feminism, movements that are dead set on freeing women and men from family-based living. This background is critical today as socialism surges in popularity and the doctrines of radical feminism take root in the minds of the rising generation. With this foundation under our feet, we will forge ahead to examine the ingenious design of the family (Part II) and then (in Part III) unmask the mechanisms of sexual radicalism which seek to destroy it.

CHAPTER THREE

FREEING WOMEN AND SOCIALISM

"**U**nseating the woman" is not a phrase that has caught on in popular culture. Instead, the terms "freeing" or "empowering" the woman are more in vogue. But what these words are often describing is the distancing of a woman from her biological position as first possessor and mentor of new human beings. The cause of unseating or freeing the woman has been taken up by governments, utopians, feminists, communist planners, Hollywood, activists, and far-reaching entities at the United Nations.

Inspiration for the modern cause of freeing the woman comes from the well-known German philosopher, Friedrich Engels. Engels was the right-hand man of Karl Marx, father of modern socialism. Marx and Engels proposed a system in which private property is abolished in the name of "equality." They theorized that non-ownership—or rather, ownership by a few select stewards who distribute resources equitably to non-owners—would facilitate widespread equality and resounding peace. The socialist theory goes that once everyone is given equal portions of everything, envy, strife, struggle, competition, and conflict will disappear from the world, and a state of equality-induced utopia will settle upon mankind.

These are noble goals. Unfortunately, this nice-sounding philosophy ignores human nature, undercuts man's motivation to produce, suffocates personal freedom, and has caused the deaths of millions of people.[1]

In 1848, Marx and Engels wrote *The Communist Manifesto*, which called for the "abolition of the family."[2] In 1884, Engels wrote another book called *The Origin of the Family, Private Property and the State*, which built upon the family abolition theme and framed the family as an unnatural entity responsible for crushing women and crippling civilization through inequality. Engels's book has since been largely dismissed by scholars "on account of its flawed anthropological foundations,"[3] but its tenets are still used widely by policymakers, activists, and influencers today. Engels's false but popular arguments are crucial to understanding the battle to unseat the woman, the rise of socialism, and the launch of the radical feminist movement.[4] Engels's three main points are:

1. Unconstrained sexual intercourse has been the norm in previous eras and must be restored today.[5]
2. All people must be freed from the care of their own children so they can fill "socially productive" roles.[6]
3. Marriage is a recent invention, based on men's lust for private wealth,[7] which accomplished the "defeat" of the entire female sex.[8]

All of these points have been challenged, if not thoroughly debunked, and yet tremors of these ideas still reverberate through society today. That being the case, each of these points deserves a closer look.

Unconstrained Intercourse Is the Desired Norm

First, Engels claims unconstrained intercourse has been the norm since the dawn of time and true love can only be found through uncommitted, passionate sex with whomever one loves at the moment.[9] For

Engels, love means sexual passion with no pretense of commitment or lifelong duration. He says that if "the consequences" of having sex (taking care of children) were taken out of the picture, women would be put at ease and there would be a wonderful rise in "unconstrained sexual intercourse."[10] The production of random children wouldn't matter, says Engels, because in socialist society "the care and education of the children becomes a public affair" and "society looks after all children alike."[11]

While Engels couched his proposals for redistributing children and decimating the family in terms of "freeing the woman," it is likely that his deeper goal was to free men. Socialist theory, if lived out to its truest form, enables men to engage in any sexual behavior they wish without incurring family responsibilities. Widespread non-monogamy would cut a man off from responsibilities to his specific children or to any woman he might impregnate, because a man would never know for certain which children were his. Engels thinks this would be fantastic.

The problem Engels does not seem to grasp or is trying to evade is that women would still be the ones to become pregnant, would still possess the children who are connected to them at birth, and that women might care about this. Socialist society could remove a woman's children from her care, but she would still know them—and most likely love them, at least to some degree—from the beginning. Men, however, would not know their posterity and would bear no responsibility—and perhaps no love—for them. Love of sex would reign supreme, while love of children would be deemphasized.

In a truly socialist climate such as Engels suggests, the mother is not expected—and perhaps eventually not allowed—to care for her own children, because her physical link to them is not considered valid, important, preexisting, or preeminent. Engels does not seem to consider that treating parenthood like a revolving door might affect the stability and development of children and, therefore, the stability and development of nations.[12]

Freeing Women to Do "Socially Productive" Work

Engels's second point is that all people should abandon parental work and instead fill "socially productive" public roles. Engels claims that children in previous ages were fathered by unspecified men and thrown into mass child-rearing groups shepherded by random women. The work these random women did was a public service, not a private service done for the love of one's own children. Engels says this is the ideal to which we must return. He declares, "The first condition for the liberation of the wife is to bring the whole female sex back into public industry, and that this in turn demands that the characteristic of the monogamous family as the economic unit of society be abolished."[13]

Communist dictator Mao Zedong[14] of China, who wholeheartedly adopted Engels's and Marx's ideals, said: "In order to build a great socialist society it is of the utmost importance to arouse the broad masses of women to join in productive activity . . . Genuine equality between the sexes can only be realized in the process of the socialist transformation of society as a whole."[15] Here, in just a few words, the work of bearing and raising human beings, which women are uniquely positioned to do, is labeled unproductive activity which women must be emancipated from in the name of equality.

Thus, the modern feminist script was in place: Socially productive work is work done in the public sphere, most often for money. Since caring for and teaching one's own children is not paid work done in the public sphere, it is not a socially productive activity and is akin to "slavery."[16] To be freed from this slavery women must abandon monogamous marriage, join the "productive" work force, and leave the raising of the next generation of humanity to someone else.

And this is exactly what ambitious socialists set off to do. Russia, under the force of Vladimir Lenin and then Joseph Stalin, embraced socialist doctrine with zeal, eventually dubbing itself the Union of Soviet Socialist Republics (USSR). One Russian socialist wrote, "Our problem now is to do away with the household and to free women from the care of children." He said this was to be accomplished by providing care centers where children would be "supervised by trained pedagogical and medical personnel."[17] He further said the socialist goal is that public acknowledgment of biological motherhood and fatherhood would wither away in favor of a system in which nobody knows who belongs to whom, and you "can't tell who is related to whom and how closely."[18] Engels says, "We are now approaching a social revolution in which the hitherto existing economic foundation of monogamy will disappear."[19] If Engels is right, if people fail to claim each other either by way of umbilical tethering or tethering through marriage, the state will be in a prime position to replace and supersede the family as the possessor and steward of all people.

The usurpation of people into state custody was the intention of Russian socialists acting on Engels's ideals when, in 1919, the Soviet of Saralof issued a decree that in order to "liberate" women and make them "equal" to men, marriage would be essentially abolished for all women ages seventeen to thirty-two. Thus women would not *belong* to anyone. Instead, all women would become "the property of the nation."[20] The "distribution and maintenance of nationalized women" then became the "prerogative" of the state. The plan was to require workers to contribute to a national fund for the support of "nationalized women" who would be given equal sums of money each month while they engaged in socially productive work. The decree further said,

> Any pregnant woman will be dispensed of her duties for four months before and three months after the birth of the child . . . One month after birth, children will be placed in an institution entrusted with their care and education. They will remain there to complete their instruction and education at the expense of the national fund until they reach the age of seventeen.[21]

Repercussions were threatened if anyone declined to comply with this socialist scheme: "All those who refuse to recognize the present decree and to cooperate with the authorities shall be declared enemies of the people, anti-anarchists, and shall suffer the consequences."[22] So, the "liberation of women" evolved into state ownership of women, and women's babies were to be forcibly placed in the iron fists of the state. This scheme ultimately crumbled, of course, but the fact that it was ever even attempted should be enough to make one nauseous at the mere mention of socialism.

While most schemes to dismantle the family and usher the possession of people into the hands of the state in the name of equality are less explicit than this, the underlying objective is the same. As Engels and Marx stated, the goal is the "abolition" of private possession[23] in all its forms, including the form of familial belonging.

"Mother Right" and the "Defeat of the Female Sex"

Engels's third point is that rich men invented monogamous marriage for their own selfish purposes which brought devastation upon womankind. He explains: "Monogamy arose from the concentration of considerable wealth in the hands of a single individual—a man—and from the need to bequeath this wealth to the children of that man and of no other."[24] Engels thinks that man became so anxious to bestow his burgeoning riches on his children that he came up with the insidious idea of monogamous marriage, so he could discern which children were his, stroke his ego by heaping riches upon those particular children, and enslave a wife in the process. Thus, the monogamous family was born based on the wretched wealth and greed of men, and capitalism took its first baby steps forward.

However, Engels hits upon a problematic point by using a term he lifted from the writings of Swiss anthropologist Johann Bachofen. Bachofen claimed that in idyllic times gone by, free-ranging sexual chaos without marriage was the common way of things.[25] Therefore, genetic inheritance was traceable only through mothers, since men never fettered themselves to the women they had sex with and fathers and children were supposedly never known to each other.[26] Bachofen calls the woman's exclusive claim over children's identity "mother right" and says mothers were held in highest esteem for their position as the only knowable parents of the children of the world.

Engels adopted the phrase "mother right" but complained that it was "ill-chosen," since the idea of basic rights had not dawned on humanity yet.[27] But the phrase is not ill-chosen. The phrase "mother right" acknowledges that the right to claim one's own children existed before greedy men invented the concept and dreamed up monogamous marriage in order to stake their claim on it. In other words, Engels doesn't like the phrase "mother right" because it validates the intrinsic, binding claim of mothers on their children and thus imperils his argument for the origins of private property–based society, which he says sprang from men. But he uses the term "mother right" anyway for two reasons: First, there is very little else to call it; mother right exists due to umbilical tethering at birth. And second, Engels needed mother right to exist so that men could overthrow it with "father right." Engels explains the catastrophic "overthrow of mother right" this way:

> [A]s wealth increased it made the man's position in the family more important than the woman's and . . . created an impulse to exploit this strengthened position to overthrow, in favor of his children, the traditional order of inheritance. This, however, was impossible so long as descent was reckoned according to mother right. Mother right, therefore, had to be overthrown, and overthrown it was.[28]

According to Engels, man found a way to wrench from woman her exclusive, private claim on her children. The instrument man chose to accomplish this theft of women's prime holdings was marriage. Engels dramatically concludes, "The overthrow of mother right was the world historical defeat of the female sex."[29] This declaration threw the females of his day into outrage about their own "defeat" and fueled a feminist fire that would burn through the decades and is still burning today.

Engels claims that if a man knows which children are his, this "over-throws mother right." Engels fails to see that *recognizing the existence of fathers does not and cannot eliminate mother right.* A woman will always have mother right because she will always know which child is hers at birth. Mother right persists because of umbilical tethering. What sexually exclusive marriage does is bring *father right* into discernible existence alongside mother right. One does not demolish the other; mother right and father right can and do exist in tandem. Marriage makes these two rights visible and legally binding.

More poignantly, the establishment of mother right and father right through sexually exclusive marriage solidifies *child right.* A child is the equitable physical synthesis of both his or her parents and inherently possesses and belongs to both of them. This is, in fact, a major purpose of marriage: Sexually exclusive marriage exposes, establishes, and equal-izes both creators in the life of the child they create. To say that including fathers in the lives of their offspring abolishes mother right is an absurd declaration that, if believed, can carry with it extreme consequences for families and societies.

Engels's position requires a belief that throughout much of human-ity's history, fathers were not the least bit interested in their own children and were not held responsible for supporting their children either by mothers, society, or their own consciences.[30] This is a significant slap in the face to the humanity of men. Engels's dream was that marriage would disappear, uncommitted "sex love" would flourish, somebody else would take care of the kids, and life would be a great big, happy utopia full of sex and plenty of shared money without any family responsibilities to worry about. This is precisely the type of society that socialists are still zealously working for today.

What Is the Origin of Private Property?

Engels purported to show how man's greed for private wealth precipitated the invention of marriage, which in turn fostered the development of systems based on private ownership rather than on communal equality. But there are chinks in Engels's theory. Men did not invent the diverse biology of man and woman; did not invent umbilical tethering; did not invent sex, chromosomes, genetic inheritance, pregnancy, birth, or a host of other physical realities. All of these spring from the anatomy of people and were in place before any man claims to have propelled private enterprise forward by inventing marriage. Anatomy is preexisting and preeminent. Mother right—based on the inherent private, anatomical possessorship of the child by its mother—existed before virtually all other rights or systems existed. Therefore, it becomes obvious that the origin of private enterprise is not the man or his money. *The origin of private enterprise is the woman.*

The family is a private entity founded on the inherently private possessorship of the woman and her anatomical claim on her own children. Every time a child is born to a mother, private possessorship is reborn with it. Either by evolutionary selection, by design, or by accident, private enterprise is built into the very sinews of the world through the anatomy of women. Individual, private possessorship is so vital that the whole system of life is based upon it. If you eliminate the biological possessorship of mothers, you eliminate private possession at its very root. And since private possession is the building block of a free society, it follows that any movement to dissolve, dilute, discount, or usurp the possessorship of mothers is also a movement to undermine free society.

Children are the ultimate possession. And women inherently possess them all. To wrench them from her grasp in the name of equality is a core objective of socialism and—as we will see—a core objective of modern feminism and sexual radicalism.

CHAPTER FOUR

FREEING WOMEN AND FEMINISM

The overarching aims of socialism as outlined by Engels and Marx included: the abolition of private property, the overthrow of governments as we know them, overthrow of belief in God, and the elimination of the family as the prime social unit.[1] They insisted all these things must be accomplished on a global level[2] in order to bring about world peace and prosperity.[3] Although the proposed goal was world peace, Marx and Engels acknowledged that the path to socialist triumph would require bloody revolution, "militant atheism," and the "overthrow" of virtually all existing social conditions including family-based living.

Seen through the lens of socialism, the belonging of things to specific people is an evil thing which leads to possessiveness and inequality. Since family bonds are bonds of belonging, the family is profoundly problematic in a socialist or communist society. Therefore, socialists seek to undo familial belonging in the name of saving the world. But if family bonds of belonging are to be fully undone, you must undo motherhood.

Ironically, the task of undoing motherhood has been undertaken by women themselves. Not all women, of course. But there is a subset of women who are vocal enough to be a major force in unseating the woman as the first and most fundamental power in the world. Feminist Linda Gordon writes, "The nuclear family must be destroyed and people must find a better way to live together."[4] Feminist Kate Millet concurs, saying, "The complete destruction of traditional marriage and the nuclear family is the revolutionary or utopian goal of feminism."[5] With such statements in circulation, it becomes clear that socialism and radical feminism are Siamese twins of a sort, united in their zeal to "free the woman" and invoke "equality" for humanity by eliminating biological belonging and disbanding the biological family.

On Feminism

Feminist history spans millennia and includes a long legacy of brilliant, determined, strong, savvy, far-sighted women who fought battles that absolutely had to be fought. And in large part, they won. Feminists of the past came in many different stripes and were not united on every point of feminist theory. However, their collective work for the good of women has corrected grotesque malformations of society that entrenched man-centric notions, insulted the capabilities and contributions of women, and limited the basic rights of many women. Women of today stand on the sturdy shoulders of feminists such as Christine de Pizan, Sojourner Truth, and Elizabeth Cady Stanton, who worked for a world in which women own property, vote, hold political office, work for pay, pursue education, act as sexual decision makers, mingle freely in society, and wear pants.

One modern feminist defines feminism as the rejection of "the notion that the masculine is superior to the feminine."[6] In that sense, the book in your hands is a profoundly feminist text. However, the radical feminist movement launched from the 1950s has a significantly different flavor and focus than most feminism of the earlier past. This latest version seeks not only to liberate women from degrading laws and practices that undercut their legal and social functioning and status, but to liberate women from their own children and from the men who are the fathers of those children. This decidedly anti-mother, anti-man, anti-child, anti-gender, anti-family form of feminism that seeks to "eroticize" human culture in a quest for equality is the type of feminism with which I do battle.

The Source of Private Property, the Family, and Free Society

I take up the sword specifically against two representative radical feminists: Shulamith Firestone and her modern disciple, Sophie Lewis.[7] In 1970, Firestone published *The Dialectic of Sex*. She commenced her text with a quotation from Engels, revealing that these two utopists are cut from the same philosophical cloth. In her book, she calls for freeing women from family-based living by eliminating the family, starting with eliminating the function of mothers.

She acknowledges failures of past socialist societies and shrewdly isolates the reason for their demise. She says previous socialist experiments have collapsed because of their "failure to sever the umbilical-cord-tying special connection between women and children."[8] This is a stunning claim. According to Firestone, the very root of the problem, the very reason that socialism has failed in virtually every instance thus far,[9] is because humanity has not been able to eliminate the bearing of specific children to specific mothers. She is right. This is the great obstacle. The woman's anatomy is the reason society remains privately oriented rather than publicly regulated. The woman's body is the thing that keeps outside powers in check and ensures that private possessorship, individual stewardship— and the systems that support such ways of living—can exert preeminence. But in Firestone's view, this is a bad thing. The connection between women and their children initiates and perpetuates the inequitable structure of family life and capitalistic society and, therefore, it must be discarded.[10]

Firestone's Four Demands

Firestone outlines four demands that must be met in order to establish the new social system made up of family-less, motherless, autonomous beings she imagines:

1. "The freeing of women from the tyranny of reproduction by
   every means possible, and the diffusion of the child-rearing
   role to the society as a whole, men as well as women."[11]

Severing blood ties established through pregnancy is Firestone's
number one priority. She explains:

> We must be aware that as long as we use natural childbirth
> methods, the [socialist] "household" could never be a totally
> liberating social form. A mother who undergoes a nine-month
> pregnancy is likely to feel that the product of all that pain and
> discomfort 'belongs' to her . . . But we want to destroy this
> possessiveness.[12]

Firestone understands that if you do not eliminate the physical and
psychological possession of children by their mothers, you will never fully
succeed in destroying private property-based society and instituting full
socialism. It is the mother who is the linchpin of the privatized system.

In the perfect, motherless world Firestone proposes, parenting—or
rather, childcare—would be diffused to society so that no one person
feels responsible for any particular child and no one gets stuck with all
the "drudgery" of caring for it. She says,

> The reproduction of the species by one sex for the benefit of
> both would be replaced by (at least the option of) artificial
> reproduction: children would be born to both sexes equally,
> or independently of either, however one chooses to look at it:
> the dependence of the child on the mother (and vice versa)
> would give way.[13]

She declares that "women have no special reproductive obligation
to the species"[14] and that children "are no more [women's] charge and

responsibility than anyone else's."[15] With these statements, Firestone is voluntarily forfeiting mother right for all women.

Firestone insists that "it has become necessary to free humanity from the tyranny of its biology"[16] and revels in the prospect that "the blood tie of the mother to the child would eventually be severed" and the triumphal "disappearance of motherhood" would follow. She says "pregnancy is barbaric"[17] and suggests that if women are no longer willing to bear children, "then artificial methods will have to be developed hurriedly, or, at the very least, satisfactory compensations . . . would have to be supplied to make it worth their while."[18] Not only does she suggest making the production of human beings a monetary transaction rather than a labor of love, she fails to realize that the child itself *is* the compensation for pregnancy, and that this compensation is incomparable, unrivaled, irreplaceable, and the envy of the entire world.

Firestone's second and third demands are closely related:

2. The political autonomy, based on economic independence, of both women and children.[19]
3. The complete integration of women and children into society.[20]

Firestone calls for a society where every person is identical under the law and has equal political clout and identical rights. She says: "With the weakening and severance of the blood ties, the power hierarchy of the family would break down . . . Children would no longer be 'minors,' under patronage of 'parents'—they would have full rights" as granted by the state.[21] Thus, in the name of total equality, the practice of parents overseeing specific children would no longer be employed or allowed. To guarantee economic independence and so-called equality for every person, Firestone offers this solution:

> People might receive a guaranteed annual income from the
> state to take care of basic physical needs. These incomes, if
> distributed equitably to men, women, and children, regardless
> of age or work status, could . . . equalize in one blow the
> economic class system.[22]

It sounds blissful, miraculous really, to eliminate inequality in one
fell swoop by handing out equal portions of money to everyone so that
everyone would be happy. But Firestone and her fellow socialist feminists
make no allowances for human nature, which would still allow for greed,
dishonesty, swindling children out of their money, misuse of funds by
some and wise use of it by others—all of which would produce differences and dreaded "inequalities." Further, Firestone makes no allowance
for the fact that if no one is taught honesty, frugality, respect for other
people's property, kindness, tolerance, delayed gratification, sharing, and
a score of other virtues by their mothers and fathers while they're young,
then few people would understand, value, or consistently live these principles.[23] It is likely that the basic principles of civilized society would be
violated with regularity, which would lead to strife, inequalities, power
struggles, and civil collapse, all of which were supposed to magically
disappear under the equalizing scepter of socialism.[24]

In order for Firestone's proposed socialist system to work, children
would need to be born autonomous. Otherwise someone would need to
occupy a position of unequal power over them, which is intolerable to
her. Since children are *not* born autonomous but are in fact born helpless,
this throws a big wrench in Firestone's plans. So, she does the only thing
that could be done: She simply declares children to be autonomous. She
says childhood is a social construct invented to validate the existence of
mothers, that history has proven that "raising" a child is tantamount to
retarding his development,[25] and that children liberated from the suf-
focating presence of their mothers are likely to become "geniuses."[26]

Firestone's final and perhaps most troubling demand for the establishment of an equality-based, socialist society is:

4. The sexual freedom of all women and children.[27]

Firestone wants a completely free sexual culture wherein adults and children engage in whatever sexual activities they wish with whomever they wish. She explains, "The incest taboo is now necessary only in order to preserve the family; then if we did away with the family . . . sexuality would be released from its straightjacket to eroticize our whole culture."[28] She says forced sexual repression of young people results in "the insecure . . . often obnoxious little person we call a child."[29] Firestone continues:

> Relations with children would include as much genital sex as the child was capable of—probably considerably more than we now believe . . . Age-ist and homosexual sex taboos would disappear, as well as non-sexual friendship . . . our concept of exclusive physical partnerships (monogamy) disappearing from our psychic structure.[30]

Engels's mantra rings loud and clear through Firestone: eliminate monogamy, invoke free sex for all, and save the world. Firestone says, "In our new society . . . all forms of sexuality would be allowed and indulged."[31] She makes no exceptions. And since children would be "equal" under the law, the law would hold no special protections or provisions for children, sexually or otherwise. Children would be at the mercy of anyone who claimed to be helping them exercise their "sexual freedom" or "sexual rights."

Firestone makes no attempt to explain how massive outbreaks of sexually transmitted diseases would be kept at bay in such a sexual climate, and one wonders how a toddler or infant would use her sexual freedom wisely and avoid becoming infected with a sexually transmitted disease from someone older and stronger than she is. It seems that disease would become commonplace in such a society, and the state would need to intervene with widespread sexual education programs starting at the earliest ages to help stem the tide of disease initiated through the toppling of monogamy.[32] It would become the task of a behemoth state to educate children and everyone else on the pleasures of free sex and how to avoid the risks inherent to indulging in those pleasures outside the naturally occurring protections of monogamous marriage.[33]

To sum up, this is Firestone's four-pronged proposal: Remove children from the tyranny of parents, give them equal sums of money to buy whatever they want, give them political power, and let them have lots of sex. Then they will become well-behaved, peaceful, secure, loving, cooperative beings who grow up to be well-adjusted, selfless adults who carry on the feminist, socialist dream of utopian equality.

It is obvious Firestone never had a child.

Firestone on Steroids

Most people might suppose Firestone's outlandish dreams were simply vapor rising off the steamy sixties and her ideas had largely dissipated into the cosmos along with so much other feminist noise. Yet nothing could be further from the truth. While most folks who read Firestone's book would dismiss it as laughable (though disturbing) nonsense, a teeming knot of feminists have ingested its philosophies over the past forty years and taken it as gospel truth. These feminists are not laughing. They have taken the founding feminists at their word and have long been at work slaughtering the family, focusing their most vehement wrath on the bond between mother and child.

One such activist is Sophie Lewis, who published her first book in May 2019. Lewis says her book, *Full Surrogacy Now: Feminism against Family*, would not have existed without Firestone's influence.[34] Lewis's disdain for the family is undiluted and her calls for its destruction are bold. Lewis casts pregnancy as a "perverse" condition[35] and declares that we must "explode notions of hereditary parentage."[36] She calls human female anatomy in all its life-giving complexity a "ghastly fluke"[37] and explains that the reason people sometimes speak of feeling joy in pregnancy and childbirth is because gestating can incite a "masochistic rush."[38]

Lewis's stance is clear evidence that the socialist-feminist agenda of family destruction is alive and well. It has been budding happily under the bower of other social movements, its roots spreading, its vines curling through society, slowly squeezing and poised to strangle the family. This lethal garden is tended by angry gardeners who resent their own anatomy and seek to literally remake the world. The world they seek has no mothers in it—only "gestators" of many genders cohabiting in arrangements of all sorts who tend the children of the world collectively.

Lewis says "polymaternalism" and "polypaternal abundance" are to replace motherhood.[39] "Redistributing the burden" of children in this way, she says, "dissolves the distinction between reproducers and nonproducers, mothers and nonmothers altogether."[40] This is unabashed feminist socialism in action, depriving people of the work of their own hands (in this case, their own children) and distributing it to others. Lewis's stated aim is that society at large will embrace "gestational communism."[41]

Lewis, like Firestone and others, pegs the family as the cornerstone of capitalism. She uses the terms nuclear family and capitalist family interchangeably.[42] She quotes the feminist adage "Our uterus is the wheel that keeps capitalism moving"[43] and admits with agitation that despite much social and political progress in demolishing the family, "the key governmental unit of capitalism really does remain the family."[44] Lewis questions "whether motherhood and pregnancy are viable cornerstones of a liveable world."[45] In her view, motherhood is decidedly not a suitable cornerstone for society; motherhood must be displaced from its cornerstone position in order to make the world infinitely more tolerable, loving, equitable, and grand.

What Lewis's Surrogacy Looks Like

Though the title of her book is *Full Surrogacy Now*, Lewis condemns modern surrogacy and its many failures and abuses. But surrogacy is a problem, she says, not because of the blurring of ties between parent and child, but because the system is cradled in capitalism. If babies were not privately claimed but rather freely offered to the world and socially gestated by its cooperating members, then *that* sort of surrogacy would be ideal. Everyone would be a surrogate, and all babies would be freely offered to humanity. She declares, "Infants don't belong to anyone, ever"[46] and that children should be "for everyone" (not for their mothers or fathers).[47]

Lewis says she is "unabashedly interested in family abolition."[48] Her definition of family abolition is fascinating. She explains, "Family abolition refers to the . . . end of the double-edged coercion whereby the babies we gestate are ours and ours alone, to guard, invest in, and prioritize."[49] In other words, family abolition is the breaking of the parent-child bond and the intense devotion that comes with it. She says the current expanding political and legal climate "in which mother-child bonds can more easily be discontinued, handed over, and multiplied" is "exciting."[50] Lewis quotes feminist philosopher Jeffner Allen, who says, "In breaking free from motherhood . . . I no longer give primacy to that which I have produced."[51] For Lewis and her comrades, the way to break capitalism, free enterprise, and free society is for parents to deprioritize their own children. And she is right.

Abolishing Parental Rights

Lewis says the concept of parental rights, which assumes children belong to their parents, is abhorrent. She says, "We need ways of counteracting the exclusivity and supremacy of 'biological' parents in children's lives."[52] Quoting an article on evolving surrogacy laws in the United Kingdom, Lewis says, "laws could be reformed to remove automatic rights from the person who gestates or genetically donates toward a baby."[53] This erosion of parental rights, of course, is poised to expand and could come to affect all parents and children, not just those involved in surrogacy.

One critic of commercial surrogacy and its inherent fracturing of the family said, "If *all* biological claims were rejected, it would be incredibly difficult to decide whose the child is." Lewis answers this with enthusiasm: "Yes, exactly, yes!"[54] This is precisely what she wants: the rejection of *all* biological claims of belonging. She says that as current social and political movements expand, they "will not so much 'smash' the nuclear family as make it unthinkable. And that's what needs to happen if we are serious about reproductive justice, which is to say, serious about [socialist] revolution."[55] (What social and political movements is Lewis referring to that are eroding biological claims and redefining parenthood to pave the way of socialist revolution? We will address this question head-on in Part III.)

Lewis admits she has little idea how to bring about or sustain the desired widespread "defeat of kinship" and the relinquishment of all children by their parents.[56] She says, "The revolutionary strategy . . . remains almost entirely unwritten."[57] Can it be done? She muses, "We must assume the answer is yes in order to find out."[58] Therefore, she is insisting we destroy the biological family and then watch in hopes that something better rises from the mayhem left behind.

The modern feminist rhetoric of reproductive rights and reproductive justice—which calls for the relinquishment of born and unborn children by their parents in the name of saving the world—is not just an isolated cause championed by a few angry females. It is spilling generously over into mainstream political, social, and educational movements. In fact, as we will see, it is poised to flood the world.

PART II

THE FAMILY

CHAPTER FIVE

INSANITY

We have briefly explored the first tactic for unseating the woman: free-ing her from family-based living as prescribed by socialist and femi-nist ideologies. This tactic will resurface in the coming pages. The second tactic for unseating the woman is state management of childbearing and rearing. We begin this leg of our journey in socialist China.

In a village in China in 1976, a woman named Chi An was pregnant with her second child.[1] She had given birth to her first child after she and her husband, Wei Xin, were granted a birth permit from the state to conceive. Their first baby was a boy. When Chi An and Wei Xin were married, the state had required them to sign a two-child agreement. Chairman Mao Zedong had instituted restrictions on childbearing, and his successor, Deng Xiaoping, continued to manage child distribution in China through increasingly strict mandates. The guidelines in Chi An and Wei Xin's area required that there be at least four years between their first and second child. This was a problem because Chi An was already pregnant, and this second baby would be born too soon. She very much wanted to have a daughter.

After the birth of her first child, a government official had come to their home and pressured Chi An to sign a one-child agreement, telling her that she would receive a cash bonus and a wash basin as a reward for signing. She would most likely need to be sterilized to ensure that the agreement would be kept. She refused to sign the one-child policy and was instructed to either begin taking birth control pills or have an IUD inserted immediately. When the population control worker in her unit discovered that Chi An was pregnant a second time, the worker confronted her and told her to "take care of her problem" and that "remedial measures" would have to be undertaken immediately.

Chi An was now involved in what was considered an illegal pregnancy. She did not have a birth permit and was carrying an illegal child. Chi An endured daily visits and increasing threats from the population control regime, inwardly resisting the mounting pressure she was under to abort her child. She and Wei Xin made plans to evade the population control personnel and give birth to their baby secretly—a baby Chi An felt sure was a girl. But their plans were foiled, and Chi An was personally escorted to the hospital to undergo an abortion against her will.

After examining Chi An, the attending physician refused to perform the abortion, because Chi An had an infection of the cervix and the harrowing caesarean section she had had the year before had not healed properly. Because of this, she was at risk of further infection and of her uterus rupturing during the abortion procedure, which could be life-threatening. The population control worker demanded the abortion be done anyway. And it was. Tears streamed down Chi An's face as the daughter she wanted was extracted from her body and discarded.

As the population control program in China became more stringent, stories such as Chi An's became commonplace, and stories even more horrific came to light. In some cases, families were able to hide their pregnancies from authorities long enough to save their babies. Chi An's sister-in-law, Aiming, had two daughters before the population regulations tightened in her area. She and her husband wanted a son, but third children had recently been outlawed. Aiming became illegally pregnant, a fact she hid until she was seven months along. When a local population control worker discovered Aiming was pregnant, the worker immediately began applying unrelenting pressure for her to undergo "remedial measures" (abortion.) However, Aiming and her husband had prepared a remote hideaway for Aiming to flee to and stay in until their baby was born.

The night before Aiming was to flee, a population control worker, flanked by five armed militiamen, pounded at their door. Aiming bolted out the back door and hid herself in a nearby pigpen. She then crept to a rice paddy where she hid for two days, being ravaged by mosquitoes, before the militiamen became weary of the hunt and disbanded. Aiming told Chi An that had she been discovered, "I was ready to fight them to the death for the life of my son."[2]

Aiming escaped to her hideout and triumphantly bore her son. A week after she returned home bearing her son in her arms, the population control brigade returned, thrust Aiming onto a cart, and hauled her to a clinic where she was forcibly sterilized. She was not alone in this fate. During Aiming's initial disappearance, the population control regime loosed their fury on nine pregnant women in the village—all more than five months along—and arrested them during midnight raids. All of them forcibly underwent abortions and were sterilized.

Birth quotas in China dipped to lower than 0.5 percent (or five births per thousand women per year) in some places, and the official family planning directive forbidding the use of force was in some cases flatly ignored. Force was invoked as "a necessary administrative measure."[3] In efforts to enforce impossibly low birth quotas "for the good of the motherland," extreme coercion was employed. Population control workers were incentivized with prizes and promotions to get pregnant women to "voluntarily" abort their babies. Workers were threatened with demotion and public humiliation if they did not enforce the assigned birth quotas.

Pregnant women were also extensively coerced. They were first invited to end their pregnancies or be sterilized voluntarily and were offered cash and items such as transistor radios and bedsheets for volunteering to terminate their pregnancies.[4] If the women resisted abortion, they were threatened with hefty fines, demotion, destruction of their homes, and denial of benefits for their illegal children once they were born. If these measures did not convince them to abort their babies, the women could be forcibly detained in storerooms or other facilities where they were physically deprived and emotionally intimidated until their resolve to keep their babies was finally broken. And at last, if women still refused to abort their unborn children, they could be taken fighting in protest or carried limp as rags to the abortionist's table, where their babies—some just weeks from being born—were forcibly taken from their wombs.

Imagine Chi An's experience multiplied millions of times. Millions of babies were crushed and extracted from the wombs of protesting mothers throughout China. Babies were born alive and suffocated, injected with formaldehyde, or left to perish in waste bins while their mothers were denied their right to claim or even console their own children as they died. Countless fathers were left to mourn their babies that would never be. Billions of single children have been raised without a single sibling, cousin, niece, nephew, aunt, or uncle. Such is the legacy of the socialist "one-child policy" in China. (The 2019 film, *One Child Nation*, documents the severe consequences of forced population suppression in China and amplifies the voices of parents like Chi An and Wei Xin.)

Heinous Crime

Forced abortion—a gruesome mix of murder, child abuse, robbery, assault, dismemberment, usurpation of free will, and disregard for life itself—is at the core of the state-ownership philosophy. Forced abortion, committed while mothers look on as their own blood and the blood of their children is spilled against their will, is the inevitable consequence of a regime comprised of socialist enforcers who see human beings as disposable liabilities rather than irreplaceable possibilities. Forced abortion is the inevitable consequence of philosophies that see private possession as an evil rather than a good. The socialist state sees itself as the rightful owner and steward of all property, including human property, which debuts in the form of babies. State ownership cannot acknowledge or allow the inherent possessorship of mothers, because that possessorship is in direct conflict with the state's power.

In a society where owning private property is not recognized as a human right, the contents of the womb can be no exception. If a government seeks to own and control all capital, it must seize control over human capital, too. Indeed, this is the most important capital it must seize.

"I Have Happiness"

In China, the phrase for saying "I'm pregnant" was once expressed as, "I have happiness,"[5] but under Communist rule the prevailing sentiment when a woman fell pregnant might more aptly have been expressed as, "I have terror." As Chi An's story illustrates, a pregnant woman without permission from the state to bear her own child could be coerced, penalized, tracked down, and finally forced onto the abortionist's table, and her baby could be violently removed. This is so because the state did not see it as her baby. The resident of her womb belonged to the agents of the state, and its fate was in their hands, not hers.

Forced limitation of childbearing, forced abortion, and forced sterility are the end result of a society that does not recognize, respect, and revere private property rights, which are rooted in the possessorship of women over their babies. Because of the supremacy of the umbilical connection between mother and child, forced abortion is one of the most heinous crimes that has ever been committed. To seize possession of a child while its mother is still physically attached to it, to extinguish a child's life while the mother's defiant body is still attempting to give it life, is perhaps the most egregious violation of the bounds of private possessorship and the worst abuse of human rights ever conceived of or carried out.

Forced abortion tramples, extinguishes, and rescinds a woman's supreme right to her own child. Because the mother–child relationship is the very heart of private possession, governments bent on totalitarian control must not only allow abortion, they must encourage, promote, normalize, and foist it upon their populaces, as China has done for decades. China's one-child policy has been adjusted to a two-child policy, which has been touted by some as a lenient and magnanimous gesture on the part of the ruling regime. But one must ask, as Chi An did, "On whose authority does the state deny couples the right to conceive and bear children in accordance with their own notion of happiness?"[6]

Planned

When Chi An and Wei Xin went to a government official to obtain a marriage application before their wedding, the official read them a document outlining the official policy on birth planning. It said,

> Our great leader Chairman Mao has said that "population must be controlled." Everyone must understand that the struggle for family planning is part of the class struggle. Planned parenthood is essential for socialist revolution and socialist construction. It is in accord with the fundamental interests of the masses. Those who oppose the policy will be criticized and punished.[7]

It is striking that the words "planned parenthood" which euphemistically encapsulate China's forced one-child policy are the very words that have been claimed as the name of a worldwide abortion organization that markets itself as a women's rights entity: International Planned Parenthood Federation. This is significant. With the historical backdrop for this parallel naming in mind, the phrase from the Chinese marriage agreement, *"Planned parenthood is essential for socialist revolution and socialist construction,"* takes on chilling meaning. Bluntly encapsulated in that sentence is the reality that *abortion is essential* for the full implementation of socialist society. Therefore, abortion facilities, a widespread abortion mentality, and permissive abortion laws are also essential. "Planned parenthood" must persist if socialist aims are to be achieved.[8] Is it any wonder that even in the face of blatant scandals, Planned Parenthood Federation of America—bearing the very name of Mao's population control program—is persistently defended and funded by socialist-leaning people in power?[9]

A population control official told Chi An and a group of assembled women:

> China is a socialist country. This means that the interests of the individual must be subordinated to the interests of the state. Where there is a conflict between the interests of the state in reducing population and the interests of the individual in having children, it must be resolved in favor of the state. *Socialism should make it possible to regulate the reproduction of human beings.*[10]

By its own admission, a key goal of the socialist state is to "regulate the reproduction of human beings." This necessitates that women be stripped of their position as the gatekeepers of life. This also means that abortion must be legal and the means to administer abortion must be widely available in order for the state to "voluntarily" impose it upon women. An all-powerful state could choose to encourage or require "voluntary" abortion in order to achieve population control goals or other objectives. Abortion is a key part of Shulamith Firestone's socialist design to "free the woman from the tyranny of reproduction by every means possible" or, in other words, to facilitate the state seizure of the woman's position and give the state command of the reins of life.

The Reins of Life

Once the reins of life are passed from the woman to anyone else (usually under the guise of giving the woman more important, liberating things to do), the entities to whom the reins are passed are in a position to turn on the woman and not only *allow* her to snuff out the lives of her own children, but also pressure, coerce, and force her to do so on their terms. As socialist philosophies expand, the situation of women in China will multiply hideously in countries across the globe. This will increasingly bring about the strangling of the family and the captivity of the woman, as the reins of life she once held in her command become the chains by which she is bound.[11]

Chi An chafed at being forced to sign a two-child agreement at the time of her marriage. "What business was it of the state how many children Wei Xin and I had?" she thought angrily as she hesitated with the pen in her hand. Of the moment when Chi An signed her name to the two-child agreement she said, "I felt a strong sense of foreboding . . . I felt as if I were signing the rights to my children away."[12] She was right. Having women sign such a document at the time of marriage implied concession on the part of the Chinese government that *the right to bear and claim children inherently belonged to women and their husbands in the first place.* The state had to take that right from them, cloaked in the guise of choice and voluntary concession. Gaining the woman's signature in writing bolstered the false authority of the state to usurp her inherent right to possess the fruit of her womb.

Young Chinese women of today know no reality in which the state did not insist on their surrendering their children. Tiny families, state regulation of children, forced contraception, and abortion are the norm. But Chi An and her contemporaries remember the time before Mao's planned parenthood initiatives, when women were free to bear children without interference from the state and they looked forward with joy to having children. These women baulked, chafed, and recoiled when intrusions into their private childbearing lives were foisted upon them. But there was little they could do to resist. The state claimed ownership of everything it wanted, leaving a bloody trail of women and children in its wake.

"Good for Women"

When planned parenthood in the form of the one-child policy was introduced in Chi An's village, the population enforcers used this line: "The new policy is not just good for China, it is good for women."[13] This strategy is key. It is the very same line used by other planned parenthood advocates today: Abortion is "good for women." If socialist coercion and control is to be most effective, the oppressed must believe their oppression is for their own good. You must convert the woman to the idea of giving up possessorship of her child voluntarily. You must get the woman to believe that the one who wishes to eliminate her child is her friend, who is defending her rights with her very best interests at heart.

The success of the women's rights movement in claiming abortion as one of its prime tenets is remarkable. While women in China have been literally running from the abortionist's tools, Western women have been flocking to them. This has been accomplished largely by means of cloaking abortion in language that appears to empower and revere women. When you hoist a banner bearing the words "Women's Rights" and roll along chanting, "We trust women," it is difficult for women not to feel compelled to jump on the bandwagon, no matter what the bandwagon is carrying. And so, on rolls this lethal bandwagon bedecked with banners and laden with menacing tools, medications, and rhetoric that assist women in eliminating their own children in the name of their own rights. And plucky women climb aboard, not realizing that they are now keeping company with the very entities who wish to unseat them—and turn a weighty profit in the process.[14]

Life and Death

It could be argued that since a mother inherently has mother right, she could presumably reject, sell, or extinguish her right to her child in whatever way she wants. But is the right to claim your own child the same as the right to extinguish your own child? Hardly. Those are two radically different things. The right to one of them does not bestow a right to the other. Women wield the power of life itself; this is grave and weighty power indeed. This power was anatomically granted to her either by the evolutionary guts of the universe or by God himself, the self-reported author of anatomy. It can be assumed that woman was granted this power because she wields it best. Those who urge a woman to take the death of her child into her own hands would make her a taker of life rather than a maker of life. They would transform the reins of life into the chains of death. To do so would breach the bounds of the woman's stewardship and would negate, trivialize, and betray the momentousness of her power.

Abortion not only unseats the woman, it unseats the child. It "severs the connection" between mother and child in a direct and gruesome fashion. Severing a mother from her child is the ultimate act of undermining private possessorship. The separation of a child and its mother should happen only under severe circumstances. Any arrangement, law, practice, or procedure that allows, encourages, or mandates the separation of the mother from her biological child, either before or after birth, carries weighty potential to affect not only the life of the child and the mother at hand, but to affect the way society perceives the contributions of mothers, the value of new people (babies), and the legitimacy of private possessorship. If a mother's claim on her own child is not legitimate, what is?

Invasion

The family has been invaded by the state in China. In China and elsewhere, when the state invades the family, women's menstrual cycles are tracked and posted on public walls, birth permits are doled out by nonfamilial entities, babies are extracted from mothers' wombs, marriages are granted on grounds of swearing to abide by state population regulations, and people's homes are ripped down as punishment for bearing illegal children. What begins as an effort said to be good for women becomes a nightmare in which women forcibly undergo abortions and sterilization "with no regard for their rights or feelings"[15] and in which women's health and comfort is called "a secondary consideration."[16]

And yet, even in China, where the state decides the fate of its citizens both born and unborn, the family has persisted. The Chinese family is smaller, more fearful, and more fragile than it used to be, but people still call the person who birthed them "mother," because she is. And that cannot be expunged. Even if the words mother and father were outlawed, mothers and fathers would still exist. They remain indestructible and invincible no matter what you call or do not call them.

As we push forward to explore the interplay of anatomy, freedom, love, government, selflessness, and parenthood, keep the story of Chi An and Wei Xin tucked in the back of your mind. Their story exposes the tragic destiny of every nation that overthrows the private possessorship of mothers in favor of government domination in the name of equality. Chi An's fate is *our* fate as we veer further into the crushing grip of socialism and stray from the safety, sanity, and supremacy of the family.

The remaining chapters here in Part II (Chapters Six through Nine) will explore why the inherent, regenerative family occupies a place of supremacy in the world, why this should remain so, and why foes of the family are doomed to failure in the face of the invincible sovereignty of anatomy.

CHAPTER SIX

THE SANITY OF ANATOMY

Either babies belong to their mothers and fathers, and mothers and fathers belong to their babies, or they do not. If they do not, then people are literally up for grabs, families can be demolished without consequence, marriage is irrelevant, mothers can be replaced by electric wombs, fathers can have as much recreational sex as they want, and the state can manage the distribution—and the very creation—of people.[1]

However, some things are more easily understood if one assumes that human anatomy was enacted on purpose rather than careening into place by accident. Anatomy and its apparent inequalities begin to make some sense if there is calculated purpose behind them. If there is purpose, this purpose could have been enacted by the wisdom of the pulsing universe itself or the wisdom of a God—whichever paradigm you prefer.

The Clumsy, Inefficient Way

If a God exists, then it seems that even in all his celestial brawn he cannot *force* people to love each other. He can only command and encourage them to love each other. It is the widely circulated claim that his two most emphatic commands are to love him and to love other people. If that is the case, it is likely he has deliberately designed virtually every aspect of life and creation with the intent of encouraging adherence to his foremost command: to love. If this is true, then human bodies are likely designed to lead each person to experience, express, understand, and become *love*.

If there is a God and he designed human bodies complete with cooperative conception, pregnancy, birth, umbilical cords, the possessorship of mothers, and the necessity of doing this whole thing over again in sexually diverse pairs every time a new person is produced, then we might deduce that he wishes to accomplish something specific. But what is accomplished through the process of conception and birth? Belonging. If a higher power exists, it seems that this power has gone to great lengths to arrange the anatomy of people in such a way that they *will* belong to each other. If the evolutionary universe, rather than the wisdom of a God, enacted the specifics of women's and men's cooperative, life-giving anatomy, then we can surmise that the wisdom of the universe wanted to accomplish the same thing: the innate belonging of people to each other.

It would have been much simpler for people to multiply asexually, like bacteria, or en masse, like fish. A female fish dumps her eggs, a male fish swims over and fertilizes them in one detached swoop, and the baby fishes swim off in bug-eyed self-sufficiency, never knowing and never needing their mothers or their fathers. Fish do not usually live in families; they travel in schools, never knowing who belongs to whom. Firestone and her fellow feminists lament the fact that human gestation is not so bereft of power dynamics and trouble for the human female as it is for the female fish. Engels and his socialist disciples detest the fact that producing children must involve men at all. What radical feminists and socialists do not realize, or perhaps do not care about, is that the reproduction of fish is also bereft of *love*. It is precisely the *belonging* accomplished through "clumsy, inefficient" human gestation and the caretaking that goes with it that makes it a superior, desirable design. Efficiency is not the goal. Love is. And love consistently begins with *belonging*.

Persuading People to Love

It is generally agreed that it is good for people to be responsible, hardworking, generous, selfless, and loving. These are, in fact, the major traits socialism hopes to arouse in people. But people are free to act otherwise; people can be irresponsible, slothful, greedy, selfish, and spiteful. So, how do you get people to be as responsible, hardworking, generous, selfless, and loving as possible? There are many answers to this question, but underpinning them all are two opposing ideas: *force people to be good*, or teach people to be good and *let them choose goodness if they will*. But how can you force someone to be good? Or if you decide to let people make choices for themselves, how can you best encourage someone to choose goodness? To be responsible? To be motivated to action? To be selfless? To love?

The anatomy of human bodies functioning in diverse, reproductive pairs is the ultimate demonstration of how to most consistently get people to choose noble, loving behavior: Let them create things and grant them private stewardship over the things they create. More specifically, grant them stewardship over things they create *that were once a part of them*. By letting people create beings that were once literally a part of them, you leverage the self-interest that is evident in almost all people by virtue of existing as a self. You help people transfer their inherent love of self to the love of something else by having that "something else" arise from their very bodies.

This works well because if something is forged *from you* and *in you*, it is, at least in part, *you*. And since people tend to love themselves at least at the level of self-preservation, you are more likely to love and preserve a thing that is or was a part of you. This is what occurs in the formation of families as we know them. This is precisely why children emerge from the bodies of their mothers and fathers: because it secures for them the greatest likelihood of being preserved and eventually loved. This reproductive design uses the potent seed of self-love to engender love of someone else; it helps humanity move from love of self to love of others. Anatomically rooted, generational life-giving is the most reliable way to initiate the engaged, responsible, responsive, attentive condition we call *love*.

Whoever or whatever enacted the anatomical system of life as we experience it seems confident that love and responsibility are most reliably born of belonging. This eternally recurring principle is evident everywhere: The owner of a house is more likely to take care of it than a renter; a person who invests in a project is more likely to work for its success; people are more careful with their own money than other people's money. Likewise, a baby who belongs to its mother is more likely to be taken care of, loved, and simply to survive than a baby who pops up spontaneously in a cabbage patch. Possessorship fosters responsible action by establishing a relationship of stewardship.

Belonging and love can occur in many circumstances, but belonging by way of anatomical designation—by giving life to someone else or receiving life from someone else—tends to be the most compelling form of belonging. Feelings of stewardship are often stronger in families than in any other dynamic because lives are at stake, and those lives spring from the lives of specific, discernable others: one's family.

Loving Everyone

But why should it matter? Should it matter who belongs to whom? You could say that it shouldn't matter if a child is yours or if a parent is yours. But it does. Belonging matters to people. But aren't we supposed to love *everyone*? Aren't we supposed to love everyone as ourselves? Isn't that the grand goal? Yes. But that's a tall order, and it takes a very long time to learn.

Learning to love works better in small, cohesive sets of people who belong to each other. The small sets of people we get to practice loving are our families. In time, when we come to realize that everyone in the world is literally part of our vast, interconnected, all-inclusive family, we love everyone better because we learned to love some people in our micro-families first. If you don't think this is so, try teaching a new person to love everybody without loving somebody first. This is a difficult task. In fact, I submit it's impossible. You cannot teach a new person to love humanity first and then move on to teaching them to love the person who is holding them. Babies love their mothers first. And mothers consistently love their babies best. This is not wrong. This is where love begins for virtually all people. Therefore, this is where love begins for the world.

Joined Existence

A child represents the equal fusing of two particular people. The child stands as a physical manifestation of those two people's joined existence, and the child possesses in its body the potential for its parents' cooperative genetic influence to persist through generations. Not only does a child stand as a manifestation of two particular people's joined existence, every child stands as a living manifestation of *all* the life-giving pairs of people who have existed before her in her ancestral line. A portion of all of them lives on in her.[2]

We are born *from* each other and *to* each other through the interplay of our bodies, which grow slowly and require years of care. It is in consistently and often inconveniently caring *for* each other that our ability to care *about* each other can deepen, expand, and make us more selfless and more capable of love.

Those who wish to abolish or denounce the possessiveness of mothers and fathers in the name of freeing children or equality for children are grossly misguided. They misunderstand the power of belonging, the supremacy of sacrificial serving, and the anatomical design of humans which fosters and demands them both. The prolonged, arduous dedication required in helping a small, incapable person become a big, capable person is a key component for growing love. Perhaps that is why fish do not love each other; they do not recognize familial belonging from the outset, nor do they serve each other. I once heard it said that being grown-up consists of being able to take care of someone else. If this is true, it seems that God or the evolutionary guts of the universe wants us all to grow up.

A Place of Connection, Not Competition

Sex is key to the whole project of life and love. But if you focus on sex exclusively or excessively, you get a lot of things wrong. Sex is primarily a means to an end. That end is producing people, establishing secure relationships between them, and keeping those people together. Cooperative male/female sex, because it is the thing that creates people in the first place, is what enables us to choose between loving and hating each other.

Sex connects us to each other inescapably and logically by forging what we have come to call family relationships. If this were not the case, and life were set up more like the classic novel *Lord of the Flies* where people are essentially airdropped into a community instead of being birthed into specific families in a community, there would be no discernible connections between people. Everyone would be starting at ground zero. Socialist utopists call this equality. What it brings is cutthroat chaos. It brings rivalries or alliances. Power will be asserted wherever multiple people exist. Family relationships launch people from a place of connection rather than competition. Starting from a place of neutrality or opposition rather than connection is more likely to result in enmity, animosity, hatred, and death. The umbilical cord ensures that everyone starts from a place of connected belonging and specific placement, which secures for them the best possible potential for surviving and experiencing love. Hatred is still possible, but inherent belonging accomplished by anatomy tips the scales in favor of love.

If human anatomy is not intentional on anyone's part, then either it is a fortunate stroke of evolutionary luck or a terrible mistake. Either we are lucky that our anatomy automatically tucks us into cozy pockets we call families, or we are horribly unlucky that we are forced to be claimed by specific people we are involuntarily connected to by our bodies at birth. Elements of radical feminism, socialist statism, and sexual radicalism insist—as Shulamith Firestone and Sophie Lewis do—that the woman's anatomy is a great and terrible mistake that must be fixed, circumvented, and reinvented because it proliferates inequality, inhibits women, impairs children, and imperils society. I vehemently disagree. A worldview in which human anatomy is seen as the handiwork of celestial sanity establishes families (and the bodies that make them) not as our enemies, but as purposeful endowments.

Perhaps the enactor of anatomy (be it God or the wisdom of the universe) believed the challenging elements of the woman's anatomical position were sufficient trade to claim and command the most coveted, dynamic, unparalleled, incomparable, magnificent possession in the universe: living souls. I'd wager that if the woman's anatomy is in fact unfair, in the long run the disparity will be in her favor.

CHAPTER SEVEN

PERFECTION, FREEDOM, AND PARENTHOOD

Wouldn't it be nice if all people used their free will wisely and loved everyone equally right from the get-go? That is, in fact, what socialist and feminist utopists claim they can accomplish. Their philosophy is that if everyone had equal portions of everything, no one would ever misbehave because they would have no reason to do so. People would not be jealous of other people's nifty stuff because everyone would have nifty stuff. Therefore, people would not act out of jealousy because they would never feel jealous. They would never act out of greed because they would never feel greedy. People would never fight because there would be nothing to fight about. And thus, we would have equality, perfection, and world peace.

In this equality-induced utopia, people would not need to strive toward becoming selfless, peaceful, thankful, or magnanimous; the system would automatically produce these qualities in people through regulated equality. People would glide through life without family obligations or financial worries; they would just be equal and content. Or so goes the theory. But utopian socialists seek the impossible. They seek to establish a society of sameness where all people are other-centered enough to share all things without envy or selfish strife, and they seek to establish it without first positioning people in small, cohesive, familial groups where they can learn and practice unselfishness in the context of love. They want a society filled with solitary, nonattached people, and yet they want to construct a system that survives on the principle of otherness, selflessness, and equality for all.

Engels and Marx imagined that only a skeleton crew of stewards would be needed to gently steer the benevolent, equal people in a socialistic society. Citizens would work to provide for random children without either familial motivation or private monetary compensation because equality would make them happy and productive. But the opposite has consistently proven to be true. Man's most immediate motivations are sex and his own hungry children. When sex is not tied to marriage and a man is not responsible for his own children, the greatest incentives for work diminish. Under such conditions production goes down, interference by the state goes up, and socialists are left wondering why their great plan isn't working. It isn't working because a man isn't working for his own children. He isn't working for his own family or even for his own flourishing. He is working for the nebulous ideal of equality wherein he is the master of nothing and the servant of the state—a state which is increasingly corrupted by the ignoble practice of taking other people's property.

Social engineers imagine that each man will use his freedom in ways that are humane, charitable, and kind not because he experiences the pull and tutoring of familial love for others, but because he feels a sense of duty to a system and a dogmatic allegiance to the doctrine of equality. This simply does not work. Allegiance to equality is rarely as compelling or sustainable as love for one's own physical creations, especially one's family.

Selfless Babies

For a socialistic society to work, selflessness must be demanded of babies as soon as they exit the womb (or whatever socialist invention is created to replace wombs). In essence, babies must be born loving their neighbors as themselves. What a fabulous plan. As soon as we get the perfect government system of planned equality in place, then babies will fall gracefully into the system, grow up as model citizens, and we will all roll forward in perfect equality and happiness, pursuing boundless pleasures and having lots of recreational sex with whomever we want without the hope or hassle of rearing children. Children will already be perfectly patient, perfectly loving, perfectly generous, and perfectly selfless because the system fosters these qualities in them by providing them with everything they want.

The socialist philosophy is essentially this: Eliminate the possibility of inequality by suspending people's exercise of free will regarding the use of their own private property, confiscate the fruits of everyone's labor to divvy out equally, and thereby secure sustenance and equality for all. The outcome sounds nice. But anyone who has ever had a two-year-old or a teenager knows this plan will never work. You cannot erase a person's desire to direct his own destiny even if you put him in a seemingly perfect, seemingly equitable system. People want to create, dream, build, try, excel, compete, conquer, explore, experiment, climb, invest, try again, rebuild, earn, save, buy, invent, inspire, and be the masters of their own destinies. You cannot erase a soul's recurring urges to excel and rebel even if you give him everything he wants. And ironically, if you give a person everything he wants, you almost always end up with a fantastically selfish, unsavory person on your hands, not the kind of person who spontaneously loves and shares.

Enormous problems arise from trying to craft a perfect *system* instead of trying to individually craft noble *people*. You cannot throw imperfect people into a perfect system and expect the system to work flawlessly. You must work to perfect *people* even in the face of imperfect circumstances, even in the face of inequalities. It can be done. But it cannot be done easily or rapidly. Babies (people) are not born selfless. They are born with the undeveloped ability to attain competence, excellence, and even magnificence, but these take a very long time to mature. At first, people are born caring about having their basic needs met and screaming when those needs are not met immediately. This self-preserving tendency could be called selfish. A baby only becomes unselfish through the long and arduous process of growing up in a small group of people who model selfless behavior and teach him how to love by loving him.

Perfect People

Life as it is currently organized, wherein families possess and shepherd new people and inequality is allowed, is meant to produce people who act nobly no matter their circumstances. And it has produced such people. Life has produced survivors, heroes, martyrs, and conquerors who have faced inequalities of all sorts and triumphed anyway. Only people who have felt the pull of greed, envy, hate, and selfishness and have mindfully chosen to live by nobler virtues can live cooperatively, peacefully, and perfectly no matter what their circumstances.

A society that is equal by force rather than by choice is not sustainable, and, even if it were, it would produce people who could only act nobly in idyllic circumstances of programmed equality. It would not produce people whose actions were consistently (and eventually unchangeably) motivated by love. It would produce people who were submerged in the philosophy of equality but who longed for autonomy. Rebellion is inevitable under such circumstances. Ignobleness must be conquered, not simply avoided or suppressed. Only perfect people, people who have conquered selfishness and ignobility in all its forms, can tolerate a utopia that demands perfection. Perfection cannot be demanded, coerced, programmed, purchased, or even bestowed. Therefore, an equalistic utopia must be chosen by the people who live in it. A perfect society will only exist when everyone in it chooses to manage themselves, their possessions, and their responsibilities in love and perfection.

The objective of life does not seem to be avoiding creating or possessing things for fear of risking inequality or ignoble behavior. Rather, the objective of life seems to be to forge loving, noble possessors by letting them practice (sometimes badly) possessing, creating, and loving.

Psychologist Urie Bronfenbrenner said, "The family is the most powerful, the most humane, and by far the most economical system known for building competence and character" in people. Competence and character must indeed be *built;* they do not just materialize as byproducts of existing in an equality-based system of non-possession. Imperfect babies roll into existence on the planet every day. Forging noble, competent, loving people out of them is a colossal task best accomplished in families.

Freedom and Parenthood

It has been said that "freedom is alarming."[1] And it is. Freedom allows vast diversity. Freedom allows inequality. Freedom allows people to be lackluster or magnificent. Modern equalism distorts the valid concept of equality and sets humanity on a quest for enforced sameness. Manufacturing false equality that overrides people's personal choices requires revoking freedom. But taking people's freedom does not make them inherently less flawed. People are free to make poor choices, and all people do at times.

For those whose top priority is manufactured equality, freedom is too alarming to risk. For those whose top priority is love, freedom is essential. Because you cannot force love out of people or into people; people must choose love. Families are the prime venues that create connection and belonging which most often lead to love, competence, and even greatness. One answer to the equality arguments gushing through society is this: *The goal is not equality. The goal is greatness, to whatever degree people are willing to choose it.* Allowing people to choose greatness or not to choose greatness is called *freedom.* Greatness is not dependent on sameness between people. People of all circumstances can and do achieve greatness.

People usually experience the highest degree of freedom in carrying out their duties as parents; parenthood is not usually closely regulated by anyone. A mother or father sees what needs to be done and either does it or does not do it. Being a mother or father entails stewardship paired with immense freedom and, remarkably, most people in these circumstances rise to the occasion, especially when their children's lives are on the line. Parenthood is a bold example of the principle that freedom paired with private responsibility consistently commands the best results. In other words, *freedom works*. Freedom generates responsibility and prosperity more reliably than any other political or social arrangement ever attempted.

Family Diversity

Because parenthood is not closely regulated by outside entities, parents can teach their children whatever they want. They can convey to their children the traditions and virtues they think are most important, and these can vary greatly from family to family. Most parents put their children fairly high on their priority list and choose to feed, clothe, bathe, read to, explore with, teach, and serve their children. But there are cruel parents. And this is indeed tragic. Some people's answer to the issue of inequality in families is to "publicize" parenthood: to move parenthood into the public sphere so that it can be regulated at the very least, and completely supplanted by outside forces at the very most.

Harvard professor and feminist Mary Jo Bane extols the socialist method of raising children equally in nonfamilial settings. She says, "If we want to talk about equality of opportunity for children, then the fact that children are raised in families means there's no equality . . . In order to raise children with equality, we must take them away from families and communally raise them."[2] Feminists such as Bane and other equality crusaders can't stand that family interactions are not regulated. Some activists go so far as to suggest that parents should be required to obtain a license from the state before being allowed to have and raise children.

One such activist is Hugh LaFollette, who wrote an essay titled, "Licensing Parents." In it he argues for governmental regulation of parenting and licensing of parents, just as society now requires doctors, lawyers, and plumbers to be licensed before performing their duties. He maintains that since parenting is the ultimate duty, the state should manage and regulate it so that no lame parents will be able to injure or damage any children.

The goal of protecting children is a noble one. However, LaFollette's proposals and others like them require extreme breaches of personal liberty and show an utter lack of understanding that parental possessorship is the very thing that provides the most reliable protection for the most children, even though it cannot protect all children all the time. (Nothing can accomplish this except not living, which is what Margaret Sanger suggested.[3]) LaFollette states outright that the belief that parents have "natural sovereignty over their children" is "abhorrent" and is an idea that must be "dislodged" and "supplanted." Perhaps most alarming of his socialistic suggestions is how to deal with parents who conceive a child without a parenting license. He says:

> How would one deal with violators and what could we do with babies so conceived? There are difficult problems here, no doubt, but they are not insurmountable. We might not punish parents at all we might just remove the children and put them up for adoption . . . If it is important enough to protect children from being maltreated by parents, then surely a reasonable enforcement procedure can be secured.[4]

After what we know of the "reasonable enforcement procedures" used in the name of regulating family formation in China, all the alarm bells in the universe should be going off. Once the natural sovereignty of parents ceases to be recognized, all bureaucratic hell breaks loose, "illegal" children become wards of the state, and society comes apart at the seams because families are no longer holding it together.

In truth, licensing of parents is done inherently by the cooperative anatomy of the woman and the man. Finding someone of the opposite sex who is willing to let his or her body work in tandem with yours to *create life* and who is willing to commit to you *for life* to raise the children you create together is a fairly stringent licensing process that demands social acuity, basic life skills, an ability to make and keep commitments, and a reasonable degree of self-mastery. In some societies of the past and in most modern societies, women have held the upper hand in mate selection, which is in essence the power to license parents. Psychologist Jordan Peterson says, "Women are choosy maters," "most men do not meet female human standards," and "women's proclivity to say no, more than any other force," has shaped human existence.[5] This being the case, women are essentially in charge of licensing parenthood. They are the gatekeepers who decide which men will potentially become parents and which men do not measure up to the task.[6]

The quality of stewardship forged in this way is superior to any government-regulated child licensing program. Parenting is already regulated through the workings of human anatomy and marriage. Licensing of parents is accomplished largely by licensing marriages. In fact, that has historically been the primary purpose of issuing marriage licenses. Licensing parents through the mechanism of marriage serves to protect new members of society: children.

Equalizing the Education of the Young and Crushing Diversity

With impassioned calls for diversity and equality ringing through society, perhaps we need to decide what it is we really want. Families themselves are the prime avenues to achieving and sustaining diversity. A state supreme court justice explains,

> Family autonomy helps to assure the diversity characteristic of a free society. There is no surer way to preserve pluralism than to allow parents maximum latitude in rearing their own children. Much of the rich variety in American culture has been transmitted from generation to generation by determined

parents who were acting against the best interest of their children, as defined by official dogma. Conversely, there is no surer way to threaten pluralism than to terminate the rights of parents who contradict officially approved values imposed by reformers empowered to determine what is in the "best interest" of someone else's child.[7]

Crushing the family inevitably crushes diversity. If the sweeping mandates of an expanding state decide what children will be taught rather than parents deciding to teach their own children, prescribed sameness will prevail, and diversity and pluralism will inevitably decline.

Efforts to regulate parenthood and equalize children's education in early childhood are continually being pushed in state and national legislatures. Schemes to increase the monitoring of young children's upbringing in the name of "improving school readiness," "children's health and development," "supporting children in early childhood," "aligning standards," and "improving high-quality comprehensive early learning standards," complete with state-appointed "early childhood commissions" and "advisory councils," are increasingly being trotted out in law-making bodies across the country.[8]

Do not be duped by such noble-sounding proposals. The care and education of young children is best done primarily in their families. While there are exceptions to this rule, the rule still stands. If the day comes when mothers and fathers are no longer willing or able to effectively raise and teach and love their own children, that is the day the world is in danger of imminent and catastrophic collapse. At that point, the world can only be salvaged by a widespread, intentional return to motherhood and fatherhood.

CHAPTER EIGHT

LOVE OR MONEY

In her passionate fury about inequality, Firestone bemoans that "culture was built on the love of women, at their expense" and that women are "the very basis" of the economy, but that these key realities are "easily overlooked."[1] She has a valid point: Because the private efforts of families and especially women in nurturing and mentoring human beings are not rewarded publicly with money or other incentives, they can be easily disregarded as the foundation upon which society stands. But society stands on these private efforts nonetheless, just as Firestone observed.

But if we all abandon private posts in order to fill public roles as Engels and Firestone demand, who will be doing the voluntary, private work that sustains the economy, fuels the flourishing of culture, and perpetuates the civil existence of humanity? In other words, who will be doing the work that is now done in and by the family? That's just it. Firestone's and Engels's modern socialist comrades want to publicize the family or dismantle the family and publicize the work that is usually done in it. This scenario would work in one of two ways: Either everyone would be paid to do what used to be considered household work or no one would be paid for such work, but it would be farmed out equally to everyone so women wouldn't be stuck with all the repulsive, unpaid "drudgery" of caring for their own children. The goal is not just to have men participate more in parenting and caring for their children, which is a worthwhile effort, but to erase the model of caring for one's own children altogether.

But notice that to do this, to publicize the work formerly done in the family, you must abandon the private sphere. You must treat what we now think of as the private parts of life as public duties, and you must believe that they can be done equally by everyone. This is exactly what Engels proposed. He said that true equality could only be accomplished when "private work in the home [is] transformed into a public industry."[2]

This strategy not only devalues private life, but it does two other things: 1) It assumes that paying a person to do certain tasks will bring about the same or even superior consequences as having someone perform a duty out of love, and 2) It lays the private sphere open to intrusion and regulation by outside forces. If there ceases to be a private familial sphere, essentially everything becomes publicly managed and monitored. This is a micromanager's dream—and most people's worst nightmare.

Anti-feminist Mallory Millet explained the cooperative functioning of the public world and private society this way: "Men are men and women are women. They are essentially different and designed for a natural division of labor."[3] She continued,

> [W]hen men ran the world and women ran society we had a chance to conduct our lives in some semblance of balance, but women have abdicated their running of society and thus, it has collapsed dramatically. . . . When women ran society power emanated from the home . . . The essential rules that Moms formed in their infants and homes radiated outwardly into streets, schools, offices, boardrooms, departments, factories, and agencies to form the framework of Western ethics.[4]

Power emanates from the private sphere—the home—only when there is a powerful and empowered being there running it. When more people are vying to run the world and fewer people are managing private society and mentoring the developing people in it, the world becomes an increasingly difficult, deviant, and decadent thing to run.

The Love of Mothers or the Love of Money?

Women have historically carried, born, and nurtured the children that come to them without being paid for the task. It started this way and remains so: Life itself is rooted in something that is not bought but bestowed. Making parenthood a paid, public service in the name of equality would undercut the economy—which the voluntary work of mothers and fathers now upholds. But it would also do something else. Since the rearing of children by a mother is based largely on that mother's love for her children and since the rearing of noble people determines the destiny of nations and the flourishing of the world, our whole system of life and society is based on love, specifically, the love of mothers. If you remove this foundation and try to build society on something else, it may be different—perhaps radically different.

Some claim that a shift from unpaid mothering to paid caregiving would not only free women but would bring about *better* outcomes because the people raising children would be paid for the task. This supposedly makes the venture of raising humanity more respectable because it doesn't "exploit" parents. However, convincing or compelling women to perform public work while putting their children—and therefore the destinies of nations—in the care of others rather than working for free to teach their children out of love displaces and debases not only parenthood, but love itself. And thus, the foundation of society begins to shift. It is built less on the love of family, and more on the love of money.

As one professional journalist and mother noted, many women do not anticipate "the degree to which they would fall in love with their new baby" and how their priorities may change when this occurs.[5] When this falling in love with one's own child happens, it is not a tragedy, it is the pivot point of life. The love of a woman for her child is the very thing that energizes, individualizes, privatizes, and stabilizes the world one child at a time.

Women who have bought in to the idea that the greatest power is tied to the greatest monetary gain in the public sphere are gravely mistaken. They have abandoned their positions of greatest influence and joined the scuffle for the coins and transient honors of misguided men. True power is not dependent upon the invented honors of earth. True power is that which guides, shapes, carves, and claims the souls of men. And the souls of men are most often won and lost at the feet of mothers.

Cooperation of the Public and Private Spheres

If the work of mothers is so vital, why is it often difficult to see and grossly undervalued? Perhaps it has something to do with camouflage. If you wanted to disguise a powerful, vital thing and keep it functioning in relative safety and privacy, you might make it intentionally difficult to discern.[6] You would do this for the purpose of keeping the pivotal piece in place and keeping it as secure as possible from outside intrusion. The world would go on quietly turning around it, largely unaware that the unassuming thing was the linchpin of creation, the thing which made its entire existence both possible and desirable. It appears this is what God or the guts of the universe may have done in the case of women.

In the familiar yin and yang symbol representing the opposing, complementary powers that compose the universe, the yang is the male principle represented in white, which signifies openness or overtness. The yin is the female principle represented in black, which signifies covertness or privateness.[7]

This expresses the reality that woman reigns in—and originally establishes—the private, covert sphere. The woman is so positioned not to disempower her, but rather to empower her. She is positioned where her power can be most comprehensive and her freedom will be least impeded because her position is least discernible, least monitored, least regulated, and least exposed to outside interference. Women can and should function openly in the public sphere on any level they choose. However, their operations *as mothers* are and should remain by and large unregulated and unimpeded by the public sphere.

The man's biological endowment allows him availability for performing administrative duties. The woman's biological endowment allows her to function as a primary creator, which affords her less flexibility to engage in administrative duties, although she is often proficient at both. Since man cannot, by edict of his anatomy, be proficient at being a primary creator *and* a public administrator, he is limited to one of those roles, which tends to give him public recognition because it is a public job. He can, however, act as a secondary creator in tandem with his wife. This is a vital function, but since it is a private function, he receives fewer accolades for it. A woman can act as a primary creator *and* a public figure. However, requiring her to do so does not result in "equality" for the woman. It requires her to bear what might be considered "unequal" responsibilities. This does not mean a mother cannot or should not engage in public actions. It simply means that doing so requires her to bear greater burdens, particularly during her childbearing and rearing years, than men.

For most people, the private sphere is more treasured than the public sphere. Work in the public sphere is where people go in order to make their private life possible. Most of us do not engage in public work just because it's a fantastic way to spend our time or because it is wondrously fulfilling and requires no unpleasantness. Although working at a paid job can be fulfilling, that is not solely why most people do it. Most people do it because they get money for doing it. And with that money they can construct for themselves a *private* pocket in the world in which they and the people they love can do what they want. The private sphere is not only the more treasured sphere but the primal one. A robust public sphere is built upon and cannot exist without a functioning private sphere wherein people are produced and then fashioned into socially competent beings by people who love them.

The Selfish Family

The "passionate determination of parents to protect and prefer their own children" is almost universally displayed by parents across the globe.[8] This preference for one's own children is not a disease, a disorder, or a disturbing inequality. Most people call it something else: love. And most people believe it is a good thing. In fact, the love of mothers and fathers has historically been the standard against which all other loves are measured. But the love of family is increasingly being attacked as selfish. The family is accused of fostering "partial beneficence" because it seeks to meet the needs of its own members. Partial beneficence is another way of saying loving some people more than others. One modern philosophy that attacks familial love as being selfish and inappropriately partial is utilitarianism. Utilitarianism and its modern sidekick, effective altruism, are currently gaining traction and publicity.[9]

One of effective altruism's guiding principles is that if you have a sum of money, you should use evidence and reason to decide how you could help the largest number of beings (human or nonhuman), no matter who they are or where they are in the world, and apply the money to that cause. For instance, if your daughter fell ill you could use $1,000 to treat her illness. But effective altruism in its purest form seems to suggest that it would be a more reasonable and equitable use of your money to help fifty girls in Africa be treated for illness if you could do so with the same $1,000. The number of beings you help is paramount. This, they say, is the best way to save the world and presumably the best way to show love.

In practice, however, even ardent utilitarians find it difficult or even objectionable to sideline their love for their own children or to outright demand that others do so. But they feel guilty for not doing so. For example, one such man wept after a child he was trying to save in his clinic died. When he realized he was weeping because he was picturing his own child dying in her place, he saw this as a "failure" and as an "inability to love other children as he loved his own."[10] On the contrary, his love of his own daughter is what enabled him to love other children and to feel the pain of their parents more deeply than perhaps he otherwise would. So it is with most people. We love others because our love for our own families carves a deep well in our souls that can then be filled with empathy, compassion, and love for others. If we had not loved and been loved by our families, it is likely the well would not run so deep.

One of effective altruism's adherents said, "The sacrosanct commitment to the family is the rationalization for all manner of greed and selfishness."[11] While members of families surely have done selfish things, the utilitarian approach to the world and the people in it essentially criminalizes familial love. It is akin to saying it's greedy to put your own oxygen mask on during a plane crash before helping others put theirs on. Helping one's own family first is not selfish; it is taking responsibility for that which is yours. That is not to say we do not or should not look beyond our own family's needs, but we should work to meet our own family's needs first and then look outward to see how our family can help others.

Exceptions to this pattern are few. If every person worked zealously to first meet the physical and emotional needs of his or her own spouse, children, parents, grandparents, cousins, etc., it would keep most people busily engaged for life and there would be a reduced need for cross-continent altruism. Familial love is not necessarily selfish or wrong. Utilitarianism's growing push for "impartial beneficence" is a push to remove love as the motivating factor in private decision-making. It pretends to be grounded in love, even using religiously based stories such as the Good Samaritan to make its points. But it talks about doing good based on evidence and reason, not one's love for the people he knows, or even on brotherly love of those who may cross his path. Evidence and reason, while valuable, are different than love.

Family-based solutions are key to solving the world's problems.[12] If we want to do the most good for the most people, we will work to strengthen, protect, repair, defend, and empower the family as the fundamental unit of society. If families help their own members, the entire world is helped because everyone is inescapably part of a family. Global efforts to solve world hunger (or world poverty or world anything), though well-intentioned, lose the motivation of attached love and therefore lose the most potent impetus in the world. In the worldview of effective altruism, the ideal of doing good to the most beings displaces the love people have for their own families. It removes love born of private belonging as a valid motivation for doing good. If the altruistic effort to distribute wealth becomes a government-dictated project executed in the name of achieving equality, the effort cuts off its own legs because it removes the most potent motivation for humankind to work and produce: the love of one's own family.

Opposition to family love is growing. Dr. Ezio Di Nucci of the University of Copenhagen writes, "A preference towards children one is biologically related to is morally illegitimate" and that the tendency to prefer one's own children is a "moral vice."[13] He says this is so because "in the context of parental love, biological considerations are normatively irrelevant." Rebecca Roache, senior lecturer in philosophy at Royal Holloway, University of London, writes, "The wish to be biologically related to one's children, like the wish to associate only within one's racial group, can have harmful effects."[14] Efforts to debase family love and to equate familial connectedness with racism are expanding.

Like Family

People often say someone is "like a mother to them" or treats them "like family." But if we torpedo the family, will other ways of living produce the same kind of love? We know how to treat people "like family" because we have families. We think we will always retain our brotherly and sisterly and motherly and fatherly graces no matter what contortions we put the family through—no matter how we strain, strangle, bend, and break it. But when the family lays broken on the scrap heap of society, there will be no one to teach us how to fix ourselves. We will have freed ourselves from the very people who might have loved us and helped us most. We will have liberated ourselves from our own past and from our familial future and in doing so, cut the umbilical cord of the human family.

The radical feminist mantra is growing louder and stronger: "The nuclear family must be destroyed and people must find a better way to live together."[15] But what if, after we destroy the family, we discover that there is no better way to live?

CHAPTER NINE

THE GOODNESS OF MEN

Engels's theory that egotistical men invented marriage as a way of greedily earmarking which children were theirs so they could heap advantages on those particular children is based on the premise that providing for one's offspring is motivated by selfishness. Pardon my simpleness, but it doesn't seem that bad to me that men would want to know which children were theirs so they could pay attention to them and give them good stuff. If every father did this, virtually every child would be cared for. And having every child cared for is, in fact, the ideal toward which almost all of humanity is striving.

After the birth of our first baby, my husband went to the store for a few needed items and returned with the items plus a tiny, pink dress with checkered bows on it and a huge smile on his face. It gave him joy to provide something good for his new daughter. This is not evil. Having just become a father, he now understood what it was like to have and to love his own child. But he also understood more deeply that every other baby girl in the world was somebody's daughter, and he valued all little girls and understood their fathers a little bit better.

If a man never cared which woman was pregnant with his child, as Engels suggests is ideal, that would leave every woman alone to bear the joint fruit of sexual intercourse. Women could comfort each other, of course, but the man who initiated each woman's condition would never be there to appreciate her sacrifices, alleviate her pains, or rejoice with her in the remarkable creation she bears that they crafted together. Women would be left abandoned in all of this. And the resulting child would be left to wonder where the other half of him came from and why this other half doesn't love him or his mother.

Notwithstanding these concerns, the idea that children are better off without fathers is running rampant in certain circles. Firestone says the only reason a father would want to know his child is for reasons of "ego."[1] Clem Gorman, communal living enthusiast, likewise says, "It is not desirable to know which male member was the father of the child, as this might encourage distinctions and possessiveness."[2] And feminist Merav Michaeli claims that a father's legal custody over his children leads to "ongoing hurt in children."[3]

Are Fathers Bad for Families?

And so, we are left with a narrative in which men are bad for families. But does current data support such a view? Certainly some fathers may fit this narrative. But even a surface-level exploration of the data reveals significant information about the influence of fathers. Research compiled by the National Fatherhood Initiative shows that children who grow up in father-absent homes are:

- Four times more likely to live in poverty
- More likely to be abused and neglected
- More likely to commit crime
- More likely to go to prison
- Twice as likely to die in infancy
- Twice as likely to drop out of high school

- Twice as likely to suffer from obesity
- More likely to abuse drugs and alcohol
- Seven times more likely to become pregnant as a teen[4]

A synthesis of numerous studies on fatherhood shows that fathers have a significant influence on their daughters. Daughters who have a loving, respectful, active relationship with their fathers are less likely to:

- Develop eating disorders
- Be raped or sexually abused
- Engage in risky sexual behaviors
- Be overly dependent on men
- Have difficulty dealing well with authority figures—especially men
- Be imprisoned
- Abuse drugs and alcohol[5]

In short, children who know, live with, and feel loved by their fathers are happier, richer, healthier, safer, more educated, more confident, less abused, and more independent than children whose fathers are absent.[6]

Weddings Are about Men

Marriage is the umbilical cord that tethers a man to his family. If you cut the cord of marriage, families unravel, men disappear, and women are left holding the bag, or rather, the child. The woman gets first and most concrete rights to her child by virtue of her anatomy, but if there is no father to help hold the bag, the result is often instability, poverty, and suffering for the woman, her child, and society. Weddings are about formalizing and solidifying a man's ability to know, claim, and care for his own children.

If men and women do not inherently possess their biological children, there is little need for a wedding other than to spend money to show people you love each other. This is what most modern marriage celebrants understand marriage to be: a state-recognized party about the sexual affection of adults—not a means of biological and legal tethering that secures possessorship of potential children to their fathers through their mothers.

If a man publicly marries a woman, signs his name in ink, and the whole village shows up to the wedding, it is difficult for a man to deny his responsibilities to the children his wife births. It would also be difficult for outside entities to deny him his unique claim to his own children. Wedding vows—publicly declared and legally binding—allow the man to be publicly and legally responsible for his children. This goes a long way to equalizing the consequences of intercourse for the man and woman and balancing their joint responsibilities to their children. Marriage tethers men to their children, and this is a good thing.

Goodness Has Always Been Possible

A common narrative is that men are brutes, woman are victims, and marriage has confined these two creatures together in a cage to fight until death do they part. Novels and movies amplify this narrative, and no doubt instances such as these have occurred at times and in certain cultures. Some may have occurred with some frequency. However, it is a faulty interpretation of history to claim that love and affection have scarcely had a place in the family. Ferdinand Mount writes, "To deduce from the sad fragments of evidence which come down to us . . . that men and women had no feelings for one another or for their children is the most callous act of historical condescension."[7] While no one can claim to know the full extent of familial affection in particular marriages gone by, there is much evidence that people actually loved each other as spouses, parents, and children in ages past.

In 1432, Leon Battista Alberti wrote:

> We may consider love of husband and wife greatest of
> all. . . . There is no one to whom you have more opportunity
> to communicate fully and reveal your mind than to your own
> wife, your constant companion. Children are born, and it
> would take a long time to expound the mutual and mighty
> bond which these provide. They surely ally their parents'
> mind in a union of will and thought.[8]

This does not sound like a brute who keeps his wife around just to do his laundry. It seems he actually loved and valued his wife and children. It has always been an option for men to be decent husbands, and a great many of them have risen to the occasion. Because some married men have chosen to be brutes does not mean men are bad or that we ought to scrap marriage altogether. Should we stop expecting men to claim and care for their own children because some men have done a shoddy job of it? Would disconnecting fathers from their children by eliminating marriage improve the state of children of the world?

People have always been free to put their best foot forward in marriage. But because life comes in sets of opposites, people in marriages are also free to put forward their worst. If we pull the plug on marriage to try to fix this problem, the same problem would exist in whatever scenario took the place of marriage. People are always free to be base, mean, and selfish. But they are also always free to be noble, selfless, and kind. Changing the scenery does not change this reality.

The answer to the quandary of lame men is not to jettison marriage. If anything should be jettisoned, it is women having sex with men who are not committed, body and soul, to their lifelong welfare. Handing out sex like bubble gum does not improve the situation of women regardless of what women's rights advocates may persuade some women to believe.[9] Sex is one of woman's greatest leverage points, because she embodies something the man wants. His pursuit of her leads to the very thing that can make a man the best kind of man he can be—family formation. It leads him to circumstances in which he is most likely to experience stewardship, sacrifice, and love, all of which abound in committed family living.

Guardians

By putting half of the human reproductive system in one set of people and the other half of the reproductive system in another set of people, both cooperation and diversity are required in order for life to continue. This anatomical pairing design accomplishes many things in addition to the creation of life. One thing it does is provide every woman and child with a personal bodyguard and physical provider bound to them by an agreement recognized by law. A bodyguard—or guardian—is a useful thing, and such a being is often bigger in size, strength, and/or firepower than the person he is protecting. This makes good sense, and this is where men usually excel by virtue of biological designation. Man is in the position to use his strength in the lifelong service of his wife and children. Whether he does so admirably is up to him.

Research indicates that fathers and husbands—despite often being depicted otherwise—consistently succeed in acting as protectors for their families. Research indicates that the absence of fathers is a prime cause of poverty and that crime is more prevalent in neighborhoods where most homes do not include fathers.[10] Studies also show that women who are married to the men they live with experience lower rates of violence than women who live with men they are not married to.[11] One study found that "women in cohabiting relationships were nine times more likely to be killed by their partners than were women who were in marital relationships."[12] Family researchers report that "single and divorced women are four to five times more likely to be victims of violent crime in any given year than are married women" and are "about three times more likely to be the victims of aggravated assault."[13] Additionally, the "rates of serious abuse of children are lowest in the intact, married family" in which a man is married to and lives with the mother of his children.[14] And further, infants born into father-absent homes are four times more likely to die in the first twenty-eight days of life than infants with involved fathers.[15] In short, men frequently and consistently function as protectors in the lives of their wives and children and in society at large.

Men's anatomical situation invites them to act as guardians of that which is most prized: the private sphere and the people in it—*the family*. It is a bit like the fabled knight with sword in hand, vigilantly guarding the Holy Grail. Man is the protector of the fountain of life (his wife) and the lives that flow from it (his children). He takes his charge seriously and fills it with valor. This is manhood at its finest. A good man is truly a grand thing. And good men may not be as scarce as we have been led to believe. A man's masculinity is not toxic; when properly applied, it is a tremendous force that leads to progress, protection, production, and prosperity. It leads a man to the proper and competent use of all that is best within him and around him.

Given the benefits that marriage brings to men, women, children, and society, how should we treat the woman and the man and the remarkable human capital they produce together? How should we treat *the family*? The Universal Declaration of Human Rights was onto something when it declared, "The family is the natural and fundamental group unit of society and is entitled to protection by society and the State." Having explored how the primal sovereignty of the family works and why it should not be abandoned or obliterated, we turn now to the mechanisms of sexual radicalism which seek to undermine it.

PART III

MOUNTING THREATS

CHAPTER TEN

SEXUAL EQUALITY AND A NEW RIGHT

The average person would probably not agree with Shulamith Firestone, Sophie Lewis, and Friedrich Engels in their belief that eliminating motherhood and alienating fathers from their children is the best way to save the world. And yet, the philosophies these three figures championed are oozing infectiously into legislative efforts, social media movements, school programs, daycare centers, political debates, dinnertime conversations, and United Nations documents. And they have been doing so for a long time.

Engels, Firestone, Lewis, and their numerous philosophical descendants have one prime goal: to dismantle the biological family and place a socialistic—and eventually communistic—state in its stead. Firestone explained specifically that the end goal of socialist feminism is "not just the elimination of male *privilege* but of the sex *distinction* itself: genital differences between human beings would no longer matter culturally."[1] This means that male and female manifestations of the human body would no longer be recognized as meaningful, which in turn means the family created through sexual diversity may no longer be recognized as meaningful. In order to dismantle the family, the differences between men and women must be erased, suppressed, ignored, or legislated away.

The foremost gender-based distinctions that must be eliminated in order for socialist-feminist societies to take hold are mother and father. When parents' ties to their children are obscured or weakened it creates an environment hospitable to government intervention and socialistic revolution. Recall that Sophie Lewis said she is excited about the current social movements that are expanding the political and legal climate "in which mother-child bonds can more easily be discontinued." If we are to avoid the social and legal disembowelment of the family and the domination of the state that follows its disembowelment, we must ask ourselves this question: What laws, practices, or social movements seek to obscure or obliterate motherhood and fatherhood, eliminate male and female designations, and loosen sexual boundaries for adults and children?

Efforts that swing momentum toward these objectives should be scrutinized and regarded as threats to the supreme rights of mothers and fathers, and therefore to the functioning of free society. Anything that dilutes, weakens, fractures, obscures, discredits, recasts, reorganizes, or undermines joint female and male reproduction and parenthood is something that enables the accomplishment of socialist designs. Any person who does not wish the family to be socially and legally annihilated and replaced with state power must recognize and resist efforts that lead society closer to the clutches of those who wish to annihilate the family.

The Road to a Nonbiologically Ordered Society

While society waits for technology and artificial wombs to rescue humanity from real mothers as Firestone suggests, other steps are being taken to free women and sever ties between children and their parents, particularly their mothers. To see this clearly, consider the following questions:

- What laws or practices are working to disavow biological relationships and "sever blood ties" between parents and their children?
- What laws or initiatives seek to loosen long-standing sexual norms?
- Who is suggesting or legislating that mothers are unnecessary to families?
- Who is suggesting or legislating that fathers are detrimental to families or, at best, optional?
- What social movements promote the concept that not knowing one's biological mother or father is normal and even a manifestation of human rights?
- What efforts are setting the stage for the state to become the gatekeeper for the distribution of children?
- Which initiatives are working to erase the differences between men and women?
- Who is working to make the care of young children a government-run endeavor?
- What entities are trying to infuse socialist, feminist, and sexually radical philosophies into the education systems of the world?
- What entities are working to advance "sexual freedom" and "sexual rights" for children?
- Who is trying to enact education programs for children that normalize a wide range of sexual behaviors including child sex?
- Who is trying to enact education programs for youth that de-normalize families in which parents claim their own children?

These are key questions. And there are clear answers.

To Found a Family

The Universal Declaration of Human Rights was drafted in 1948 under the direction of a newly formed United Nations. Article 16 of this declaration says in part, "Men and women . . . have the right to marry and to found a family." In 1948, when the declaration was drafted and the United Nations adopted it, the assumption was that men and women would marry each other in sexually diverse pairs. Today, however, there is no such assumption. In the United States and other countries, the marriage of men to men and women to women has been legalized. Because marriage is now legally available to sexually non-diverse couples, many activists assert that "founding a family" encompasses the right to have children. Thus, couples of all sexual combinations legally claim the right to have children. This is key. Because sexually non-diverse couples can now marry, parenthood has become a right.

If parenthood is a right for all people and not all kinds of human couplings can produce children, then either babies do not inherently belong to anyone in particular from the outset, or their inherent belonging can be transferred to other parties with no impact on the child, on the parents, or on society. This position requires that babies should be available to virtually anyone who wishes to exercise his right to child equality on the basis of his right to marry.

Sexually non-diverse marriage between two men removes a woman from the foundational unit of the family. Removing women from the foundational unit of a family unlinks women from their children. It inserts other entities in the place of the mother and legally grants them the rights that she biologically holds. The same is true of fathers; removing men from the foundational unit of a family displaces fathers and unlinks men from their children. Perhaps most poignantly, if people have a right to be parents regardless of their biological sex or the sex of their marriage partner, then as they acquire a child, *the right of that child* to know and possess his or her own biological creators is negated.

The Right of the Child to Know His or Her Parents

This new right to have children precipitated by sexually non-diverse marriage becomes problematic in light of international documents regarding children's human rights. At least three UN documents, including the Convention on the Rights of the Child, the Beijing Declaration of 1995, and the Convention on the Rights of Persons with Disabilities of 2006, declare and defend every child's right "*to know and be cared for by his or her parents*."[2] The right of a child to know and be cared for by his or her parents as stated in these documents takes precedence over the desire of any other entity to procure a child in order to fulfill a perceived right to parenthood or for any other reason.

It cannot be reasonably argued that these documents intend to protect the rights of commissioning or adoptive parents to secure a child for themselves. It is the *child's* right to know his literal parents that is being asserted and defended in these documents. The child's right to know and be cared for by his literal parents supersedes any purchase, exchange, or transfer of his person to the care of entities other than his own biological creators. Sexually non-diverse marriage philosophically undoes this right for all children, and literally undoes this right for a child who is commissioned for the purpose of fulfilling a person's or couples' right to parenthood.[3]

Adoptive adults may benefit from and find joy in raising a child, but the intention of adoption has never historically been to support adults' rights to have children. Further, the intention of adoption has never been to allow adults to *commission the creation of a child* with the intent to place him in circumstances where he will automatically forfeit knowing and being cared for by one or both of his literal parents. Rather, the intention of adoption has historically been *to best care for existing children whose parents cannot care for them*. Even in cases of adoption or other circumstances where a child's relationship with his parents is suspended, it could be argued that a child's right to know his birth parents should be preserved whenever possible, even if he cannot be cared for by them.

With this in mind, the sticking point with sexually non-diverse marriage is not that it publicly legitimizes same-sex couples' loving feelings for each other. Those feelings may be very real and deeply felt. The problem is that when marriage becomes a right for virtually all people, then parenthood—in the popular psyche and in law—also becomes a right. In a society where parenthood is a right for all people (individuals, couples, or all groups of people), mothers' rights as the universally recognized possessors of children are weakened. If there is an inherent right to parenthood for all people, then there is no inherent right for babies to possess their own mothers and fathers. You cannot have it both ways.

False Rights

It is true that not all rights asserted in United Nations documents or other official declarations are true rights. The encroachment of false rights into the dialogue of human rights is ongoing. Various entities fight to get specific statements enshrined in international documents so their particular viewpoints will be recognized as human rights, giving them international clout and funding. So, is the right of children to know and be cared for by their biological parents a false right that should be expunged? Or should children retain their right to know and be cared for by their parents? Same-sex marriage demands an answer to this question.[4]

At the crux of the sexual equality movement, sexually non-diverse marriage is center stage. It is propped up as a human right, which in turn allows the ushering of children into the care of virtually anyone, severs biological ties, and recasts the family as a nonbiological entity. If parenthood is indeed a right, then it would be a human rights violation not to let people have babies. So, in order for equality to reign in matters of child-getting, there has to be redistribution of babies at least at some level. Same-sex marriage law and its attendant right to parenthood accomplishes and even requires this.

Same-sex marriage law leaves unprotected that which has been fiercely protected for millennia. It seeks to invalidate the belonging of specific children to their biological parents. It lends legal strength to the idea that mothers and fathers are inconsequential to their own children. Legalization of same-sex marriage requires the state to take the position that mothers and fathers (either biological or adoptive) are inconsequential to children and that biological parents can be replaced by any other people as long as the other people are loving.

Theoretically, the way to make the lack of a mother or a father not matter to a child is by removing the "stigma" associated with families. To do this, you must de-normalize the existence of families in which there is both a father and a mother present. Many school programs now aim to de-normalize the reality that children have literal parents, one of whom is a man and one of whom is a woman, and that knowing and possessing one's own parents is normative and desirable.[5] This effort to challenge heteronormativity is increasingly common in elementary and secondary school curricula.[6] One educator admitted gleefully that the goal of the Educate & Celebrate program and others like it is to "completely smash heteronormativity."[7] Smashing heteronormativity includes smashing the notion that people have literal parents who inherently belong to them.

The United Nations Educational, Scientific and Cultural Organization (UNESCO) also advances initiatives that fight heteronormativity. As one example, UNESCO's guidelines for teaching sexuality include this instruction for children ages five through eight: "All people regardless of their health status, religion, origin, race or sexual status can raise a child and give it the love it deserves."[8] This statement implies that literal mothers and fathers are irrelevant. It implies that any person (or group of people) can acquire any child and love it exactly the same as if they were the child's parent. This unilateral declaration that *all people* can give any child the love it deserves might be combated with the UN's own documents which clearly state that a child deserves the love and care of its own parents.

Creating Life

The creation of children and the perpetuation of human life depends on sexual diversity. Every person who has ever lived—regardless of his sexual attractions—is the product of reproductively diverse cooperation. Therefore, treating all sexual relationships as if they are equal is problematic because sexually non-diverse families are dependent on reproductively diverse involvement for their existence. This is an inconvenient truth that marriage equality proponents try hard to obscure.

On the other hand, sexually diverse, fertile couples have historically been and remain independent of the state or any other entity in their ability to found families that include children. Children were created by way of sex and inherently belonged to their parents long before any king, monarch, parliament, or court spread its authoritative robes over any section of humanity. The sexually diverse family is preexistent and primary.

Non-creators will always seek to claim the creations of creators. This is the operating principle behind socialist governments, wealth redistribution programs, and the marriage equality movement that demands having children. In each of these cases, things are taken from those who produce and given to those who do not produce. Redistributing children according to the dictates of the state is, of necessity, a core tenet of both socialism and same-sex marriage. Relinquishment of children by mothers is not just *part* of these two paradigms; it is essential to them. This development—the widespread, legalized, and celebrated disavowal of mother right—is stunning. Since father right is inseparably connected to mother right through marriage, mother right and father right are both sawn asunder by the legalization of same-sex marriage. And child right—or the right of a child to his or her own parents—disappears.

The goal of the current sexual equality movement is not to have a few alternatively formed families nestled in amongst the throng of heterosexual families, while the mother-father family is regarded and legally upheld as the inherently occurring norm that serves to secure children to their creators. The goal is to de-normalize heterosexual family living on a massive scale and enforce acceptance of nonbiological equality by force of law. The question has often been posed, "How could legalizing same-sex marriage possibly affect straight marriage?" A prime answer is this: Same-sex marriage affects all relationships in society by eliminating the normalness of claiming one's own biological family. This is a seismic shift.

The Path Going Forward

Sexually non-diverse marriage is not the only thing working to dismember the biological family (no-fault divorce, sex outside marriage, rampant selfishness, drug and alcohol addiction, pornography, and other factors are all playing their part), but it is among the most effective. It is what most readily changes people's beliefs about the family because it comes cloaked as the family itself. It makes people believe that if they believe in love, they must believe that the inherently biological organization of the world is an enemy to some people's human rights.

Since same-sex marriage law will be in place for some time, it is essential that we understand the implications these laws bring to the forefront. Do ancestry, posterity, marriage, biology, and genetics matter, and do they warrant recognition in law? The plot thickens as we look more closely at the children who hang in the balance.

CHAPTER ELEVEN

COMMERCIALIZING PARENTHOOD

Placing a child for adoption for the good of the child is fundamentally different than *producing* a child in exchange for money to serve the desires of adults. Women traditionally have not been paid when placing their children for adoption for two reasons: 1) so that humans do not become products to be bought and sold, and 2) to prevent women's bodies from becoming an exploitable resource. However, this position is losing ground.

Some people in single-sex marriages express a strong desire to have a biological child, a descendant or heir, who exists because they exist; who belongs to them not by way of assimilation but by way of creation.[1] For many, this is a fundamental human desire. But if biological parenthood is accepted as a human right for everyone, then surrogacy must be legalized in order for men in same-sex marriages to exercise that right because they cannot accomplish it without the help of a woman. Calls for biological parenthood as a right are increasing, and enthusiasm for surrogacy is growing (see menhavingbabies.org). As this trend continues, one or both of the following may happen: women's and children's bodies will enter the private sector as legally accepted commodities, or the state will regulate parenthood to ensure equality in child distribution. The latter is what happened in China when it enacted the one-child policy.

Men Having Babies

Couples that do not include a woman can obtain children in essentially one of five ways:

1. Adopting a preexisting child who is placed for adoption by its birth parents
2. Hiring a woman to gestate a child who is her own biological child and the biological offspring of one of the men in the marriage
3. Hiring a woman to gestate a child who is created from an egg acquired from an egg donor and from sperm belonging to one of the men in the marriage
4. Hiring a woman to gestate a child who is created from an egg acquired from an egg donor and from sperm acquired from a sperm donor
5. Instead of hiring a woman to perform one of the above services, find a woman who will perform these services for free

In all five of these scenarios, a woman must be involved. In all five scenarios, the child is removed from the care of its mother, and the relationship of the mother and child is often suspended. In three of the five scenarios above, the baby is no longer the crowning compensation for the rigors of pregnancy. Money becomes the motivation for and the crowning compensation for pregnancy, just as Shulamith Firestone said it should be. Our transition to a widely accepted reproductive model wherein people are purchased or donated to non-related people instead of being born and claimed by biological endowment is underway, driven largely by same-sex marriage.[2] This situation is reminiscent of the wide-spread severing of blood ties for which Firestone eagerly campaigned.

Surrogacy

Money in exchange for children is a thriving business. A system of impregnating women with foreign eggs and donated sperm has boomed across the globe.[3] Advocates of the practice claim that surrogacy improves the lives of surrogates since most of them are poor and could, theoretically, earn more in nine months than they could in nine years. However, the financial and other realities of surrogacy are often not as rosy as promised.[4] Miscarriages or stillbirths can result in no payment; forced abortions can be ordered if the baby is not developing according to the commissioning parents' wishes or if too many embryos develop; complications can threaten the health or life of the surrogate or the baby; the commissioning couple or person can reject the baby after it is born; or the surrogate may have difficulty giving up the child she carried inside her body. Surrogacy and egg donation introduce discord into the relationships established by the umbilical cord. Babies who develop in and are born from a certain woman's womb are *supposed* to be hers and her body knows this.

But even if none of the above complications occurs and the surrogate receives nine years' pay for nine months' work and goes home with bags of money in her arms instead of a baby, does that make it okay? Is it okay to equate the value of a baby with the value of money because it makes some poor people richer? Is it okay to found families on monetary exchange instead of on the love of mothers, and to do so in the name of love?

In recent years, India and other countries have placed restrictions on surrogacy. But surrogacy is still thriving in many areas of the world, and homosexual men seeking the unique services of women is an expanding business. (For instance, in spite of other areas banning paid surrogacy because it facilitates the egregious commodification of women and babies, New York State legalized commercial surrogacy in April 2020.[5]) One woman who operates a surrogacy agency in Illinois says male couples in particular tend to seek the help of a fertility service in commissioning a child because, "Everything is new to them. They don't even understand the woman's body and how things are going to work."[6] This is troubling. Male couples seek to tap woman's unique power without understanding her or her body and without jointly shouldering the risks inherent to that power. They want to buy the benefits of creation without buying into relationships that initiate creation. They seek to secure the child without securing the child to its mother. Heterosexual couples who purchase certain reproductive services must face the same questions regarding the purchase and reassigning of children's biological and social identities.

Gay Opposition to Surrogacy

Gary Powell, a gay man and longtime gay rights campaigner, opposes the notion that surrogacy is a right for LGBT people—or for any people. In his article "Why the Gay and Lesbian Equality Movement Must Oppose Surrogacy," he highlights the exploitive nature of surrogacy, the fracturing of children's rights it necessitates, and the bodily risks to women it entails. He says, "In surrogacy, the perceived 'right' to have a child competes with the right of women and the right of children to freedom from exploitation, instrumentalization and commodification, which are violated by surrogacy arrangements. Any claim to an 'LGBT right' here could not prevail over the rights of the women and children that are affected so negatively."[7]

Powell highlights the demotion of motherhood surrogacy brings about, saying the growing media insistence that two men having a baby is identical to a man and a woman having a baby "results in the birth mother and the biological mother increasingly being airbrushed" out of the picture "by the unrelenting rainbow spray can."[8] He says that in such situations "mothers become no more than an inconvenient, politically embarrassing, and dispensable means to an end."[9]

Powell addresses another crucial piece of the third-party reproductive puzzle involving the protection of children. Egg donation, sperm donation, surrogacy, and other reproductive services allow virtually any adult to procure a child under conditions that lack either the screenings and safeguards of adoption or the benefits of joint biological connection. Powell explains, "Once the legal surrogacy gate gets opened, all kinds of people walk through it, not just those who genuinely care about children and will provide them with unconditional love and excellent parenting. [In surrogacy] the rigorous vetting procedures for adoption do not apply."[10] This applies to essentially all forms of third-party reproduction. Such developments should be approached with extreme caution.

Children of Third-Party Reproduction

In order for marriage equality involving the acquisition of children to be a valid and lawful option in society we must accept the thinking that it does not matter how children are created, who creates them, or who raises them. But even as society bends to this line of thinking, many children beg to differ. Alana Newman is a donor-conceived person who has collected the stories of other donor-conceived people through the Anonymous Us Project (anonymousus.org). She says of donor-conceived people, "We are troubled by the exchange of money in our conception. To many of us, donor payment reeks of baby selling, prostitution, and human trafficking. It's much harder to accept yourself and to respect your parents (both genetic and social) when money is involved in your conception."[11]

While a portion of donor-conceived people may be largely indifferent to their origins, most donor-conceived people care deeply about the circumstances of their creation. Here is what a small sampling of donor-conceived people have had to say:

- "If I could have one wish it would be to just hear the donor's voice. I would love to ask him the most basic questions about himself. I wonder why he did it. It bothers me that there was money involved in my conception."[12]

- "I am a human being, yet I was conceived with a technique that had its origins in animal husbandry. Worst of all, farmers kept better records of their cattle's genealogy than assisted reproductive clinics had kept for the donor-conceived people of my era. It also made me feel strange to think that my genes were spliced together from two people who were never in love, never danced together, had never met one another."[13]

- "How could my donor help create me, and then abandon me without even leaving his name? . . . My donor was young and focused on 'doing a good deed.' He believed the clinics who told him that the biological link can be extinguished by signing a contract."[14]

- "I hate being donor-conceived. I think it is ridiculous and bizarre that the two people that made me have never met and never will meet. I think it's creepy that my dad was paid. I think it's creepier that agents and salespeople and commercial doctors worked so hard to create me and now that I'm an adult have no interest in my opinion."[15]

- "Who are you? . . . I grieve for you and for the part of myself that I will never truly know. I feel as though half of me is missing alongside my family, because that's what you are: Family . . . Do you honestly care about the poor couples out there unable to conceive? Or did you just need the money?"[16]

- "When I asked my mom for info about my donor, she said it was [my uncle.] It feels weird and incestuous and NOT cool . . . You can't just decide you want to raise some of your kids, and donate the others . . . What about me? I feel

like a freak show, and I don't hate gays. I loved my moms
and I appreciate they wanted me, but if they loved me why
the hell didn't they consider how I felt about all this
stuff?"[17]

A key element of this last story is that this girl realized *her father
disowned her to make his sister happy.* This statement sums up the
problem with the marriage equality paradigm for children: the child cares
that she was disowned by someone even though she was lovingly cared
for by someone else.

Children conceived in circumstances wherein their biological parents—for whatever reason—were not committed to each other at the
time of conception can weather the potential storms of being conceived
outside committed circumstances, and many people have. People born
under such circumstances are as valuable as any other people, and living
can bring them benefits and opportunities just as it does to people conceived in any circumstance. But the question is whether a child should
be *purposely* subjected to the storms of uncommitted conception, or
whether conception of a child between two people who do not intend to
permanently join their lives together should be averted whenever possible,
whether the adults involved are homosexual or heterosexual.[18] Sexual
equalism, which claims that virtually all sexual relationships and all ways
of forming families are equal, does not honor the rights of human beings
to know and claim their originating parents.

Sexual Exclusivity

The sexual exclusivity historically required by marriage has been
the long-standing means of governing which sperm makes its way to
which womb. Sexually exclusive, opposite sex-marriage has consistently
established two core pieces of information a person has a right to
know—and most often hungers to know—about himself: who created

him. Adultery—having sex with someone you are not married to—has been blackballed from the beginning of time not because God or the law-giving guts of the universe wanted to restrict people's expressions of love but because sexual exclusivity directly enables biological connections to be forged and claimed. Sexual exclusivity establishes the ancestry of every person ever born and locates him or her as a specific fruit firmly attached to the family tree of humanity, cradled in relationships of inherent stewardship.

The same-sex arguments for sexually exclusive marriage are different than the arguments for sexual exclusivity in opposite-sex marriage. For same-sex people in a marriage, their sexual exclusivity with each other is not connected to creating a biological child, establishing who that child's literal parents are, establishing an umbilical claim of stewardship over a certain child, or maintaining a child's ancestral, cultural, or genetic inheritance as it is in sexually exclusive, opposite-sex marriage.

Lifelong exclusivity of *a man and a man* does not ensure that a child will know both of his parents. In fact, male marriage makes it possible to obscure a mother's existence from a child almost entirely or to simply acknowledge her as a peripheral player in the drama of two men's love for each other. The same is true for female marriage; a father becomes simply a donor who can be honored for his contribution to the formation of a child, or essentially erased.

A major purpose of marriage has historically been to establish and protect biological relationships between parents and children and ultimately between all of humanity by way of sex. But since same-sex marriages do not accomplish this, it is not necessary to maintain sexual exclusivity within same-sex relationships for those same reasons. No one's biological identity is on the line. Same-sex couples are certainly able to exercise sexual exclusivity in order to show commitment to each other, to reduce their risk of contracting sexually transmitted diseases, to avoid damaging emotional entanglements, or for other reasons. But sexual exclusivity is not required for them in order to safeguard anyone's biological identity.[19] And so, it turns out it is not as necessary to maintain the prime characteristic of marriage—sexual exclusivity—when the marriage involves two people of the same sex.[20]

It is important to note that it was necessary for extramarital sex to be accepted by the heterosexual majority before moving on to other plateaus in the sexual revolution. Sex had to be separated from marriage and childbearing before homosexual marriage would be rational in the public mind. For millennia and up until about the 1960s, marriage had meant *permission to have sex* and agreeing to have sex only with each other. Although not every individual adhered to this rule, the rule still stood. This way of doing things largely maintained biological connections and required claiming responsibility for one's own offspring. But if sex regularly happens outside marriage and a marriage contract no longer means *permission to have sex with each other* but instead means *I love you*, that changes the game entirely. And the game has most certainly changed. If marriage today still meant permission to have sex in order to produce and preserve biologically inherent relationships, sexually non-diverse marriage would make little sense, because it cannot accomplish this. It can only claim *love*.

The New Racism

We are currently witnessing a paradigm shift in which the family is regarded less as a biological entity born and claimed by women, and more as a nonbiological entity that is purchased by contract as a matter of fulfilling adults' rights. In this process, children become not the naturally bestowed assets of mothers and fathers, but the legally contracted possessions of other parties, or in the case of true statism, property of the state. Will this affect the stability of nations, the stability of people, the stability of the world? If you remove the foundation that holds a thing up and replace it with a foundation made of something else, will the stability of the thing it is holding up be affected? It depends on whether the new foundational material is better or worse than the first.

Can children born of surrogacy or gamete donation be loved by their commissioning parents no matter the sexual orientation of the commissioning parents? Of course they can. But at its core, marriage equality (and its attendant right to parenthood) is not about love making a family or love winning. While those are sincere sentiments, same-sex marriage law has the effect of legally unseating the love of mothers and replacing it with something else. It dismantles the natural sovereignty of women and displaces the rights of children to know and claim their own parents. It normalizes the absence of mothers and fathers and endorses the stance that the link between children and their literal parents is irrelevant, disposable, and exchangeable. It hastens a social order in which mothers and fathers are less likely to claim or raise their own children.

The doctrines of socialism, radical feminism, and sexual equalism all supplant the love of mothers as the foundation of society. Sexual equalism in the form of marriage equality has gained the widest public acceptance because it claims to be built on love. Love is the most powerful argument; that's why the marriage equality campaign took it as its mantra. But the shift from love to money is quite literal in the marriage equality sphere. Instead of a woman bearing a child in consequence of the love she shares with a man, two men purchase the existence of a child from a woman for money. The purchase is presumably based on the two men's love for each other, but this scenario unavoidably brings money into the equation of creation and discounts the rights of children whose birthrights are being bought and sold.

The umbilical cord goes both ways. Not only does a mother have claim upon her child but the child has claim upon his mother; his mother is *his*. Sexually non-diverse partnerships that purchase reproductive services ignore a child's possessorship of his own mother or father. A child cannot consent to giving his own mother or father away. It is baffling why two men suppose that because they like to have sex with each other, that means a child somewhere does not need a mother.

They recklessly assume that their affection for each other trumps the joint possessorship of mother and child.

When women trade their children for money it is a sign that the foundation of society is crumbling beneath our feet. In the philosophical and legal environment emerging around us—wherein children's rights to know and be raised by their creators is de-prioritized and support for selling children's rights is expanding—claiming one's own biological heritage, ancestors, family history, and family members is in danger of becoming the new racism.

Selling people is something that, amongst all the nefarious practices of the world, has managed to maintain a bad reputation. Human trafficking, especially trafficking of children, is a cause almost the whole world theoretically condemns. How, then, do you make the commodification of children—and of women's wombs—a celebrated development? You enact marriage equality, which claims parenthood as a right.

We have now covered the third tactic for unseating the woman: commercializing parenthood and making children purchasable commodities.

The Natural and Fundamental Unit of Society

If surrogacy and marriage laws continue to disavow the validity of the rights of children to claim their biological parents, it may not be long until the validity of the biological rights of parents to claim their children are also called into question. Because these are, of course, the same connective relationships.

In 1948, when the Universal Declaration of Human Rights asserted that "The family is the natural and fundamental group unit of society and is entitled to protection by society and the State," it is unlikely that the drafters of the declaration intended to suggest that two married American men who contract with a surrogacy agency to hire a woman from India to gestate a child created from an egg donor in Russia is "the natural and fundamental group unit of society." But we now find ourselves in the situation where non-regenerative sexual partnerships that intentionally sever the biological ties of children in order to found families are being legally recognized as the fundamental and natural fountains of life and the wellsprings of humanity. This is a deception of enormous proportions.

But the deceptions are just beginning.

CHAPTER TWELVE

TRANS-FORMING THE ARGUMENT

Establishing the LGBT initialism was key to unseating the woman and uprooting the family. The teeth of this four-letter movement is same-sex marriage, but the tail—the "T" in LGBT—is potentially the most lethal element in the LGBT construct.

To see how the mechanism of transgenderism works to unseat the woman and dismember the family, we must consider the major argument that propels the LGBT movement. It is the catchphrase "born that way." Most arguments for homosexuality and same-sex marriage rest on the assertion that homosexuality is biologically inherent. By the LGBT community's own assertion, biological determination—the way someone is born—is supremely important and must be honored above all else. This is defensible because biological realities are considered immutable and a person's biological inheritance is considered key to his or her very identity.[1]

With the born-that-way message nestled in the minds of the masses and firmly connected to all four letters in LGBT, men don dresses, claiming that they were born women, and humanity feels it must embrace their narrative. But one might ask, where is the biological, bodily evidence that people born with male genitalia and bearing unchangeable XY chromosomes are not males? Where is the biological evidence that they are women and that they were, in fact, "born that way"? Instead of citing biological evidence, transgender activists often ignore biological realities and declare that they were "born in the wrong body" and that their own bodies betray them.

Notice the bait and switch here: *"Born in the wrong body"* is an entirely new and different argument than biologically *"born that way."* This new argument changes the body from the expert to the enemy. The born-in-the-wrong-body argument insists that instead of the body acting as the final biological authority, the body of the transgender person is totally and utterly wrong and must be discarded as evidence. When transgender persons say that the way they were born is erroneous and must be changed in order to fit *a biological reality other than their own body*, it has to give the thoughtful person pause. It becomes painfully obvious that the L, G, B, and T all claim the same argument to validate their position, but the biologically born-that-way argument begins to crack under the weight of transgenderism.

However, society at large has taken the born-that-way bait attached to the entire LGBT hook, and we now find ourselves in a society where it is considered deplorable, incendiary,[2] and perhaps even criminal[3] to suggest that females and males exist as biologically distinct beings[4] and that one can, except in rare cases of disorder, discern which is which by observing the biological structure of the person.[5]

Transgenderism and Simone de Beauvoir

Transgenderism insists that woman and man are not realities evidenced by the anatomy of the body. This is a radical departure from physically observable reality that has been honored for millennia. How did so many people come to widely accept this radically altered version of reality so quickly? A core player in the development of this idea was Simone de Beauvoir in the mid-twentieth century, as touched on in Part I. The crux of Beauvoir's thesis is this famous sentence: "One is not born, but rather becomes, a woman."[6] It has been noted that "Beauvoir's thought is the first to provide intellectual justification for divorcing sex from gender and for holding that culture alone had determined the meaning of sex and the body."[7]

The concept of transcendence is at the heart of Beauvoir's argument. She insists that people can transcend their bodily existence and create any reality they desire despite their physical anatomy; the physical body does not determine the person. In responding to the notion that the distinctive body structure inherent to being born either male or female may influence one's reality, Beauvoir says, "The situation does not depend on the body; the reverse is true."[8] She discounts the body as an authority on the person.

A simplified summation of Beauvoir's philosophy might be called "the Think System." Beauvoir implies that if you think you are a woman, you are one. Or, if you think you are a man, you are one. In this paradigm, anatomy is meaningless. You can create yourself to be whatever you wish to be. As applied to human gender, this has proven to be one of the most seismic ideas of our time. As the transgender movement sweeps through society with terrific speed, devastating consequences are befalling those who become convinced that their very bodies betray them and surgically altering their anatomy is the only way to live authentically as Beauvoir insists. The word transgender encapsulates Beauvoir's core thesis: Biological sex can be transcended, and one's bodily anatomy is inherently meaningless.

What You Think You Are

With transgenderism comes the idea that being a woman is not a state of body; rather it is a state of something else. In this worldview, if someone does not feel like a woman, then she isn't one. If a woman is not a being that can be discerned and defined by the anatomy of her body, then what is she? The first answer to that question from the transgender movement was "She's a man," because those seemed to be the only two available choices. But this has since evolved. If one is whatever one wishes to be as Beauvoir says, then the possibilities are endless. And yet, male and female anatomy is preexisting, persistent, and nearly impossible to suppress. The continued use of the words feminine and masculine even by those in the transgender community perpetuates and underscores the almost inescapable existence of two opposing, appealing realities.

Of course, there have always been different ways of dressing or displaying gender. Through the centuries, trends for hairstyles, shoes, clothing, jewelry, and other trappings for the body have varied widely and fluctuated between the sexes. Gender-specific clothing norms are *social constructions* which have historically helped people distinguish at a glance between the two sexes that exist. In a society where men and women seek to marry in sexually diverse pairs, it is helpful to know which people are men and which people are women right off the bat. This is accomplished largely through clothing and grooming social constructions. In a society where men and women *do not* necessarily seek to marry each other in sexually diverse pairs, such social constructions become less relevant. Reciprocally, when social constructions differentiating women and men decay and become less evident in society, this helps drive a culture wherein people do not seek to unite in sexually diverse pairs.

It is entirely possible that people might desire to wear clothing or other trappings for the body that do not fit with current social constructions. Revolutions in clothing, grooming, and accessories have occurred and will continue to occur. The world has proven that it can withstand such revolutions. It would be one thing if the transgender movement simply wanted to encourage the breaking or changing of clothing norms. But much more is at work here, and much more is at stake.

Tragic Consequences

In the transgender atmosphere that now surrounds us, there can be sobering consequences for those who attempt to alter their biology in the name of living authentically.[9] One anguished mother described her teenage daughter's descent into transgenderism after presumably being exposed to transgender ideology online. She says, "Her personality changed almost overnight and she went from being a sweet, loving girl to being a foul-mouthed, hateful pansexual male."[10] At sixteen her daughter ran away from home and reported to authorities that she felt unsafe living at home because her mother did not embrace her revised identity. Shortly thereafter, without the knowledge of her mother, a pediatric endocrinologist taught the girl how to inject herself with testosterone. The mother reports that her daughter then fled to Oregon "where state law allowed her at the age of 17 without my consent or knowledge . . . to undergo a double mastectomy and a radical hysterectomy."[11] The mother says, "My once beautiful daughter is now 19 years old, homeless, bearded, in extreme poverty, sterilized, not receiving mental health services, extremely mentally ill" and planning on undergoing genital surgery to complete her transition to becoming her "true" male self.[12] The mother laments, "The level of heartbreak and rage I am experiencing as a mother is indescribable."[13]

Regardless of the divergent arguments cascading around this issue, gender dysphoria is a very real condition deeply affecting a portion of the population and their families. Gender dysphoria can be diagnosed when there is conflict between a person's physical sex and the person's feelings of maleness or femaleness. This conflict can be dealt with in a number of ways. In all cases, responding to this real and often troubling condition requires compassion. Despite the dominant media messaging related to transgenderism in minors, studies show that often the most effective means of bringing the mind and body into harmony with each other is to let time and puberty—in concert with loving support—run their course without radical or even modest medical intervention.[14]

The *Diagnostic and Statistical Manual of Mental Disorders*, 5th ed. (DSM-5), published by the American Psychiatric Association, indicates that the majority of children who experience gender confusion do not persist in living as the opposite sex into adulthood. It states: "Rates of

people and rarely shined on the troubling business of surrogacy, the selling of children's rights, the weakening of mother right and father right, and the eventual obliteration of the distinctions between women and men that would come with the restructuring of marriage.

The LGBT strategy to unhinge gender and the family never would have worked had it been attempted in the opposite order: TBGL. It would not have worked to initially, directly market the idea that people are not born male or female and that biological sex is a figment of our collective imagination. It wouldn't have worked because people *are* born male or female, and humanity has intuitively known and physically observed this for millennia. Most people would have flatly rejected this idea on its face. So, in order for the transgender, genderless version of reality to be adopted, it had to ride on the coattails of another more appealing philosophy, which dubbed itself marriage equality. With L and G in the lead, B trailing awkwardly in tow, and T pasted at the end like an exclamation mark, all the letters and their supporting philosophies were meant to be accepted almost automatically en masse upon the legalization of sexually non-diverse marriage, and they were. This strategy has proven almost invincible.

The Punch of the Think System

The current trend is to say that instead of gender-specific clothing and other embellishments being regarded as social constructs (which they are), male and female themselves are social constructs. One definition of social construct is "an idea that has been created and accepted by the people in a society."[20] A social construct is an *idea*. This is where the true cunning of Beauvoir's "Think System" comes into play. If woman is a state of mind rather than a physical state of body as transgender activists insist, then "woman" *does* fit the definition of a social construct because woman is simply an *idea*, not a physical reality with material substance that can be discerned by her physical structure and properties. And if woman is not a physical reality with material substance that can be discerned by her physical structure and properties, then woman is not a tangible thing. She is an idea.

If woman is merely an idea, she will have difficulty maintaining her status because social constructs change. And if no general consensus persists concerning what a woman is, then the woman is in grave danger of being socially construed right out of existence. And when this happens, the woman slips from the protection of laws that were instituted to protect her unique standing in the first place. When women no longer exist as a physically discernible and defensible class of people, they slip from their prime place in society, and they semantically and legally disappear.

If you have climbed aboard the LGBT movement because you are sympathetic to arguments for homosexuality, you do not have to climb aboard the transgender express. Though they both lead away from the biological family, they are different trains entirely. Their philosophies are divergent, contradictory, incompatible, and in direct discord with each other. It is not too late to disembark from the transgender express; growing numbers of people are doing so as displacement of women advances and gender chaos explodes exponentially around us.

Not Everyone Likes the T in LGBT

I am, of course, not the only one to note the glaring differences between homosexual philosophy purportedly based on the body and transgender philosophy not based on the body; and I am not the only one to perceive the grave consequences this presents for women.[21] There is a strong sub-movement—including some feminists and some within the LGBT community itself—that sees incompatible differences between these two divergent philosophies and wishes to disentangle them. One woman from this protesting sub-group is lesbian activist Miriam Ben-Shalom. Addressing the discord between homosexual philosophy and transgender philosophy, Ben-Shalom said, "There are a great many people who are lesbian, who are gay men, who are bisexuals who are not happy with this and who wish the "T" would just go away. Transgender issues are not our issues."[22] When Ben-Shalom was accused of making transphobic and trans-exclusionary statements on her Facebook page she said, "I'll be damned if I'm going to let them co-opt the word 'woman.'"[23] "Don't say I can't use the proper words for my body, because I will." She concluded, "Biology isn't bigotry. Biology is the truth."[24]

Ben-Shalom is joined in this opinion by Mary Lou Singleton, a feminist, pro-abortion activist, and board member of the Women's Liberation Front. Singleton says, "I'm very upset that the gender identity movement has stolen from me a comprehensive name for that group of people that I fight for. Because now I'm being told that it's transphobic to call those people women and girls."[25] Singleton explains, "What we are seeing is the legal erasure of the material reality of sex" and the "complete eradication of any material meaning of female" which leads to the "legal erasure of women and girls."[26] She warns, "If we lose this fight as women, we have lost everything in terms of our legal protections."[27] Singleton concludes, "We are a sexually dimorphic species and that's material reality, and to become untethered from material reality is the definition of insanity."[28] Another woman put it this way, "When gender identity wins, women always lose . . . 'Woman' means something."[29]

According to these women, it appears we are on the cusp of referring to biological females as *the group of people formerly known as women*.[30] The women quoted above assert that crafting laws which unbind the definition of woman from the material body of the woman is an affront to both women and men and serves to remove legal acknowledgment of the two inherent sexes altogether and thus remove legal protections that apply specifically to women. And they are right. All these things can happen when you cease to recognize binary biological sex as manifested by human bodies. But it goes further than that.

Erasing Women

Some have asserted that women themselves are anti-woman and bigoted for daring to question a biological male's status as a woman.[31]

So in the current social climate, not only is claiming one's own genetic ancestry on the cusp of being considered racist, but claiming the parameters of one's own biological sex is now considered bigoted. Transgenderism is fundamentally changing the definition of what it means to be a woman. Or a man. The old definition was the body itself. In the new definition the body is a pliable stage on which to perform what the mind wishes to enact.[32]

It is alarming that the foundational substance of womanhood—the female body—could be so easily dismissed and philosophically discarded. What is often overlooked in the mania of transgenderism, however, is that if women disappear, so do mothers. If there are not two specific, perceivable sexes that can be definitively recognized by law, then it becomes difficult to define or defend mothers in legal terms. Legal movements surrounding transgenderism are setting the stage for the legal marginalization of mothers, fathers, and biological families by force of law.

If maleness and femaleness are not distinct or definable, then neither are fathers or mothers. Mother is a gender-specific word and so is father. If maleness or femaleness don't matter or are, at the very least, fluid, then any title or position that is gender-specific is inconsequential and also fluid. If gender blindness is to be legislated, then gender-specific relationships and the words used to describe them can become discriminatory. If it is legally inappropriate to recognize bodily sex and the ways in which it establishes and defines biological relationships, then family relationships as we know them are not only legally irrelevant but verging on illegal or, at the very least, politically incorrect. And so, what started out masquerading as a celebration of gender turns out to be an edict for the elimination of the sex distinction itself, just as Shulamith Firestone jubilantly proposed.

Disharmony

Eliminating the intrinsic opposition which asserts and perpetuates itself in the form of male and female bodies undercuts the natural voltage that propels and balances the world. As mentioned before, this two-pronged, complementary voltage is often referred to as "yin and yang." The yin and yang philosophy is relevant to transgenderism. It says:

> All things exist as inseparable and contradictory opposites, for example female-male, dark-light and old-young. The two opposites attract and complement each other and, as their symbol illustrates, each side has at its core an element of the other (represented by the small dots). Neither pole is superior to the other and, as an increase in one brings a corresponding decrease in the other, a correct balance between the two poles must be reached in order to achieve harmony.[33]

It could be argued that legally and socially eliminating male and female as the fundamental opposing physical realities in the world is likely to throw the world into a state of disharmony or deep contention. To steep the world in the temperament of contention, it is most effective not only to pit people against each other, but to pit the individual person *against him or herself.* A key way to accomplish this is through the rejection of one's own inborn, physical sex.

Abdication of Posterity

Puberty blockers administered in concert with cross-sex hormones can cause permanent sterility.[34] Thus, the permanent abdication of posterity by young people, who have no way of fully comprehending what that means, is in full swing.[35] Living "authentically" as prescribed by modern transgender sophists can require the surrender of literal parenthood before it even has a chance to begin. This is a jolting turn of events which excludes people from producing or claiming their own posterity and exempts them from experiencing biological parenthood.

This abdication of posterity, in turn, loosens the need for marriage by which women and men are bound to each other and to their literal children as mother and father. "Mother" loses legal meaning because that role is no longer sex-specific and can be filled by anyone. Further, if one's sex and the sex of others is philosophically in flux, marrying someone of the opposite sex or the same sex becomes elusive and increasingly meaningless. Thus, by eliminating the legal and theoretical existence of men and women through gender theory, biological sex is neutralized, marriage is negated, children can be claimed by virtually anyone, and the biological family is disemboweled. Transgenderism accomplishes this by legally and socially redefining the woman—and the man—right out of existence.

Same-sex marriage discounts the sexual diversity that has historically and rationally existed in marriages, but by its very definition same-sex marriage maintains that there is such a thing as "the same" and "the opposite" sex. It maintains that women and men exist inherently and can be discerned from one another. It does *not* maintain that the two diverse sexes are complementary, but it *does* maintain and insist upon the sexual binary. Transgender philosophy on the other hand, balks at binary notions of bodily sex or gender. It discounts and unhinges the veracity of the body and works to accomplish the legal and social abolition of sex distinctions in human beings.[36] In short, same-sex marriage annihilates the idea that men and women are complementary. But transgenderism annihilates the idea that men and women inherently exist at all.

Firestone dreamed that a day would come when "transsexuality would be the norm."[37]

That day is upon us.

CHAPTER THIRTEEN

SOCIALIST FEMINISM AND SAME-SEX MARRIAGE

Most people do not bend the knee to homosexual philosophy or transgender theory with the intent to annihilate the family or explode notions of biological connectedness and belonging. Most people who climb aboard the LGBT express do so with noble intentions. Most fall into one of these categories:

1. They want to be seen as loving people.
2. They want to support the idea of equality.
3. They experience same-sex attraction or gender dysphoria themselves.
4. They have loved ones who experience same-sex attraction or gender dysphoria.
5. They see the family as an oppressive institution and are working to hasten its destruction and pave the way for socialist rule and sexual chaos.

I believe this last group is relatively miniscule. Most people have started down the path of family destruction not fully realizing where the path would lead. I don't believe there are large numbers of people who earnestly believe that motherhood and fatherhood are evil, marriage should be destroyed, sexual chaos is ideal, men are actually women, or children would be better off severing connections to their biological parents and living a sexually free lifestyle rather than living in families. At least not yet.

However, there are some who do passionately believe these things and are working and paying to promote them. And their influence is significant. But where are they? Who are they? Most of the time the engineers behind society-altering movements that seek to annihilate civilized life as we know it prefer to retain a man-behind-the-curtain persona.[1]

Engels and Firestone Resurface Together

One person who is a useful cog in the machinery of the anti-family movement and who has bought into Engels's and Firestone's philosophies hook, line, and sinker is radical feminist and member of the Israeli Parliament Merav Michaeli. Michaeli was included on a panel of six participants in a nationally televised debate in September 2017 concerning whether Australia should adopt same-sex marriage.[2] I cite her here because her arguments bring Engels and Firestone squarely back into the conversation and because her views are representative of the modern feminist, anti-family, anti-marriage movement.

Michaeli openly calls for all governments, religions, and principalities everywhere to "cancel the very concept of marriage."[3] Prompted by the first question in the same-sex marriage debate, Michaeli launched into a retelling of Engels's familiar fable that *men invented marriage to serve their own selfish purposes.* Her next major point was straight from Shulamith Firestone: *Children should have autonomous free choice especially in matters of sex.* She then berates the family as being a place of domination and danger:

> The core family as we know it, unfortunately, it is the least safe place for children. . . . It is exactly those parental rights . . . the total custody that we have in this structure of marriage, which still gives men domination, complete domination over their children . . . [that] is a part of the ongoing hurt in children.[4]

Michaeli continued, "First and foremost, I want to say that I'm all for love . . . but it does not necessarily have to do with who you make a child with, or who you bring it up with. That's one of the things that we need to start breaking apart."[5] It was Shulamith speaking from the grave: *Breaking apart biological ties and the love between mothers and children is the primary objective society must accomplish.* Michaeli said that instead of marriage, the state should endorse child custody agreements wherein "[a] child can have more than two parents; they don't necessarily have to be his biological parents or her biological parents. The person who takes responsibility for the child . . . needs to be obligated for certain criteria that the state should actually decide on."[6]

Three key things must be noted about Michaeli's proposal for child custody agreements. First and foremost, notice that Michaeli is calling for the revocation of mothers' rights to their own children. If you must apply to acquire a child and receive permission from the state to do so, then mothers no longer inherently possess the fruits of their wombs. Likewise, fathers have no recognized claim on the children they produce. In Michaeli's proposed society, mothers' and fathers' inherent biological claims on their children are not recognized by the powers of the state.

Second, Michaeli wants to deregulate marriage while increasing regulation in other areas of life. It's intriguing that early on in the debate Michaeli balked at state registration of marriages, and yet she says that those who want to raise children would need to register with the state and be "obligated for certain criteria that the state should decide on."[7] This would, in fact, be necessary if the family were broken apart as Michaeli and her comrades suggest. If the private sanctuary of family was torn down, virtually everything would become a publicly regulated matter.

Third, Michaeli is redefining the word parent. She wants *parent* to become a nonbiological label. She wants the concepts of mother and father to be replaced by concepts like "custodians," and she wants parental rights to disappear. She wants literal parenthood to be forgotten, abolished, or forbidden. As Michaeli delivers such passionate sermons against the family, Firestone and Engels must be doing synchronized high kicks from the grave and Lewis must be gleefully shaking pom-poms somewhere.

Registering Our Love with the State

The debate about same-sex marriage has been staged in terms of love (*Love Makes a Family, Love Equals Love, Love Wins.*) Michaeli, like others, has criticized marriage because it makes us "register our love" for each other. However, when two people marry, they're not registering that they love each other. We might hope that they love each other, and it might work out best if they do. But this is not why the state has historically required that people publicly register their marriages.

Historically, people who marry have been publicly declaring and registering that they are going to participate in the activity which has the potential to make a child: heterosexual sex. The reason they are required to officially register this information is so that any child they may bring into the world will be most likely to know and be cared for by his or her creators, and the state can hold parents legally responsible for the care of their own children. So, yes, it is good to publicly register marriages before heterosexual sex occurs. That way the majority of children will be born into situations where both of their creators claim them and are publicly committed to caring for them. Therefore, society survives and thrives because babies survive and thrive.

Calculated Convergence

If we look closely, we notice that feminism, socialism, and marriage equality were all symbolically onstage together at this debate. The participants and their cooperating philosophies didn't draw undue attention to themselves. They just got people to clap. Most of the clapping people didn't realize they were clapping for socialism because they don't know that modern feminism, as brazenly embraced by Michaeli's band of sisters, is based largely on the flawed theories of the cofounder of socialism himself, Friedrich Engels. They also apparently don't know that true socialism explicitly calls for the abandonment of marriage, the mandated entrance of women into the workforce, the care of children by the state, and the total estrangement of fathers from their children. They just think it's about equality.

And most people at the debate didn't know that when they were clapping for marriage equality they were clapping for the revocation of children's rights to know their parents, the expansion of surrogacy entailing the purchase of women's bodies for the benefit of men, and the collapse of marriage itself—detonated from the inside.[8] This public convergence of feminism, socialism, and sexually non-diverse marriage on the public stage was no mere happenstance. Michaeli's inclusion on the panel of a national same-sex marriage debate appears to be a carefully orchestrated move meant to further the cluster of philosophies that all desire and require the same thing: the cessation, eradication, cancellation, and annihilation of marriage and the biological family. You will notice that, fortuitously, from the outset of the same-sex marriage debate, the idea was sprung that marriage itself was evil. But for now, if we're going to allow marriage for some people, we have to allow it for all people as a simple matter of human rights.

The Great Question of Civilization

Radical feminism, socialism, and sexual equalism all insist that biological family relationships must be deprioritized or redesigned in order for society to achieve its greatest potential.[9] All three of these cooperating movements require us to answer the same key questions: Should biological relationships initiated through sex, conception, birth, and marriage be recognized and legally protected? Does private possessorship born of umbilical tethering hold the world together, or does it bind, strangle, and choke the life out of humanity?

Philosopher Ludwig von Mises observed, "If history could teach us anything, it would be that private property is inextricably linked with civilization."[10] Socialism, radical feminism, and sexual equalism all call for the restriction and relinquishment of private property starting at its very root: the mother and her child. This being the case, will diminishing the exclusive private rights of the mothers, fathers, and children of the world affect the stability of civilization? This is the grand question. It seems we are on the verge of finding out the answer as we steer increasingly away from biological possessorship and plunge headlong toward nonbiologically engineered families and societies.

But some sages are willing to declare the outcome right now. Mark Dreyfus, another panelist on the Australian same-sex marriage debate, said reassuringly, "I don't think that any dire consequences have befallen any of those countries which have already long since achieved marriage equality."[11] It's possible this man will one day be likened unto a smiling chap on the deck of the *Titanic* saying smugly, "I don't think that any dire consequences have befallen our ship which has long since been hit by a giant iceberg."

CHAPTER FOURTEEN

THE SANITY OF FAMILY

Merav Michaeli insists that a child's own biological family is the most dangerous place for him or her to exist. In her TED Talk, "Cancel Marriage," she said,

> If you thought that this arrangement [marriage] is the best thing for children, think again. I know we live under the impression that the outside world is hostile and dangerous . . . but the truth is that children are most likely to [be] abused sexually, mentally, and physically in their homes, inside their core families formed by marriage where men are patrons over their wives and children.[1]

Similarly, in the same-sex marriage debate Michaeli said, "The core family as we know it, unfortunately, is the least safe place for children . . . The data speaks about every fifth child that goes through some kind of abuse—sexual, physical, emotional." She then says that "the core family is the place" where abuse happens because of "parental rights" and because of "this total custody that we have in this structure of marriage." She concludes that domination by fathers "is part of the ongoing hurt" in the children of the world.

The Least Safe Place for Children?

The purpose of this book is not to explore all data relevant to all the topics raised but rather to expose the underpinnings of philosophies attempting to alter the destiny of humanity by altering the structure of the family. However, even a glance at credible data addressing family structure and child abuse reveals a different picture than the dark and foreboding one Michaeli paints. Dr. Paul Sullins, who has spent his career studying families, observes, "The proposition that the natural family comprising joint married biological parents offers the best context for child well-being and development is among the most strongly attested assertions in all of the social sciences."[2] He continues, "National health surveillance surveys have repeatedly found that children in alternate family arrangements are subject to a wide range of emotional and behavioral problems at higher rates than are children in conjugal families."[3]

In a 2015 cooperative report from Princeton University and the Brookings Institution, David Ribar, from the University of Melbourne, writes:

> Reams of social science and medical research convincingly show that children who are raised by their married, biological parents enjoy better physical, cognitive and emotional outcomes, on average, than children raised in other circumstances. . . . [R]esearchers have been able to make a strong case that marriage has causal impacts on outcomes such as children's schooling, their social and emotional adjustment, and their employment, marriage and mental health as adults.[4]

In 2010, demographers from the Centers for Disease Control reported findings from National Health Information Surveys from 2001 to 2007. They report: "On every indicator examined, children being raised in single mother or blended families exhibited poorer health than those in nuclear families."[5]

Specifically regarding abuse, the 2005 National Incidence Survey reported that children living with married biological parents experienced significantly less physical, sexual, and emotional abuse than children in any other family living situation.[6] In fact, instances of abuse were "three to ten times higher for children not living with married biological parents."[7]

Other studies suggest that one of the most dangerous places for a child to live is with a man who is not the child's biological father. According to a federal study of child abuse and neglect published in 2010:

> Children living with their mother and her boyfriend are about 11 times more likely to be sexually, physically, or emotionally abused than children living with their married biological parents. Likewise, children living with their mother and her boyfriend are six times more likely to be physically, emotionally, or educationally neglected than children living with their married biological parents. In other words, one of the most dangerous places for a child in America to find himself in is a home that includes an unrelated male boyfriend—especially when that boyfriend is left to care for a child by himself.[8]

Children are more likely to stay alive if they are raised by their married parents. Death by killing significantly increases when children live in alternate situations. Social science researcher Dr. W. Bradford Wilcox reports,

> Children are not only more likely to thrive but are also more likely to simply survive when they are raised in an intact home headed by their married parents, rather than in a home headed by a cohabiting couple. For instance, a 2005 study of

fatal child abuse in Missouri found that children living with
their mother's boyfriends were more than 45 times more likely
to be killed than were children living with their married
mother and father.[9]

Scholars from UC Berkeley, Rutgers University, and the Universities
of Texas, Virginia, Minnesota, Chicago, Maryland, and Washington
reported that children who live with their own married parents
generally:

- Live longer, healthier lives both physically and
  psychologically
- Do better in school
- Are more likely to graduate from high school and attend
  college
- Are less likely to live in poverty
- Are less likely to be in trouble with the law
- Are less likely to drink or do drugs
- Are less likely to be violent or sexually active
- Are less likely to be victims of sexual or physical violence
- Are more likely to have a successful marriage when they
  are older[10]

According to Sara McLanahan of Princeton University, evidence
strongly demonstrates that biological parenthood matters to children
regardless of other factors:

Children who grow up in a household with only one biological parent are worse off, on average, than children who grow
up in a household with both of their biological parents,
regardless of the parents' race or educational background,
regardless of whether the parents are married when the child

is born, and regardless of whether the resident parent remarries.[11]

McLanahan further explains,

> If we were asked to design a system for making sure that children's basic needs were met, we would probably come up with something quite similar to the two-parent ideal. Such a design, in theory, would not only ensure that children had access to the time and money of two adults, it also would provide a system of checks and balances that promoted quality parenting. The fact that both parents have a biological connection to the child would increase the likelihood that the parents would identify with the child and be willing to sacrifice for that child, and it would reduce the likelihood that either parent would abuse the child.[12]

These examples barely scratch the surface of the ever-expanding body of evidence demonstrating that living with one's own married, biological parents is consistently the most stable, most prosperous, safest place for a child to live. Family structure does not make "no difference" to a child.[13] The difference is staggering.

Rates of abuse are often low in adoptive families as they are in biologically inherent families. Rates of abuse and neglect in stepparent and foster families are often notably higher. My contention is not that gay or transgender people will be more abusive than other parents. Many gay and transgender people are committed, loving parents. My contention is that abuse and neglect of children will increase generally the more the biologically inherent family model is rejected both in law and by the rising generation.

Further, the question is not whether biology is *all* that matters in families, but rather whether biological connections matter *at all*. Of course, a host of other factors also matter. Simply existing in a biological family is no guarantee against difficulty or abuse, nor does it promise love or happiness. And yet, studies show that biological, married families have consistently produced the best outcomes for men, women, and children on virtually every measurable indicator.[14]

Diamonds

Why do marital and biological connections consistently seem to forge the strongest, most enduring social structures?[15] *Because belonging matters.* Exactly *why* belonging matters is an elusive question. The almost inexplicable phenomenon of marital and biological connectedness and the positive outcomes consistently associated with them are difficult to explain. But perhaps the case of common graphite and diamonds can shed some light on the question. Graphite and diamonds are both made of identical carbon atoms, and yet they are vastly different substances with vastly different properties. One is brittle, and one is almost unbreakable. It has been observed that the divergent properties of graphite and diamonds "do not reside in the carbon atoms; they reside in the *interconnections* between the carbon atoms, or at least arise *because of* the interconnections between the carbon atoms. So similarly, the pattern of connections among people confers upon groups of people different properties."[16]

The pattern of connections around us can include friendships, teams, clubs, religious groups, political parties, critique groups, and support groups. But the family—in its preprogrammed possessiveness, complete with all the pressures and pleasures that come with marital and biological connectedness—is the bond that seems to matter the most. These tenacious bonds extend through, strengthen, and bind all of humanity together, past, present, and future. The biological family is the overarching and undergirding force that forges, fashions, and fires entire societies. If we dislodge, erode, or explode the connections that tie families together or prevent family bonds from forming in the first place—especially bonds between mothers and their children—the structure of the world is laid vulnerable to extraordinary, unprecedented, and astonishing collapse.

Against a landslide of data in favor of the family, modern feminists, socialists, and sexual radicals stubbornly insist that if the biological family is abandoned completely, equality-induced euphoria will engulf the globe. As these zealous disciples continue to toil for the disappearance of motherhood, one is left to wonder what the state of the world might be when mothers are finally thrown on the scrap heap of history. I can imagine no greater hell than a world without mothers.

PART IV

GLOBAL ONSLAUGHT

CHAPTER FIFTEEN

TAKING IT TO THE TOP

The common person does not respond well to direct doses of Shulamith Firestone, Sophie Lewis, or Friedrich Engels. Most people don't think families are the root of all evil, childbearing by women should be eliminated, men should not shoulder any familial responsibilities, redistribution and management of children by the state is a great idea, children should have more sex, or that the only way to save humanity from itself is to annihilate family relationships.

So, if you are a radical feminist, an avowed socialist, or a sexual activist who earnestly believes these things, what can you do? How can you save humanity against its will? If the common person will not listen to you, how can you fundamentally change society? If you cannot start a grassroots movement because the principles you're peddling tend to poison the grass down to the roots, what do you do?

You go to the top. If you cannot start a movement from the bottom up, you enact it from the top down. You could take your caustic ideology to a mayor or a governor or even a president. But if you wanted to wield the widest possible influence, you would go even farther up the chain of command. You would go to where heads of state and their emissaries put their heads together and think great, detached thoughts. You would go there and you would adorn your ideas in the highest and holiest language. You would drape your philosophies with pleasing words and cast them in the most appealing light possible. Then you would introduce your philosophies solemnly to heads of state and you would seat them strategically beside equality, tolerance, and love. You would foster a special friendship between your ideas and women's rights.

The Highest, Holiest Language

The highest and holiest public language of our day is the language of rights. And rights are increasingly regarded as things that emanate from the hallowed halls of the United Nations. If a thing can be officially christened an international human right, then any opposition to that thing is almost automatically seen as barbaric, inhumane, and backward. The appellation of "human right" is among the most persuasive labels in the world, and this designation is sought by virtually any entity that seriously wishes to change the world, especially those who have difficulty doing so by gaining the allegiance of ordinary people.

So, if you wanted to change the world and could not do so on the fruits of your own principles, you would go to the United Nations. And you would begin to leverage the weight of the world's nations—and the money they dispense—in your favor. You would weave your philosophies into every document, treaty, statement, program, and declaration you possibly could. You would ally yourself comfortably with as many diplomats, decision makers, and self-supposed demigods as possible. People intoxicated with the limelight of public service are often easily entreated, and so this is the perfect place to persuade people to your way of thinking, especially if it paints them as progressive, crusaders for women, or champions of equality.

This is precisely where the Shulamith Firestones and Friedrich Engelses of our day have gone. They have taken their cause to the United Nations. And after decades of careful grooming and calculated collusion, they have secured a commanding seat at the global helm and are pulling at the reins of the world. The take-it-to-the-top strategy has been executed with precision, and it's working like a charm.

Unpaid Work and the United Nations

Though many people are largely unaware of the complex workings of the United Nations, the influence of these workings is profound. Massive funding and attention are channeled to particular causes through the UN system, and those causes tend to prosper in the societies of the world.[1] Every spring at the United Nations headquarters in New York City, the Commission on the Status of Women (CSW) negotiates and finalizes an official outcome document. The document is supposed to represent the attitude of the world in regard to women. Women come to the UN from around the globe, absorb the doctrines that are taught, and take these doctrines back to their homelands to advocate for them. The outcome document, though technically nonbinding, is regarded by many as the consensus of the world on the status of women and is imbued with significant influence.

One of the positions UN entities consistently push is that unpaid work constitutes inequality and oppression. As one example of how the socialist, feminist, and equalist movements have infected the UN system and are working to disband family-based living, in March 2017 a paragraph labeled "Unpaid care and domestic work" was proposed for inclusion in the CSW outcome document. It said in part:

> Consider undertaking targeted measures to recognize, reduce and redistribute women's and girls' disproportionate burden of unpaid care and domestic work, by promoting policies and initiatives regarding the construction of national care systems with a gender perspective including reconciliation of work and family life, equal and democratic sharing of responsibilities between women and men, flexibility in

> working arrangements without reductions in labour and
> social protections . . . as well as accessible, affordable and
> quality childcare and care facilities for older persons, per-
> sons with disabilities, persons living with HIV and AIDS
> and all others in need of care, and by challenging social
> norms and gender stereotypes that limit women's roles to
> being mothers and caregivers and promote men's participa-
> tion and responsibilities as fathers and caregivers.[2]

Woven into the sentences above is the deconstruction of the family in the name of freeing the woman. Amongst all the legalese, notice the intent to "redistribute women's and girls' disproportionate burden of unpaid care and domestic work." What does this mean and how is this redistribution to be done? The rest of the paragraph provides answers: by constructing "national care systems" including "quality childcare and care facilities for older persons" and care centers for "all others in need of care." All people needing care (which would include all children) would potentially be redistributed away from private homes and into state-run facilities to receive "quality care." In this way, the private, unregulated sphere of life shrinks away while the publicly planned and scrutinized sphere of life expands exponentially.

Regulating Caring

The task of caretaking is to be transferred from the private sphere to the public sphere, where it is transformed from a work based on love to a work based on money or, at the very least, assignment. In this scenario, every child would theoretically receive care; it would just be cared for by people other than its parents. The same would be true for anyone who needs care. They would likely be put in the care of nonrelatives and monitored by state employees in a state-run facility so "women's and girls' disproportionate burden of unpaid care and domestic work" could be redistributed.

When was the last time you went to a state-run facility and wished you could stay there forever? Do you crave the feelings of warmth, joy, and love you feel when you go to the Department of Motor Vehicles? This is the grand future of the world if the UN gets its way. If the UN gets its way, childhood will become a mammoth stint at the DMV. And so will old age. Caring for the young and the old will not be done out of love, but rather out of a duty to equality and to liberate women from their own children and families.

Of course, care facilities already exist in the free-market system, and people can put their family members in care facilities if they choose. The difference is whether those facilities will be run socialistically by the world's governments or if they will be run by private businesses (functioning on the principle of private belonging established by mothers) wherein competition keeps costs down and quality up. Further, care centers are currently entered into by the choice of the individuals and families involved. There is a strong possibility that putting one's children or others into state care would become mandatory in a planned economy in which socially productive work does not include caring for one's own children.

Familiar Fingerprints

On the topic of unpaid caregiving, Michaeli said, "We need to stop one of the most devastating parts of marriage, which is the unrecognized work that women do in the house and caretaking of children. It is still not recognized in the economy." She echoed this elsewhere, saying, "Above all, we have to . . . abolish marriage because we must make our governments rethink economy to include housework and childcare. This is the fundamental thing that we must change in our lives."[3] She and her like-minded sisters at the UN always get applause from women when they talk this way. Most women applaud because they would like their work to be more appreciated and recognized. And they are not wrong for wanting this; their contributions should be more noticed and more noted. Most women who engage in caregiving sense that the work they do holds the world together. But they scarcely realize that what Michaeli and her fellow crusaders are proposing is not simply recognition for the woman, but abolition of her private position in society, the removal of her own children from her care, the expansion of state regulation, and the shrinking of the private sphere.

What the globalist socialists at the United Nations and elsewhere are talking about when they refer to "redistributing women's and girls' disproportionate burden of unpaid care" is making virtually all roles in society public roles so that all people contribute directly to the economy and to the gross domestic product. They want the public and private spheres to be "reconciled," or in other words equalized, and to fall under the same scrutiny and control.[4] They want to essentially eliminate the private-ness of the private sphere.

Be assured that those who push these positions at the United Nations seek not only to dismantle the privately functioning man-woman-child family as the fundamental unit of society, but to dismantle it and replace it with something else. That something else is global regulation. And if the family ceases to function as the self-regulating, autonomous, productive, private cell within societies, there will indeed be a gaping void in the world, and a global state will attempt to fill it. The United Nations has gathered its weighty coils and is poised to strike at every opportunity to usurp the mighty power that currently rests within the families of the world. When natural disasters, economic crashes, or other calamities occur and the United Nations (or any of its allies) begins to lean in with solutions that reek of socialist domination in the guise of salvation, we can be sure that the snake is about to strike. And we must escape the bite at all costs.

Discussions of unpaid work begin to look benign when compared to other causes United Nations agencies are advancing. The picture becomes more troubling as we move from the realm of work to the realm of sex.

CHAPTER SIXTEEN

SEXUAL RIGHTS AND GENDER EQUALITY

The term "sexual rights" was coined during the latter half of the twentieth century and has been eerily stalking the halls of the UN ever since. Before then, almost no one had heard of sexual rights (also called sexual and reproductive health and rights, and other variations), but now nearly every major event at the Commission on the Status of Women seems to be built around the issue of sexual rights.

Just what exactly are sexual rights? There is no international consensus on what sexual rights are, or if they are even valid rights at all. And yet, the talking heads continue to speak of sexual rights as a noble concept that must be honored by all UN member states and all people everywhere because it supposedly honors, exalts, and empowers women.

International Planned Parenthood Federation (IPPF) is a major player at the United Nations. IPPF pushes for the expansion and endorsement of sexual rights ideology worldwide. IPPF functions in over 170 countries, maintains 65,000 service points, and regularly partners with UN agencies.[1] IPPF says sexual rights "are an evolving set of entitlements related to sexuality that contribute to the freedom, equality and dignity of all people."[2] This lofty-sounding but vague definition leaves the doors wide open for claims as to what sexual rights actually entail. This vagueness is intentional so the phrase sexual rights can be reinterpreted later to mean whatever those at the helm want it to mean.

Although the definition of sexual rights is elusive, these three major elements of the sexual rights agenda consistently surface in UN initiatives and elsewhere:

- The right to *sexual pleasure*[3]
- The right to *sexual information*
- The right to *contraception and abortion*

These sexual rights are promoted in the name of "gender equality." When I first went to the Commission on the Status of Women at the United Nations, this symbol was everywhere:

One might think this symbol simply means men and women should be valued, paid, and respected equally, which they should. But after listening to a few sexual rights presentations at the UN, it became clear that gender equality as represented by this symbol does not mean women and men should be valued equally for their unique and complementary contributions to the world, but rather that women and men have no unique contributions to make. The message is that woman *equals* man, or more pointedly, that woman *is* man. This is problematic because women are not, in fact, men. The fact that there is a huge annual conference at the United Nations convened for the purpose of deliberating on the *status of women* underscores the fact that women are distinct and different from men.

Becoming Like Men

The clearest differences between men and women—and therefore the things that must be crushed so gender equality can be achieved—are the woman's ability to conceive, gestate, bear, and nurse children. These, of course, are the very things that give women natural sovereignty over the people of the world. If humans are to achieve the UN's version of gender equality, it is clear what must happen: the capacities of the woman must be *reduced*. The only way to abolish the inequality created by sexually diverse anatomy is to reduce or eliminate a woman's ability to conceive and bear life so that she becomes barren, just like men.

If taken to its extreme, this position would obliterate human life. But there truly is no other viable option. If equality means sameness, then making women like men is the only avenue to equality. Because you cannot make men like women. Women's ability to harbor and create life can be arrested, suppressed, aborted, and surgically removed so they are more like men, but it is extremely difficult for men to be made into reliable harbors and ports for life.[4]

Those who see women as somehow inferior to men because women can bear children are either oblivious to the obvious or intentionally discounting the production and flourishing of human life as relevant when, in fact, it is a factor so dominant in its importance that it eclipses almost all else. But few women wandering among the endless gender equality banners at the UN realize this fact. They continue to battle ferociously to be like men instead of expecting and demanding that the world see, value, and respond to them as they are: naturally empowered beings who rule civilization through their direct custody of everyone who is ever born.[5]

Elimination of the Sex Distinction through Gender Equality

You will remember that Shulamith Firestone said, "The end goal of feminist revolution must be . . . not just the elimination of male *privilege* but of the sex *distinction* itself."[6] Many efforts at the UN and elsewhere are pushing the world toward legally and culturally eliminating sex distinctions between men and women, propelled by transgender activism and gender equality initiatives. The international push for *gender equality* rather than *women's equality* or *women's and men's equality* is intentional. For decades the terms gender and gender equality have been inserted into numerous UN initiatives, and for decades most everyone assumed that these words simply meant equality between men and women. If this was ever the case, it is no longer the case now. Due to the mainstreaming and increasing codification of transgenderism, the word gender can now be used to encompass gender identity which promotes and protects the ability of individuals to claim they are a gender that is not manifested by their physical bodies.

The international agenda to decimate the distinctions between men and women by co-opting the word gender became clear in March 2019 at the Commission on the Status of Women. South Africa put forward a resolution which claimed to protect the rights of intersex athletes to participate in women's sports.[7] However, the wording in the document could be inclusive of not only intersex persons, but of virtually all men.[8] Revisions to the document that would have clarified that its language would apply *only* to intersex athletes rather than men wishing to infiltrate women's sports in the name of transgenderism were rejected by those pushing the document. This revealed that their true intentions had little to do with intersex people or with sports; the resolution casts a much wider net.

The resolution names numerous UN documents and initiatives that include the word "gender" including: the Universal Declaration of Human Rights and the Convention on the Elimination of All Forms of Discrimination against Women. It also invokes a laundry list of Human Rights Council resolutions, the 2030 Agenda for Sustainable Development, the Sustainable Development Goals, and virtually every UN document that has ever used the word "gender" or addressed "gender discrimination" in any way or form. And this is where it gets tricky.

In listing all these human rights instruments, this resolution seeks to retroactively infuse virtually every previous reference to gender with the meaning of *gender identity*. This means that instead of these instruments protecting the interests of women and girls under the banner of gender equality as they were originally intended to do, they would now protect the interests of men presenting as women and women presenting as men, not only in sports but in virtually every conceivable circumstance. Every country that supports this resolution would essentially be conceding that every document which previously addressed gender was really addressing gender identity. This would serve to forcefully "transgender" any society that adopted the resolution and might subject those societies to gender monitoring by the Human Rights Council.

This is a fantastic bait and switch that weaponizes the word gender—and turns the weapon on women. And thus, under the guise of gender equality, the meaning of woman is disfigured, and women are marginalized in the name of what everyone thought was equality for women.

But perhaps even more stunning than this attempt to turn all previous references to gender on their heads and undo the significance of biological realities is the dramatic transformation of UN Women itself. UN Women is the UN's official body dedicated to advancing women's rights around the globe. But in July 2019, UN Women announced it would no longer focus solely on women's rights, but will focus on "equality of all genders."[9] A representative clarified that this included lesbian, bisexual, gay, transgender, questioning or queer, intersex, pansexual, gender nonconforming, nonbinary, and "the full range of gender diversities that exist."[10]

The UN Women executive director further said that sexual orientation and gender identity are core values of the UN's Sustainable Development Goals. This means that millions of dollars earmarked to further the rights and well-being of women and girls worldwide will likely be hijacked and redistributed to support the cause of transgenderism and gender activism. This bold course change by UN Women represents the official abandonment of women's rights at the highest UN levels and signals the attempted obliteration of biological sex as a meaningful or defensible designation in society.

Gender Equality beyond the UN

Other potent examples of gender abolition in the name of gender equality are popping up everywhere. One is the "rainbow voting agreement" entered into by leaders in the Netherlands. This agreement calls for (among other things) "the registration of gender to be abolished wherever possible."[11] Another example is the banning of the words "he" and "she" by the California state senate committee and instead compelling people to use the pronoun "they" to refer to anyone during committee hearings.[12] Developments such as this are surfacing so frequently now that it is difficult to keep pace with legal and social efforts that seek to forcibly suppress gender.[13]

Another legislative example of gender equality gone awry is a bill introduced in the United States House of Representatives in the spring of 2019. HR5, known as the Equality Act, seeks to amend several previous acts, including the Civil Rights Act of 1964. The Civil Rights Act banned discrimination based on race, color, religion, sex, national origin, and other characteristics. Much like the UN resolution on women's sports, the Equality Act seeks to redefine the meaning of "sex" to include gender identity and seeks to make this definition retroactively effective in a number of previously adopted pieces of legislation.

The Equality Act would work to disallow the legal recognition of biologically female and male people. A member of the House Judiciary Committee made this comment regarding the Equality Act: "HR5 nullifies women and girls as a coherent legal category worthy of legal protection. It ignores fairness and denies science. It exploits stereotypes. Women and children are the collateral damage of HR5."[14] Another critic said that if US law changes according to the dictates of the Equality Act, "[W]e can no longer distinguish females from women with testes for any purpose."[15] This may truly be the case. The Equality Act, which has essentially unanimous support on the Democratic side of the aisle and some support on the Republican side, is so sweeping in its potential effect that it (or future measures like it) could make bodily sex legally irrelevant, negate protections and benefits for women, ensure on-demand abortion sponsored by the state, curtail parental rights, and upend a host of basic societal dynamics.[16]

The Equality Act is essentially an ugly stepsister to the Equal Rights Amendment (ERA) of the 1970s. The ERA has reemerged in the current political landscape and, if adopted at any point in the future, would initiate many of the same outcomes the Equality Act threatens to set in motion. Yet another initiative that could accomplish similar (or perhaps more severe) outcomes is the Convention on the Elimination of all forms of Discrimination Against Women (CEDAW), presented to the United Nations General Assembly in 1979.[17] The United States has thus far chosen not to ratify CEDAW. However, individual cities in the US are beginning to adopt it.

Although these initiatives have been given nice-sounding names ringing of equality, equal rights, and non-discrimination, they all hack at the root of the family: the diversity, complementarity, and necessity of women and men. These examples and others like them represent the ongoing erasure of physical sex as a relevant category in society, which is unavoidably leading to legal erasure not just of women and men, but of mothers and fathers. The legal and social embrace of transgenderism encapsulates the rejection of the human body as inherently manifested in two distinct, complementary forms and can act as a precursor to the legal eradication of the family as the fundamental unit of society.

Do Sexual Rights Achieve Equality for Women Anyway?

Even if there were no nefarious global agenda to unseat womanhood and manhood in the name of gender equality, the supposed rights to abortion and contraception pushed by UN agencies and their partners do not achieve equality for women. The claim that contraception and abortion achieve equality for women is marred by at least two facts. First, abortion and contraception involve risks to women, not men. And second, abortion and contraception are promoted by organizations which earn money from selling abortions and contraception to women; this presents a significant conflict of interests between women and abortion providers wishing to become rich off women's bodies.

What risks does abortion present to women? The risks include hemorrhage, uterine rupture, tearing of the cervix, heart attack, damage to internal organs, future miscarriage, placenta previa in future pregnancies, stillbirth in future pregnancies, sterility, anxiety, depression, increased suicidality,[18] infection, blood clots, and, in rare cases, death.[19] But those who stand to profit from abortion[20] (including abortion clinics, abortionists, and companies that manufacture abortion devices) downplay these risks, insisting that the phrase "safe abortion" be used in UN documents and initiatives.[21] But the fact remains that abortion requires grave risks on the part of women, while men's situation remains largely unchanged. This is not equality.

In addition to the physical risks inherent to abortion and some forms of contraception,[22] easy availability of abortion gives men greater license to sexually dominate women. When abortion is readily available, a man can rest easy knowing that if a woman becomes pregnant because of his actions she can simply have an abortion, and in so doing exercise one of her most celebrated rights—and he will be off the hook. This serves to sexually embolden men and sexually disempower women. This is not equality.

Further, women are situated differently toward their children than men are. A woman cannot simply walk away from her unborn child like a reprobate man can. A woman must act decisively to eliminate her child. Walking away and initiating violent annihilation through abortion are not the same thing. Initiating a fatal act against one's own child can leave a woman with feelings of desolation and emptiness rather than the promised feelings of empowerment.[23] A man who walks away from his unborn baby and his pregnant sexual partner may have a change of heart later in the pregnancy or later in life and decide to return and embrace his child. But for a woman who aborts her child, the consequence of her choice is permanent. There is no going back. Her child is not just out of sight, her child is dead. This is not equality.

Abortion advocates such as International Planned Parenthood Federation assure women it is their empowering right to engage freely in sex with uncommitted men. This is helpful to IPPF's cause because sex must occur in order for babies to be conceived, so that babies can be aborted, so that abortion providers can become rich. And the chance of abortion is often higher if the father is not committed to the baby's mother. Women have been convinced to buy into this system which normalizes sex with uncommitted men and at the same time expects non-fertility and non-childbearing on the part of women. Such a system works against the woman's life-giving anatomy and her innate inclinations to seek stable emotional commitment. It also encourages irresponsibility and promiscuity in men. This is not equality.

Celebrating Coerced Abortion and Population Control

Germaine Greer is one feminist who confronts legalized abortion for what it is. She says,

> What women "won" was the right to undergo invasive procedures in order to terminate unwanted pregnancies, unwanted not just by them but by their parents, their sexual partners, the governments who would not support mothers . . . The crowning insult is that this ordeal is represented to her as some kind of a privilege. Her sad and onerous duty is garbed in the rhetoric of a civil right.[24]

Greer is right. Legalized abortion opens the door for coercion to be loosed on women from outside parties, including the state. Research indicates that nearly two-thirds of abortions in America occur under situations of coercion wherein sexual partners, family members, sexual abusers, or other entities pressure the pregnant woman to abort her child.[25]

The passing of New York's libertine abortion law in January 2019, which essentially allows the extermination of babies up until the moment of birth, (and the lighting of the New York skyline in pink to commemorate the macabre event) was an eerie reminder that the noose of socialistic control is tightening around us while we're celebrating in the name of liberating women. Abortion must be legal in order for governments to foist it upon women in their jurisdictions. Greer predicted the state could and would do so if abortion were legalized. If a truly socialist administration seizes the White House or the highest house of any country, *"regulation of the reproduction of human beings"* through coerced abortion is likely to find its way onto the national agenda as it has in China and elsewhere.[26]

When one excuse to exterminate humans expires or is exposed as dubious, a new idea is invoked in its place. Gender equality, overpopulation, racial superiority, political expediency, saving the whales/owls/trees/ ice caps/polar bears, and women's empowerment all take turns vying for the best reason for limiting, prohibiting, and extinguishing the lives of people and convincing women to be the ones to extinguish it. The most popular reason currently proffered for eliminating humans is the threat of climate change. In fact, "family planning" is near the top of the list of most effective ways to save the world from climate disaster.[27] Family planning, of course, is interpreted by many to include abortion.[28] So the developing agenda is to save the world by killing the people being born into it, which is exactly what China did.

Because of the horrific stories coming from China and elsewhere, most entities are wise enough not to openly promote coercive population control measures or the elimination of babies as a way to save the world. Instead, most activists smile and speak of expanding "family planning" and "educating women."[29] No doubt family planning initiatives going forward will educate girls and women on their responsibility to save the world by eliminating their own children. Some claim that such initiatives would be noncoercive; but as expected, women are already reporting that one of the reasons they are choosing not to bear children is mounting social pressure and social concern about climate change.[30] There is more than one way to coerce a woman onto the abortionist's table.

I said most entities are wise enough not to openly promote coercive population control measures, but the United Nations is not one of them. Every year, the UN bestows Population Awards on people and institutions who champion the United Nations Population Fund's (UNFPA) objectives for managing the world's population.[31] In 2018, the Guttmacher Institute—the pro-abortion research entity that works in cooperation with Planned Parenthood and is named for one of its first presidents—received the award.[32] In 2016, the former executive director of International Planned Parenthood Federation for the Western Hemisphere Region received the award.[33]

But digging into the history of this award a little further, it gets worse. In the mid-1980s, the UN Population Award was given to Prime Minister Indira Gandhi of India and China's family planning chief, Qian Xinzhong. Gandhi's government "was accused of forcing men in villages to undergo sterilization," while China, under Qian Xinzhong's supervision, reportedly used "a system of punishment for couples who have two or more children" wherein women carrying a second child who refused an abortion could lose 20 percent of their pay or perhaps worse.[34] These are the individuals chosen for highest honors by the UN system.[35] The bestowal of these awards gives weighty kudos to those who use coercive measures to force abortion on the women of the world.

In contrast, the Trump administration came out against abortion and continued on that course. In addition to appointing a staunchly pro-life judge to the Supreme Court, in his first days in office President Trump reversed the so-called Mexico City policy, cutting US funding to foreign NGOs that perform or promote abortions. Then, in March 2019, the administration expanded the ban to include NGOs that provide financial support to other groups who provide abortion services or counseling.[36] This essentially shut the back door through which US money was flowing to abortion providers worldwide, including Planned Parenthood. These actions will contribute to the true sexual equalization of women and men, save children, preserve families, and thwart the lethal work of Planned Parenthood.

True Sexual Rights

Do women really have sexual rights? If so, what are they? Since women possess the preeminent right and power to populate, possess, and fundamentally influence the world, women *do* have unique rights related to sex. You will rarely hear these rights discussed at United Nations events, but the women of the world should know what these rights are and should reap the benefits of exercising them. The true sexual rights every woman has are:

- The right to refuse any person sexual access to her body who does not have her immediate and lifelong well-being in mind
- The right to expect a man who desires sexual access to her body to publicly commit to her for life
- The right to hold the man who accesses her womb accountable for claiming and supporting any children who emerge from it
- The right to avoid sexually transmitted diseases, unsupported pregnancies, and damaging emotional entanglements by reserving sexual intimacy for one man who reserves sexual intimacy for her within the parameters of a publicly recognized, lifelong marriage
- The right to expect her fertility, health, and happiness to be top considerations in her sexual relationship with her spouse[37]

- The right to conceive, bear, possess, and raise the children she and her husband create together

These sexual rights best protect women from exploitation, disease, poverty, unsupported pregnancy, and a host of other negative outcomes.[38]

CHAPTER SEVENTEEN

CHILDREN'S SEXUAL RIGHTS

U N agencies have done much good for the children of the world in the decades since the UN was organized, and many UN diplomats and employees oppose the sexualization of children. However, evidence suggests that several key UN agencies have been significantly influenced by the children's sexual rights movement and are, in fact, promoting it.

When most people think of children's rights, they think of protective rights or rights that are meant to protect children. However, there is another view of children's rights heavily promoted by some entities at the United Nations. This position advocates for *autonomous* rights for children. A major element of the children's autonomous rights movement is children's so-called sexual rights.

Children's Sexual Rights & International Planned Parenthood Federation

International Planned Parenthood Federation actively promotes sexual rights for children in cooperation with UNESCO and UNICEF.[1] When I first went to the United Nations, I attended an event sponsored in part by IPPF. In this meeting, there was a post–middle-aged woman with bifocals and short-cropped salt-and-pepper hair sitting a few yards from me. I glanced at her name placard and knew her at once. I had researched IPPF, and this woman was a top player in the organization. I marveled that it was likely this very woman and her IPPF cohorts who created and promoted the 2011 document entitled *Exclaim! Young People's Guide to 'Sexual Rights: An IPPF Declaration.'*[2] I had studied this document in depth. In fact, it was this document that brought me into the arena of children's sexual rights in the first place. It lavishly dresses sexuality and sexual pleasure for children in the high and holy language of rights. Here are some excerpts from that document:

- "Young people are sexual beings. They have sexual needs, desires, fantasies and dreams. It is important for all young people around the world to be able to explore, experience and express their sexualities in healthy, positive, pleasurable and safe ways. This can only happen when young people's sexual rights are guaranteed."[3]
- "Sexuality and sexual pleasure are important parts of being human for everyone—no matter what age, no matter if you're married or not and no matter if you want to have children or not."[4]
- "There is a common misconception that young people are not or should not be sexual beings with the exception of certain groups, such as married young people or young people above a certain age. Sexuality is a central aspect of being human during all phases of each person's life."[5]
- "Governments and leaders have a duty to respect, protect and fulfill all sexual rights for everyone."[6]

You will notice that these statements use the words "everyone," "all people," and "all phases of life" in reference to sexuality. This document does not define the term young people and specifically says that sexual pleasure is an important part of being human "for everyone—no matter what age." This could include minors, young children, and babies. Further, "protect[ing] and fulfil[ling] all sexual rights for everyone" as stated in the document would likely require an overhaul of the sex crime laws of most nations, including abolishment of the age of consent, decriminalizing adult–child sex, legalization of child pornography, legalization of prostitution, and other measures. These developments are in line with Shulamith Firestone's goals for achieving a sexually free and equal society.

Perhaps it doesn't seem plausible that smart, professional human beings would put time and money into promoting sexual rights for children. And yet, the names and logos of top-tier UN agencies including UNICEF, UNFPA, WHO, and UNAIDS all appear on the front cover of *International Technical Guidance on Sexuality Education*, updated by UNESCO in January 2018.[7] This document is laced with references to sexual rights for children, including these statements:

- "[Y]oung people want and need sexuality and sexual health information as early and comprehensively as possible . . ."[8]
- "[E]ach person's decision to be sexually active is a personal one, which can change over time and should be respected *at all times.*"[9]
- Children should have "agency in their own sexual practices and relationships."[10]
- Comprehensive sexuality education can "help children . . . form respectful and healthy relationships with . . . sexual partners."[11]

Contrary to these purportedly rights-based declarations, most parents do not want their children engaging in sex acts or forming relationships with sexual partners because of the physical and psychological risks involved. Further, most major religions teach against engaging in sexual acts outside of marriage. This is where the Convention on the Rights of the Child comes slinking in. I will show you how this works.

The Convention on the Rights of the Child

The Convention on the Rights of the Child (CRC) was drafted at the United Nations in 1989 in the name of protecting the children of the world. However, the CRC provides footing for arguments in favor of children's autonomous rights. The CRC asserts children's rights to:

- "Seek, receive, and impart information and ideas of all kinds"
- Exercise "freedom of association"
- Refuse "arbitrary or unlawful interference with his or her privacy . . . or correspondence"
- Access "information and material from a diversity of national and international sources"
- Access to "the highest attainable standard of health" and "health care services"[12]

While some of these elements can be interpreted in ways that may be beneficial to children, many of them can limit parental influence, endanger children, and advance the cause of children's sexual rights. For instance, if children are to *"receive and impart information and ideas of all kinds through any media of the child's choice"* and are to have *"access to information and material from a diversity of national and international sources,"* this could include a wide variety of troubling and potentially dangerous material, such as pornographic and sexual resources and youth recruiters of all sorts, including terrorist groups and sex-trafficking rings. Further, if children are granted unfettered *"freedom of association"* along with prohibitions on *"interferences with his or her privacy,"* then parents' authority to limit their children's access to certain materials or their association with people they deem detrimental or dangerous to their children would be diminished or demolished in the name of children's rights.

Exploiting Children's Health

The CRC's references to health care services become problematic in an environment that promotes sexual rights for children. Most people would agree that promoting children's health is a worthy goal. But much depends on *who* is deciding *what* is healthy for children. If children have a right to access health care services, then it could be said that children have a right to access anything that is labeled a health care service, including sexual and reproductive health services. The term "sexual and reproductive health and rights" (SRHR) is used repeatedly in UN initiatives. Most entities that promote SRHR support an interpretation of that term that includes abortion and access to virtually all kinds of sexual information.[13] If a child has a right to sexual health services and also has a right to privacy, this can be interpreted to mean that children have the right to access abortion, contraception, and a wide range of sexual information *without the knowledge or interference of their parents.* This is precisely the stance most children's sexual rights activists take.

However, as I said before, most parents do not want their children engaging in sex acts, and most of the world's religions prohibit engaging in sexual acts outside of marriage. Article 24 of the CRC addresses this problem. It says: "States Parties shall take all effective and appropriate measures with a view to abolishing traditional practices prejudicial to the health of children." If experiencing sexual pleasure is important for the health and well-being of children as IPPF and its partners claim it is, then according to the CRC, familial and religious attitudes and practices that place limits on sexual activity for children are prime candidates for being "abolished." The UN's World Health Organization's 2017 framework for sexuality educators specifically says sexuality educators should "demonstrate a positive attitude and respect towards sexuality in children,"[14] "be willing to challenge . . . different cultural and religious backgrounds," and be willing to challenge "parents and colleagues."[15]

Attacks on Parental Rights

UNICEF is a prime partner in the effort to challenge parental rights. UNICEF is the UN agency tasked with protecting the well-being of the world's children, especially children in crisis. In 2016, UNICEF published a document called *Legal Minimum Ages and the Realization of Adolescents' Rights*, which says:

- "States should review and consider allowing children to consent to certain medical treatments and interventions *without the permission of a parent*, caregiver, or guardian, such as HIV testing and sexual and reproductive health services, including education and guidance on sexual health, contraception, and safe abortion."[16]
- "In the area of sexual and reproductive health, the *requirement of parental consent*, especially for information, counseling and testing, *can constitute a significant obstacle to accessing health services.*"[17]
- "When setting a minimum age for medical treatment without parental consent, laws should provide for mechanisms to *waive the minimum* if the adolescent demonstrates adequate maturity and understanding of the implications of the medical decision."[18]

These statements position parents as obstacles to their children's health, make minimum ages essentially meaningless, and negate parents' involvement in their children's medical treatment, especially as related to sexuality.

The UN's World Health Organization (WHO) also advocates for eliminating parental consent in regard to abortion, contraception, and other sexual services for young people. Their 2015 document, *Sexual Health, Human Rights and the Law*, asserts that human rights standards protect "adolescents under 18 from discrimination in accessing both information and services for sexual health" and "require states to guarantee adolescents' rights to privacy and confidentiality by providing sexual and reproductive health services without parental consent."[19]

The United Nations and Child Sex Scandals

Who are the people writing documents and pushing initiatives that advance sexual freedom for children? It is not always easy to connect names and faces to the controversial cause of children's sexual rights, but faces periodically surface in the form of mug shots. In the wake of the #MeToo movement, sexual scandals at the United Nations seem to have erupted at an unusual rate.

Before we delve briefly into the history of UN-connected sexual scandals, it should be stated that not every organization found to have a pedophile or pedophiles in its midst is a pedophilic organization at large, and it could be argued that these examples and others in the UN's history are isolated cases wherein sexual renegades infiltrated the otherwise saintly UN network. However, the ongoing push for children's sexual rights by UNICEF, UNESCO, UNFPA, WHO, and their partners, along with the veritable torrent of sexual abuse allegations gushing from the United Nations, suggests that the problem is systemic, has existed for a very long time, and may be getting worse.

In February 2018, Peter Newell, a children's-rights campaigner who worked extensively for UNICEF, was convicted of three counts of indecent assault and two counts of buggery (sodomy) and sentenced to over six years in jail.[20] In years previous to his employment at UNICEF, Newell reportedly raped a boy over the course of three years beginning when the boy was thirteen; Newell plead guilty to charges against him.[21]

Newell is one of two people listed as authors on UNICEF's *Implementation Handbook for the Convention on the Rights of the Child*.[22] This means that the UN handbook instructing policymakers worldwide on how to implement the Convention on the Rights of the Child was written by a man who committed child rape. This should be a clue, if not a damning indictment, concerning the true nature of the CRC and the intent of at least some of the people promoting it and promoting sexual rights for children.

Additionally, in April 2018 Peter Dalglish, a former senior United Nations official, was arrested in Nepal on suspicion of pedophilia. Dalglish reportedly worked for a number of United Nations agencies over the course of years, including as a child protection advisor for the International Labour Organization.[23] Reports claim Dalglish "offered children foreign trips and better education before sexually abusing them."[24] A statement lodged by one alleged victim indicates that Dalglish may have been exploiting children for a very long period of time.[25] Dalglish was charged with child rape and could face over a decade in prison.[26] However, as of yet it appears no effort has been made by UN entities to discover if there are victims whom Dalglish abused during his tenure at the United Nations.

One of the most egregious incidents of child sex abuse and inadequate response of UN officials to it occurred in the Central African Republic beginning in 2014. An organization called Code Blue Campaign, which works to end impunity for UN-connected sexual abusers, reports that in May 2014 several displaced children disclosed that they and their friends were being raped by international forces in exchange for food.[27] An eleven-year-old boy reported that "a French soldier promised him food in exchange for . . . sex, negotiated with a guard to bring him onto the base, raped him, and then gave him biscuits and cash."[28] One thirteen-year-old boy said he "couldn't number all the times he'd been forced to perform [sex acts] on soldiers."[29] UNICEF staff members in this area found that forced rape of boys ages eight to fifteen had occurred.[30] This disturbing information was allegedly relayed to superiors on multiple occasions as more victims were identified, but Code Blue Campaign reports that little to nothing appears to have been done to stop soldiers from raping children or warn the people in the camp "that sexual predators were disguised as protectors and posed imminent danger to children and other civilians."[31]

One UN official—disturbed by the lack of response by the UN hierarchy to the blatant sexual abuse of children by French peacekeepers—notified French authorities of the alleged abuse so they could pursue appropriate action against the perpetrators and put a stop to the ongoing rape and abuse of children. But incredibly, he was suspended by senior UN figures for allegedly "leaking confidential UN documents and breaching protocols."[32] This scandal along with others has led former UN investigator Peter Gallo to conclude, "There is a shocking disregard for the sexual abuse of children in the UN system at large."[33]

Another UN-related sexual scandal erupted in Haiti, where at least 134 UN peacekeepers from Sri Lanka were accused of sexually abusing nine children in a sex ring from 2004 to 2007.[34] Officers reportedly required sex in exchange for food or money. Investigators reported that one boy said he had sex with more than twenty Sri Lankan peacekeepers. Another boy reported having sex with more than 100 peacekeepers, averaging about four a day over the course of three years beginning when the boy was fifteen.[35]

Further, a series of "food-for-sex" scandals erupted in the early 2000s and the scope of that tragedy continued to unfold through 2006, when UN peacekeepers in Liberia were accused of selling food for sex from girls as young as eight.[36]

In April 2017, news broke of what was dubbed yet another UN child sex ring.[37] A report on the scandal said criminal sexual activity impacting at least twenty-three countries had been discovered, and that "U.N. missions during the past 12 years found nearly 2,000 allegations of sexual abuse and exploitation by peacekeepers and other personnel around the world . . . More than 300 of the allegations involved children."[38]

Another glaring instance of sexual abuse committed by a UN official is the case of Didier Bourguet. Bourguet is a Frenchman who worked for the United Nations in the Democratic Republic of Congo in 2004. Bourguet was head of logistics for peacekeeping efforts in his area and allegedly victimized local children. Bourguet reportedly said it was easy to ensnare his victims because they were starving, and he would give them money in exchange for sex.[39] This situation was not unique to Bourguet. He described a culture of UN workers having sex with prostitutes, young women, and children.[40] And yet, almost unbelievably, reports indicate that "Bourguet remains the only civilian peacekeeper to have been jailed for sexual abuse while working abroad for the UN."[41]

And finally, over thirty years ago, the director of UNICEF for an entire European nation along with his associates was allegedly running a child porn studio—using children they were supposed to be helping—in the basement of a UNICEF facility.[42]

These are just a few incidents in the long and seemingly endless string of sexual allegations against UN-related personnel showing a decades-long pattern of child rape and sexual abuse and lack of substantive action against it by the United Nations. When considering the number of children who may have been victimized worldwide (and who are likely still being exploited now), bear in mind that sexual abuse and rape are consistently underreported. This is especially true in areas of crisis where victims feel their lives may be at stake if they refuse to participate in abuse or if they report those in authority who are abusing them. Some estimate that sexual abuses committed by humanitarian aid workers including UN-connected personnel over the past decade may number in the tens of thousands.[43]

Anthony Banbury, former UN assistant secretary-general for field support, is deeply committed to the UN objectives but has become disenchanted with the UN system due to the mismanagement, disfunction, inefficiency, and sexual corruption he witnessed while working there. His most serious complaint against the UN is the "persistent pattern of rape and abuse" committed by UN peacekeeping troops and the insufficient UN response to it.[44] UN watchdogs at Code Blue Campaign report that "unjust UN policies and practices have, over decades, resulted in a culture of impunity for sexual 'misconduct' ranging from breaches of UN rules to grave crimes."[45] Similarly, Gallo says of some UN personnel, "They're paid enormous salaries for what they do and they're comfortable in their immunity, knowing they won't be caught."[46] Another former UN official who is associated with HearThierCries.org has gone so far as to say, "The United Nations is by far the biggest harborer of pedophiles in the world. They prey on children with alarming regularity during their many years of UN employment throughout the world."[47]

This sinister coalescing of minimal accountability, huge financial reserves, fondness for child sex, and ever-increasing political power at the UN has done harm to the children of the world and threatens to do more.

Diplomatic Immunity

Sadly, the UN system may be a logical place for people interested in sexually victimizing children to place themselves. If a sexual predator wants easy access to helpless victims, an appealing option is to become an official child advocate and put on a blue UN uniform that makes starving, homeless children trust you. A bonus of joining the UN team is not just easy access to victims, but the high probability of escaping punishment due to endless, bureaucratic red tape. The UN can excuse itself from responsibility for the actions of the troops it uses to carry out its peacekeeping missions on the grounds that they are not technically UN employees; they are only soldiers assigned from various countries to fill missions under the umbrella of UN operations. Troops are accountable to the military discipline systems of their own countries for crimes they may commit. To what degree this occurs depends on many factors, including internal corruption.

While peacekeeping troops cannot technically claim immunity for their actions under the auspices of the UN, official UN personnel can. A founding UN document called the Convention on the Privileges and Immunities of the United Nations says UN officials shall "be immune from legal process in respect of words spoken or written and all acts performed by them in their official capacity."[48] Diplomatic immunity is a necessary part of carrying out some political initiatives. However, Gallo believes the immunity loophole is "being grossly abused" in the UN system, allowing offenders at many levels to escape accountability for their actions.[49]

With accusations of child exploitation running rampant and the reputation of the United Nations increasingly in peril, in 2017 UN secretary-general Antonio Guterres admitted, "[S]exual exploitation and abuse is not a problem of peacekeeping, it is a problem of the entire United Nations."[50] To his credit, he then spoke strongly against sexual exploitation and outlined a strategy for combatting it. Unfortunately, critics point out that for at least twenty years the leadership of the UN has known child rape and other sexual offences were being committed by UN personnel and UN partners and have failed to act effectively against it.

Although elements of it sound promising, the strategy going forward offers little in the way of concrete policy changes such as screenings to weed out child predators before they join the UN system or robust protection for whistleblowers. There has been no commitment to permanently waive immunity for child sex crimes or to grant outside entities the power to criminally charge UN staff, peacekeepers, and international NGO staff for crimes involving children. Because these ongoing deficiencies continue to enable abuse of children across the globe, one former UN official says, "The failure to put in place the best possible training, prevention, detection and prosecution mechanisms" is an "inexcusable command failure at the most senior level in the UN."[51]

Commenting on the history of sexual abuse in United Nations peacekeeping efforts, representatives from Code Blue Campaign state,

> Member States have not yet come to the realization that the day of reckoning is approaching. If they do not take the initiative to fully recognize, understand, and solve a problem that

has become an attention-getting Achilles heel, the UN's sexual abuse crisis is likely to reach a pinnacle soon that could hobble the United Nations' ability and authority to perform any of its functions.[52]

The UN's history of sexual scandals involving children is so egregious and is persisting at such a rate that it is threatening the stability and credibility of the entire United Nations system. And yet, as we will see in the coming pages, the UN and its partners continue to relentlessly and recklessly pursue a public campaign to advance sexual rights for children.

CHAPTER EIGHTEEN

COMPREHENSIVE SEXUALITY EDUCATION

After attending several sexual rights events at the UN's Commission on the Status of Women, it becomes clear that a prime weapon in the hands of children's sexual rights advocates is *comprehensive sexuality education*. Many UN agencies are on board with the children's sexual rights movement and seek to advance this movement through comprehensive sexuality education programs. The UNESCO publication *International Technical Guidance on Sexuality Education* unequivocally promotes comprehensive sexuality education for children. This document is endorsed by UNICEF, UNFPA, UNAIDS, and WHO. International Planned Parenthood Federation—the major international entity promoting comprehensive sexuality education for children of all ages—openly partners with UN agencies on sexual rights issues including UNFPA, UNAIDS, UNICEF, UN Women, WHO, and UNESCO.[1]

What *is* the comprehensive sexuality education the UN and its partners are so fond of, and why should we care?[2] The common person might suppose comprehensive sexuality education (CSE) is simply a type of sex ed program that does a thorough job of explaining the biological workings of sex to teenagers with some solid cheers for condoms and STD

The Invincible Family

prevention thrown in. That is how CSE is often marketed, and many people might be just fine with that approach to sex ed. While those things are elements of comprehensive sexuality education, they are only the tip of the iceberg.[3] Although CSE is often wrapped in appealing claims (such as being an age-appropriate sexual disease prevention tool), virtually all CSE programs include some or all of the following elements:[4]

- Present sexual activity to children as their right
- Teach children various ways to obtain sexual pleasure
- Teach children to sexually stimulate themselves
- Present non-vaginal forms of sex to children and teach them these behaviors are safe
- Promote abortion as a right
- Teach gender fluidity and gender theory, wherein the physical body does not indicate maleness or femaleness
- Invite children to question the religious, cultural, and sexual values of their parents and/or community
- Instruct children on how to obtain sexual information and services without parental consent

Because CSE often sounds harmless—and even heroic in many documents that promote it—leaders, legislators, and school officials often adopt CSE programs before fully understanding what CSE curricula contain or the behaviors they promote. CSE programs are sometimes presented under names like human rights education, sexual abuse prevention, life-skills education, or sexual and reproductive health education,[5] but their core philosophies and content remain consistent.

Age-Appropriate?

Those who advocate for CSE often seek to placate parents and policymakers by claiming that CSE is unfailingly age-appropriate. But the things sexual rights advocates consider age-appropriate may surprise you.

For example, the *International Guidelines on Sexuality Education* published by UNESCO in 2009 was intended to guide sex education programs in schools globally. The learning objectives listed in the guidelines for children *ages five through eight* include statements describing how to sexually stimulate one's self.[6] They also teach children, "All people regardless of their health status, religion, origin, race or sexual status can raise a child and give it the love it deserves."[7]

The learning objectives for children *ages nine through twelve* include positive discussion of sexual self-stimulation,[8] give graphic descriptions of various sexual responses,[9] give instruction on condom use,[10] and present legalized abortion as "safe."[11]

The learning objectives for children *ages twelve through fifteen* teach children to "respect" different gender identities,[12] continue positive discussion on abortion,[13] address sexual pleasure with same-sex and opposite-sex partners,[14] and discuss a wide range of sexual behaviors and sex acts including various forms of non-vaginal intercourse.[15] (For a complete review of these guidelines, go to StopCSE.org. I have declined to include actual quotations from the guidelines because of their graphic nature.)

Where did these guidelines come from? One of the authors of the UNESCO guidelines was Nanette Ecker, a former executive at the Sexuality Information and Education Council of the United States (SIECUS).[16] It is worth noting the relationships between SIECUS, Planned Parenthood, UNESCO, and other entities. SIECUS was founded by Mary Calderone, who was previously a medical director at Planned Parenthood Federation of America.[17] A man named Wardell Pomeroy served as an early president of SIECUS.[18] Pomeroy was a colleague of infamous sex researcher Alfred Kinsey and co-authored "Sexual Behavior in the Human Male," which included data on infants and toddlers who were sexually stimulated in the name of research.[19] Pomeroy was dubbed part of the "pro-incest lobby" by *Time* magazine in the 1980s.[20] He made statements such as, "It is time to admit that incest need not be a perversion" and that incest "can sometimes be beneficial."[21] These are some of the people and organizations whose fingerprints are all over the UNESCO guidelines for teaching sexuality to the children of the world through comprehensive sexuality education.

Teaching Consent

Comprehensive sexuality education programs are often promoted on grounds that they teach sexual consent, which will presumably help reduce sexual violence. Many policymakers, school boards, parents, and other gatekeepers assume that sexual consent curriculum focuses on refusal skills that will enable young people to refute unwanted sexual advances. However, teaching *positive consent* is often a major focus of CSE instruction. In other words, CSE often teaches children how to say *yes* to sex and shows them how to negotiate sexual situations. A common classroom strategy is to have a teacher or another student pose as a sexual aggressor or sexual partner, while another student practices giving and getting consent. One worksheet titled "Making Consent Clear" used in a ninth grade CSE class at Acalanes High School in California offered numerous statements such as "Can I take your shirt off?" as good examples of getting or giving sexual consent.[22]

Planned Parenthood Federation of America produced a suite of videos about sexual consent.[23] These consent scenarios communicate that progressing from first kiss to possible sexual engagement in five minutes is healthy and normal, promote homosexual sex, show that sexual activity without long-term familiarity or long-term commitment is the norm, and portray that seeking pleasure is paramount—you just have to make sure your partner consents. These kinds of materials are probably not what most parents and policymakers have in mind when they hear that CSE teaches sexual consent.

Three CSE Programs

It will be helpful at this point to look at excerpts from three CSE programs. The three programs we will briefly review are *It's All One*;

You, Your Life, Your Dreams; and *Rights, Respect, Responsibility (The 3Rs)*.[24] For all three CSE programs reviewed here, I have declined to include the most troubling content so as to spare readers (especially younger readers) from exposure to graphic material. As a resource to help parents and others understand and expose the content of CSE curricula, ProtectChildHealth.org and StopCSE.org offer extensive information on many CSE programs. These sites also include an essential documentary titled *The War on Children* which exposes the international effort to advance CSE and shows what can be done about it.

It's All One

The *It's All One* comprehensive sexuality education program was developed in cooperation with International Planned Parenthood Federation and has been promoted by UNESCO and UNFPA as a premiere model for sexuality education.[25] The stated goal of the program is "to enable young people to enjoy—and advocate for their rights to—dignity, equality, and healthy, responsible, and satisfying sexual lives."[26] *It's All One* is intended for youth aged fifteen and older and includes suggestions for adapting the lessons to children as young as ten.

The *It's All One* curriculum:

- Has an intensive focus on sexual pleasure, mentioning sexual pleasure over sixty times, and consistently presenting sexual pleasure as a right. The curriculum says "there is no right age to have sex" and that each person can determine when he or she "feels ready" for sex.
- Aggressively promotes abortion, mentioning abortion over one hundred times. It frames pregnancy as a dangerous condition while portraying abortion as "safe." One activity titled "Walking in Her Shoes" requires students to read case studies wherein women chose to abort their babies.[27]
- Includes extensive instruction on positive sexual consent.[28]

- Includes graphic instructions for condom use featuring sex between unmarried partners.[29]
- Extensively promotes sexual self-stimulation as a positive, healthy, normal, expected, and frequent behavior.[30]
- Normalizes a wide range of sexual behaviors and sex acts including various forms of non-vaginal sex.[31]
- States that it "provides a basis for extending sexuality . . . education into civics, social studies, and language-arts classrooms." This means that CSE is designed to be taught not only in health classes but addressed and reinforced in virtually all school subjects through sexually focused and sexually inclusive literature, examples, and role-plays.

One section on sexual expression and enjoyment in *It's All One* says: "Public health and rights organizations have issued declarations regarding the rights of all persons to sexual expression. These rights include the right to seek pleasure in the context of safety and of mutual and meaningful consent."[32]

It's All One ends with a section titled "Advocating for Sexual and Reproductive Health, Rights, and Gender Equality," which trains young people to become sexual rights activists. The Additional Resources section refers to the most aggressive abortion and sexual rights and CSE advocacy groups in the world including IPPF and SIECUS.

In March 2018 Christopher Castle, UNESCO chief of section for Health and Education, enthusiastically recommended the *It's All One* curriculum and said the updated 2018 UNESCO *International Technical Guidance on Sexuality Education* is specifically designed to align with *It's All One*.[33] Castle further said that it is a common misconception that CSE-type programs "would lead to increased sexual activity and risk taking" in youth.[34] However, during the same event Castle said, "We cannot just provide knowledge without having youth-friendly sexual and reproductive health services available. We are going to create demand by doing comprehensive sexuality education. So, these services have to be available."[35] Similarly, UNESCO's 2018 *International Technical Guidance on Sexuality Education* says: "There is a need to generate evidence to demonstrate . . . the demand creation potential of CSE and the provision of youth-friendly SRHR services."[36] Comprehensive sexuality education will most assuredly create demand for the very services IPPF and other sexual rights organizations just happen to provide. That's why they promote CSE so enthusiastically. Expanding their revenue depends on it.

IPPF says it "puts young people at the centre of everything we do"[37] and explains that doing so "provides a unique opportunity to shape the behaviour and attitudes" of young people "for life."[38] IPPF further says, "IPPF is putting young people at the heart of its services: with them, *we want to change social norms and guarantee their rights.*"[39] Steeping children in sexual rights rhetoric while they are young is indeed the best way to change the sexual norms in society. And if you are a sexual services provider like IPPF, it is also the best way to profit off children as early as possible and gain sexual clients for life. The sooner a child becomes sexually active the sooner he or she will seek the services IPPF and its member associations offer, including contraceptives, STI testing, and abortion.[40] Further, the new lucrative opportunity for IPPF and its member associations is dispensing cross-sex hormones to those who have been spoon-fed transgender ideology in their youth and rejected their own bodies.[41]

You, Your Life, Your Dreams

A second example of CSE curriculum is *You, Your Life, Your Dreams*. This program is a recommended resource for Caribbean countries as part of the Health & Family Life Education project, whose partners include UNFPA, UNICEF, and UNESCO. *You, Your Life, Your Dreams* is designed for adolescents aged ten to nineteen.

The *You, Your Life, Your Dreams* curriculum:

- Normalizes engaging with multiple sex partners and encourages calculated risk-taking:[42] "Taking risks is not necessarily bad, but it is important that we take calculated risks that we can handle. To do this, we must have enough information to evaluate the risk, try to anticipate the consequences of our decisions, and trust in our own capacities to respond responsibly . . . One important sign of maturity is to be aware of our abilities and limits, and to take calculated risks."[43]

- States, "Every person is a sexual being from birth until death" and describes with numerous examples what it can mean to be "sexual."[44]
- Promotes contraception, emergency contraception, and abortion as safe without discussing risks and possible side effects."[45]
- Includes extensive promotion of sexual self-stimulation as a safe-sex technique and offers explicit descriptions of physical sexual responses and sexual behaviors.[46]
- Introduces a wide range of sexual practices to children: "Did you know that there are other types of sex and intercourse besides vaginal sex? Vaginal sex is the best-known type of sexual practice. But there are other kinds such as. . . ." The curriculum then provides graphic descriptions of non-vaginal sex acts.[47]
- Includes graphic illustrations of people without clothing on and condom use.
- Promotes sexual and reproductive rights for minors: "All adolescents should be able to make decisions about their sexuality and decide without pressure whether or not to have sex, and when and whether or not to have children. To do this, young people need access to information, counseling, and health care services."[48] "Our sexual and reproductive rights include having access to this information and to appropriate health services."[49]

Rights, Respect, Responsibility (The 3Rs)

The 3Rs curriculum is designed for children grades K–12 and is produced by Advocates for Youth, which refers youth directly to Planned Parenthood to obtain services.

The 3Rs curriculum:

- Includes role-plays that portray and promote sexual relationships between unmarried young people. Here is one example: "Andrea and Diana are two girls who just met last weekend at a party. They had fun together, and now they've hooked up again this weekend. They're alone in Andrea's basement. Plan a role-play in which Diana asks Andrea about having sex and they make a decision."[50]

- Actively teaches gender ideology. It states that one core objective of the curriculum is to help children "challenge the gender norms that have been taught to them from their earliest ages."[51] It explains that using the words male and female is incorrect. It teaches: "You may commonly hear people refer to just being 'male' or 'female,' but the correct term is 'cisgender.' For some people, what they see in the mirror and how they feel on the inside are different. This is called being 'transgender.'"[52]

- Reinforces children's rights to privacy involving sexual choices and services, reiterating that "You have a right to privacy and confidential sexual health care."[53]

Among a wide range of other things—which, for the sake of discretion, we will not explore here—the 3Rs contains the top two elements the United Nations Fund for Population Activities says are essential components of comprehensive sexuality education:

1. "A basis in the core universal values of human rights."
2. "An integrated focus on gender."[54]

Teaching sex from a human rights perspective can include teaching children that it is their "human right" to access virtually all forms of sexual information, sexual pleasure, and sexual services. Teaching sexuality with "an integrated focus on gender" can include instruction that promulgates decimation of gender norms and the rejection of the concept of male and female as manifested by the physical body. In short, these two components are designed to promote the position that sex should be presented to children as a human right and that the sexual and other differences between males and females should be explored, obscured, and, finally, obliterated in the name of inclusiveness and equality.

No matter what other elements CSE programs do or do not contain, the inclusion of these two components in CSE curriculum is sufficient to radically influence the mindset of the rising generation such that they are likely to: 1) Demand sex and sexual services as their right (which will enrich sexual service providers, proliferate disease, and weaken families), and 2) Reject biological sex as a relevant characteristic indicative of one's identity. At its core, this mindset rejects the biological family—based on physiologically oppositional sex—as the fundamental unit of society.

Both IPPF and SIECUS support human rights–based CSE programs such as *It's All One*; *You, Your Life, Your Dreams*; and *Rights, Respect, Responsibility* because they are key to helping them achieve their core objective. SIECUS's stated objective for society is to "dismantle the systems of power and oppression which perpetuate . . . stigma and shame around sex and sexuality across the intersections of age, race, size, gender, gender identity and expression, class, sexual orientation, and ability."[55] In other words, SIECUS supports teaching sexual education to children from a sexual rights perspective in order to dismantle virtually all sexual boundaries in society. The systems that best hold these sexual boundaries in place include families, religious institutions, cultural traditions, and laws. All of these can be and often are framed as enemies to children's sexual rights.

CSE as a Vehicle to Social Change

The aggressive form of CSE currently emerging is meant to address much more than just sexual education or sexual health. SIECUS interim president and CEO Christine Soyong Harley says, "Sex ed is a vehicle for social change," and explains the intended, long-term social impact of CSE:

> While sex education is a necessary sexual health tool, it can (and should) be so much more than that. With sex education, we have a golden opportunity to create a culture shift—tackling the misinformation, shame, and stigma that create the basis for many of today's sexual and reproductive health and rights issues, like: reproductive justice, LGBTQ equality, sexual violence prevention, gender equity, dismantling white supremacy.[56]

She continues, "[CSE] is more than just teaching young people how to have safer sex. It's also key to dismantling the systems of power, oppression, and misinformation that allow today's biggest sexual and reproductive health and rights injustices to exist in the first place."[57] Another advocate for CSE said, "If everyone received CSE, we would see a world where systems of patriarchy, white supremacy, and cisheterosexism cannot continue to thrive."[58]

The phrases "dismantling the systems of power and oppression" and eliminating "systems of patriarchy" are veiled references to the destruction of the family, as well as a host of other things including the decimation of capitalistic economies and the freedoms that come with them. According to Firestone—and her devoted descendants at SIECUS and Planned Parenthood—the biological, heterosexual family operating under circumstances of economic freedom is the root of all oppression and injustice. And, by their own admission, they intend to push this philosophical position to the youth of the world through comprehensive sexuality education, and thus effect radical social change.

One key social change the UN's World Health Organization and other organizations are advocating for is the decriminalization of "sex work" (i.e., prostitution.)[59] A closely related social change Planned Parenthood and other entities advocate for is lowering the age of sexual consent for children.[60] If pursued, these two intersecting efforts could lead to legalized prostitution for children in the name of equality and children's sexual rights.

Conflicting Claims about CSE

Many entities including UNFPA claim that receiving CSE is a human right for all children. UNFPA says, "The right to comprehensive and non-discriminatory sexuality education is based on rights protected by several human rights agreements."[61] However, despite repeated claims that CSE is a human right, at present *there are no binding UN documents or treaties that provide a right to CSE*. The documents cited by UNFPA in support of CSE are not binding treaties ratified by the UN body. They are either nonbinding resolutions that were negotiated by a subset of UN member states or nonbinding references to CSE by various entities.[62] In 2010, the report of the UN Special Rapporteur on the right to education to the General Assembly unilaterally and grandiosely declared sexuality education a "human right in itself."[63] And predictably, UNFPA has specifically used the Convention on the Rights of the Child to claim that children have a human right to CSE based on their right to health services.[64]

Advocates of CSE often claim that it is a surefire way to reduce sexually transmitted diseases, reduce pregnancy, and increase consistent condom use. But a report issued by the Institute for Research and Evaluation (IRE) examining sixty studies of US school-based CSE programs shows overwhelming evidence that CSE programs frequently fail to achieve their core objectives.[65] The IRE report says:

> For U.S. school-based CSE programs, we found no evidence of effectiveness at producing sustained reductions in teen

pregnancy (0 programs) or STDs (0 programs). . . . CSE failure rates at producing sustained effects on targeted outcomes included 88% failure to delay teen sexual initiation and 94% failure to reduce unprotected sex.[66]

Further, UNESCO's own 2018 *International Technical Guidance on Sexuality Education* reports that over 50 percent of CSE programs reviewed for their research had "no significant impact" whatsoever on the following factors: delayed initiation of sex, frequency of sex, number of sexual partners, condom use, and contraception use.[67] UNESCO further admits that the studies utilized for their research used small sample sizes, allowed for participants up to age twenty-four in some cases, measured outcomes of CSE programs for as little as three months after program participation, and had other significant weaknesses.[68] This information is buried in Appendix IV, surrounded by pages of dense language.

But most concerning of all is that despite widespread claims that CSE will reduce sexual disease in youth, UNESCO itself admits there is virtually no evidence base for this claim. The UNESCO sexuality education document itself says, "It is difficult to draw strong conclusions about the impact of CSE on biological outcomes such as STI or HIV rates, as there are still relatively few high-quality trials available." The strongest statement UNESCO is able to muster about CSE and rates of sexual disease is that CSE is "likely to have the desired positive effect on young people's health."[69] In other words, arguably the top promoter of CSE in the world with millions of dollars at its disposal and enormous influence worldwide cannot demonstrate with credible data that CSE consistently reduces sexually transmitted infections. Despite conflicting claims and data, many UN member states have adopted CSE and are firmly on board with the children's sexual rights movement.[70]

To be fair, not *all* material in CSE programs is objectionable or harmful. Some elements of it can be appropriate or helpful. However, the fact that it is laced with children's sexual rights rhetoric, graphic sexual content, gender ideology, and promotion of sexual risk-taking makes it unsuitable for consumption by children.

Despite the advancement of CSE on many fronts, it must be noted that many informed, unwavering United Nations diplomats from countries around the world oppose the sexualization of children. They have been working tirelessly for years—along with the NGOs who support them—to keep language out of consensus documents that would foist early sexualization on children through CSE, undercut parental rights, and erode the family unit. We owe them a great deal for their persistence in holding the international tide of sexual rights at bay, which is becoming an increasingly ferocious battle.[71]

The United States and CSE at the United Nations

Under the Obama administration, the United States was one of the strongest advocates *for* comprehensive sexuality education at the United Nations table. Under the Trump administration this changed dramatically, with the US taking a firm stance *against* CSE at the United Nations and in domestic policy. From 2017 onward, the administration favored sexual risk avoidance (SRA) programs that stress the well-documented benefits of sexual abstinence for teens and children.[72] Further, the Trump administration's expansion of the Mexico City policy which defunds NGOs that provide or promote abortion strikes a direct blow to the biggest promoter and provider of comprehensive sexuality education in the world: International Planned Parenthood Federation. This is among the most effective actions the US administration could have taken to impede the spread of comprehensive sexuality education and, with it, gender ideology, promotion of abortion, and promulgation of a sexual-rights mentality to children around the globe. Additionally, the Trump administration transformed the US' relationship with the United Nations by seeking to remove funding for programs that run afoul of US interests, withdrawing the US from UNESCO, and appointing a pro-life UN delegation.

Five Things

The unabashed endorsement of sexual rights for children by UN agencies and their partners, the UN-backed push for CSE to be administered to every child, the UNICEF assault on parental rights, and the troubling history of child sexual abuse oozing forth from the United Nations should galvanize us to do the following five things:

- Withdraw funding for all UN agencies and NGOs that produce or promote materials that seek to advance sexual rights for children, including International Planned Parenthood Federation
- Support the US Congress in declining to ratify the Convention on the Rights of the Child
- Remove sexual rights advocates and sexual service providers—including International Planned Parenthood Federation and its affiliates—from all school programs
- Bring UN child predators to justice and support reforms that will reduce the likelihood of sexual abuses being committed by UN-connected personnel
- Reject comprehensive sexuality education in all forms, from local schools to national programs to the United Nations. Support and fund sexual risk avoidance (SRA) programing for youth.

If UNESCO, UNICEF, UNFPA, or other UN agencies wish to clarify that they do not support the children's sexual rights agenda—including the right of non-parental entities to teach children to sexually stimulate themselves, to teach children various ways to experience sexual pleasure, and to administer medical procedures to children without their parents' consent—they will swiftly and completely withdraw all UN statements, programs, and initiatives that promote sexual rights for children and will cut all ties with entities that promote children's sexual rights.

Don't hold your breath. Gaining intellectual and sexual control of the youth of the world is at the very core of their agenda.

CHAPTER NINETEEN

THE GLOBAL HIJACKING OF EDUCATION

Since my introduction to the children's sexual rights movement some years ago, I have become increasingly aware of the global machinery in place to advance it. There are numerous ways the UN laces its fingers through the workings of the world and reaches into the minds of children. This chapter exposes only one. It just happens to be an especially insidious and effective one. UN agencies and their partners are working to infiltrate and dominate the education systems of the world, which will enable them to deliver comprehensive sexuality education—in tandem with socialist and feminist philosophies— to youth around the globe.

This chart shows the formidable delivery line running from the United Nations to your child's classroom:[1]

UN agencies promote sexual rights for children

⬇

UN Sustainable Development Goals

⬇

Organization for Economic Cooperation and Development
Reinforces UN ideologies

⬇

Incheon Declaration

⬇

Global Partnership for Education

⬇

Your child's school
Entities above partner with national and local organizations
to bring UN-based education to your community

UN Agencies, the Sustainable Development Goals, and Comprehensive Sexuality Education

The UN infiltration of the education systems of the world is a complex issue with many intertwining tentacles; we will explore only a few strands of the tangled mix. First, I must make an important clarification. Technology and the global connection it brings is a good thing, even a wondrous thing. The shrinking of the world and the softening of the natural barriers in it through technology is a brilliant and liberating advancement that enhances and enriches the world. Education through *global connection* is good. Education through *global direction* is bad. And there is a big difference between the two.

This chapter will address the elements in the chart above from the top down. At the top of the global education regime is UNESCO, the United Nations Educational, Scientific, and Cultural Organization.

UNESCO considers itself the education czar of the world. UNESCO is one of the prime supporters of comprehensive sexuality education for children and, as mentioned before, partners with the International Planned Parenthood Federation.[2] UNESCO has formed other partnerships with entities worldwide with the intent to implement the UN's Sustainable Development Goals on a massive scale.

The Sustainable Development Goals (second tier down on the chart above) are the objectives UN member states agree upon that will guide their efforts and direct their funding for the next fifteen years. The current Sustainable Development Goals (SDGs) were renegotiated in 2015, and the UN and its partners are working to accomplish them by 2030.[3] In large part, the SDGs are noble goals (zero hunger, no poverty, quality education, clean water, etc.). However, the manner in which the goals will be pursued is the question. Will they be pursued by giving individuals, families, and nations the greatest degree of freedom and personal stewardship possible in meeting their own needs? Or will the SDGs be pursued through the globalization and domination of virtually all systems of civilization in the name of global equality?

After ferocious negotiations, the phrase "comprehensive sexuality education" was kept out of the SDGs. However, CSE is being promoted through SDG goals like "Good Health and Well-being." This goal states in part: "By 2030, ensure universal access to sexual and reproductive health-care services, including for family planning, information and education, and the integration of reproductive health into national strategies and programmes."[4] This is interpreted by many to mean ensuring universal access to abortion, contraception, and comprehensive sexuality education. Another goal is, "Quality Education: Ensure inclusive and equitable quality education and promote lifelong opportunities for all."[5] Many are claiming that CSE is a crucial part of children's quality education; therefore, children have a right to receive CSE through the education systems of the world,[6] and the sexual rights entourage, with UNESCO in the lead, is prepared to give it to them.

The Organization for Economic Cooperation and Development (OECD)

We are down to tier three on the delivery line from UNESCO to your child's school. This third level involves multiple initiatives including global data collection; individualized student assessments; social and emotional manipulation of students; the fracturing of familial loyalties; the encroachment of socialist, feminist, and globalist ideologies; and the global spread of CSE.

How is UNESCO going to educate the entire world and fulfill all children's purported rights to comprehensive sexuality education? The broad answer is: through technology-based, global curriculum and testing. A more specific answer is: through the Organization for Economic Cooperation and Development (OECD). The OECD is a group of over thirty-five nations, including the United States, that ostensibly works to improve the economic well-being of the world. The OECD has done this, in the decades since it was organized, in the name of helping countries recover from the devastation of World War II. However, the focus of the OECD has changed significantly in recent decades. The OECD is a member of the UN Global Compact and is accordingly committed to "take strategic actions to advance . . . the UN Sustainable Development Goals."[7] The OECD openly partners with at least seven UN entities, including UNESCO.[8] Additionally, the OECD has reportedly collaborated with International Planned Parenthood Federation[9] and with the Open Society Foundations founded by billionaire and leftist political activist George Soros.[10] It has also reportedly received funding from the Bill and Melinda Gates Foundation.[11]

The OECD has traditionally claimed to support democracy and free markets. However, as it deepens its ties with the United Nations and other partners, its aims appear to be evolving. The OECD's *The Future of Education and Skills: Education 2030* document, published in 2018, says, "Children entering school in 2018 . . . will need to value common prosperity, sustainability and well-being" above other concerns and "curricula should continue to evolve, perhaps in radical ways" that "reflect evolving societal requirements." The OECD cites three major issues global education will focus on:

1. **Environmentalism** focusing on "climate change and the depletion of natural resources which require urgent action and adaptation."
2. **Economic change** requiring "new economic, social and institutional models."
3. **Social evolution** arising from "cultural diversity."[12]

Encapsulated in these three points are the seeds of the global takeover of energy resources and population regulation, transition from capitalism to more "equitable" economic models (i.e., socialism), and the intentional rise of sexually diverse culture.[13] The OECD declares that it "contributes to the UN 2030 Global Goals for Sustainable Development aiming to ensure the sustainability of people, profit, planet and peace, through partnership."[14] One does not need to read between the lines to see the socialist equality rhetoric dripping from the mouth of the global education regime.[15]

Andreas Schleicher, director of the OECD Directorate for Education and Skills, says that achieving the SDGs "will depend on today's classrooms; and it is educators who hold the key to ensuring that the SDGs become a real social contract with citizens."[16] Further, in its *Global Competency for an Inclusive World* document, the OECD says the following:[17]

- "The skills, attitudes and values that shape human behavior should be rethought, to counter the *discriminatory behaviors picked up at school and in the family*."[18]
- "All young people should be able to challenge cultural and gender stereotypes, to reflect on the causes and solutions of racial, religious and hate violence and to help create tolerant, integrated societies."[19]

This is a stunning admission. The OECD intends to foster widespread rethinking of the values children learn in their families in order to uproot gender and cultural stereotypes. The OECD specifically says it has made LGBT inclusivity a priority[20] and is working to create tools for measuring (and reducing) "homo-, trans- and intersexphobia" across the globe.[21]

Programme for International Student Assessment & Social and Emotional Learning

One of the OECD's major initiatives is facilitating assessments and data collection in schools all over the world. The data it collects can be used to assess how inclusive and equitable education systems are and how inclusive and equitable individual students are in their attitudes and actions.[22] This information can then be utilized in crafting individualized online interactions that incrementally craft students into good global citizens. Good global citizens are those who display the values and attitudes the global system would like them to display. This, of course, can include the sexual attitudes UN agencies promote.

Schleicher says the OECD student assessment tool known as PISA (Programme for International Student Assessment) was inspired by SDG 4 (Ensure inclusive and equitable quality education for all), and its aim is to pursue "global competence" and promote "living together sustainably."[23] These are nice-sounding phrases. However, they are used to push globally aligned initiatives designed to ensure children are taught the same things, believe the same things, and act the same way so as to ensure socialistic equity and inclusiveness for everyone according to what the UN global education czars deem equitable and inclusive.

Understanding the impact and the strategy behind OECD-led assessments such as PISA is key. PISA assessments are administered to schoolchildren throughout the world at certain ages. The results are then made public and the nations of the world can be ranked on their PISA standings. When OECD's PISA testing initiative was first implemented in 2000, it was strictly an academic skills yardstick. It would assess the academic achievement of students in various nations so as to promote greater academic achievement across the board. However, in 2015 the OECD switched its emphasis.[24] PISA testing began assessing not only the academic progress of children but the social and emotional skills of children.[25]

This switch from academic testing to social and emotional testing was a wily move on the part of the OECD and its UN partners. Since virtually everyone is in favor of increasing children's social and emotional skills, that line was sold to schools with relative ease. Most everyone thought the goal was simply to emphasize kindness and social acuity in children. But then the OECD's definition of social and emotional skills began to evolve. Instead of referring to universal things such as kindness, empathy, and relating well to others in your peer group, the term *social and emotional skills* also began to refer to what were dubbed *global social skills* including students' "attitudes and values" in relation to social issues.[26] As the scope of UN-defined "global social skills" expands, it is primed to include attitudes on environmentalism, weapons control, the role of government, family structure, sexual rights, gender expression, national sovereignty, parental rights, religion, equality, and virtually any other social issue. This cunning expansion to assessing social attitudes in addition to social skills enables the grooming of UN-proscribed socialist, feminist, sexual equalist attitudes in children worldwide.

In addition to PISA tests, the OECD also uses other tools, such as the Study on Social and Emotional Skills (SSES).[27] The OECD says of its SSES international survey:

> Apart from examining the level of children's socio-emotional skills, the study will gather information on their family, school and community learning contexts, thus aiming to provide information about the conditions and practices that foster or hinder the development of these critical skills.[28]

This statement discloses that the OECD intends to ask children questions that will enable the "gathering [of] information on their family." This data can be used to help socialist education monitors dissect how elements of a child's family life foster or hinder the development of the global skills and attitudes the UN and the OECD wish to foster in children. This tactic of asking students probing questions to assess elements of their family life is a classic socialist technique. It is often used to pit children against their families, fracture cultural alliances, and expose religious loyalties.

Defining Social and Emotional Skills

The OECD's measurements for social and emotional competency are:

- Openness to experience (open-mindedness)
- Conscientiousness (task performance)
- Emotional stability (emotional regulation)
- Extraversion (engaging with others)
- Agreeableness (collaboration)[29]

These benchmarks are common in psychological circles, and proper, balanced mastery of these factors could lead a person to much success and satisfaction in life. However, a great deal depends on *who is defining these terms* and *how they are measured*. If open-mindedness in matters of sex, religion, moral dilemmas, and social norms is to be assessed, then the definition of open-mindedness becomes key. For instance, if people or organizations who favor a sexually open society and wish to advance sexual rights for children are at the helm, openness could mean something very different for them than it would for, say, most parents. Likewise, agreeableness can mean different things to different people. It might seem disagreeable for a student to maintain his convictions on a particular issue—for instance, the role and definition of marriage in society—in the face of opposition, derision, or conflict.

Like open-mindedness and agreeableness, equitable and inclusive are elastic terms open to a wide range of interpretations. If deference to equity or equality is required, then young people who embrace the concept of free market systems wherein inequalities are allowed may be tagged as harboring attitudes that are unacceptably inequitable and targeted for reeducation. If inclusiveness is applied to matters of sex, then holding specific beliefs about sexual conduct may be assessed as noninclusive and therefore undesirable. In fact, "inclusivity" is commonly used to express acceptance of sexual variance.

Assessing the Terms through Data Collection

A partnership between UNESCO, Cisco, Intel, Microsoft, and the International Society for Technology in Education (ISTE) is poised to extend the reach of the United Nations through personalized data collection in schools.[30] The CEO of ISTE says personalized curriculum-embedded assessments in schools can collect "hundreds of thousands" of data points on every child.[31] Data-gathering assessments and curricula can be personalized to track and influence each student over his or her lifetime.

Computer-adaptive data assessments can be useful. They can respond to each individual student's academic footprint and track each student over time. These adaptive systems can tell if a student is struggling with a certain concept and can help him or her master the concept by repeating it or presenting it in different ways. For instance, if a student consistently hesitates before answering 8×12 or consistently answers it incorrectly, a personalized learning system can reintroduce the problem in a different form until the student assimilates the concept and can respond quickly and correctly. This is useful. However, the same thing could be done with other skills, values, or attitudes the designers of systems wish to impact. For instance, if a student consistently answers "incorrectly" on questions that require deference to an economic equality mindset or a sexual rights mindset or any mindset the learning system prescribes, then the system can subtly or not so subtly reintroduce those concepts in different forms or different contexts until the student answers "correctly" and internalizes the desired ideal. The student must conform in order to get the answer "right." This in turn helps his or her school and nation get good marks on the global report card.

If a nation's schools want to be labeled (and perhaps funded) as equitable and inclusive along with other high-ranking countries of the world, it is likely children will have to conform their views to fit those reinforced by the global testing regime, regardless of what they personally think is right or what their families teach them. As schools, districts, and nations vie for top marks on PISA, SSES, and other assessments, the race to keep up with the global neighbors drives fundamental social change by conditioning the minds of the children of the world.[32]

The self-appointed educational and social engineers housed at the United Nations and the OECD started the quest to infiltrate the classrooms of the world at the natural soft entry point: academic testing in the name of "common" standards. Once they entered classrooms in the name of online academic assessments, they could then modify the programs they administer with relative ease and minimal opposition because the questions, readings, curriculum, and assessments students see are often (conveniently) not seen by anyone else. Even the teacher in a classroom may not be aware of the personalized digital curriculum each student is being taught, and the specific digital curriculum is almost never available to or chosen by parents.

To Measure or to Alter?

The OECD seeks not just to *measure* the values and attitudes held by the people of the world, but to *change* them. In 2012, Schleicher offered a clear example of how the OECD not only measures attitudes but has changed them through data collection. He said,

Data transformed some of the beliefs and paradigms underlying German education. For example, traditionally the education of the very young children was seen as the business of
families and you would have cases where women were seen
as neglecting their family responsibilities when they sent their
children to [preschool].[33] PISA has transformed that debate
and pushed early childhood education right at the center of
public policy in Germany.[34]

Consider that carefully. Schleicher gives PISA and the OECD credit
for changing Germany's attitudes and policies regarding the education
of very young children. Education of young children was previously seen
as the purview of families, especially mothers. Now, thanks largely to
PISA, the education of the very young in Germany is seen as a state
responsibility. The OECD holds this up as a shining example of the
fundamental change its assessments can bring to pass.

The Incheon Declaration

We now descend to the fourth level on the line running from the UN
to the classroom: the Incheon Declaration. In 2015, UNESCO convened
the World Education Forum in Incheon, Republic of Korea, in cooperation with UN agencies and other entities. Over 1,600 participants from
160 countries were invited to the event. The outcome document of the
forum is the Incheon Declaration for Education 2030. It will be used as
a reference platform for the advancement of UN education initiatives
throughout the world through 2030 and beyond.

The Incheon Declaration calls for globalized education, massive
school-based data collection, and mandatory schooling "for all" built
around the specifications the UN and its partners decree. The Incheon
Declaration specifically states, "We entrust UNESCO, in consultation
with Member States, the WEF 2015 co-conveners and other partners,
to develop an appropriate global coordination mechanism."[35] Essentially,

UNESCO convened a big meeting at which it re-crowned itself the global emperor of education and declared its tech-driven intentions for the children of the world.

The framework accompanying the Incheon Declaration calls specifically for a representative of the OECD to serve on the steering committee. And tucked in the "Indicative Strategies" section on page 49, the Incheon Declaration says it aims to promulgate the "knowledge, skills, *values and attitudes* required by citizens" and to address "human rights, gender equality, health, *comprehensive sexuality education*, climate change, sustainable livelihoods and responsible and engaged citizenship."[36] This is a direct injunction to influence the values and attitudes of citizens and to bring comprehensive sexuality education to the world.

The Incheon Declaration and Framework for Action further states that "free and compulsory" education is a "right" for all people.[37] It's intriguing that according to this declaration all people have the "right" to be compelled to receive globally mandated education even if they disagree with what is being taught. It appears that UNESCO and its partners are prepared to thrust unwanted instruction upon *all* people at *all stages of life* in the name of global competency, which is a nicer way of saying global compliance.

Global Partnership for Education

Descending to tier five on the delivery line, the Incheon Declaration also specifically declares that the Global Partnership for Education (GPE) should be part of the "global coordination mechanism."[38] What is the Global Partnership for Education which UNESCO has granted a prime seat at the world's educational table? For starters, GPE says it has adopted SDG Goal 4 (quality and inclusive education for all) as its guidepost.[39] Additionally, UNESCO, UNICEF, and World Bank all currently sit on the board of directors for GPE.[40] GPE promotes schools that are one-stop sites fulfilling virtually all children's needs. GPE aims to establish schools that are educational facilities, nutrition facilities, and medical facilities (providing "adolescent-friendly health services") all under one roof.[41]

This scenario of providing full-service, state-directed facilities for children will sound familiar. It is the very scenario early Russian socialists promoted, saying that to "do away with the household and to free women from the care of children" the state must provide full-service facilities "supervised by trained pedagogical and medical personnel" where children would receive comprehensive care.[42] Anti-family feminist Sophie Lewis suggests the same thing, noting, "There have lately been powerful calls for counter-familial institutions and communist centers of social reproduction" to "meet all humans' basic needs for the first two decades of their lives."[43]

An online infographic showcasing GPE's grand vision for full-service schools of the near future specifically cites *comprehensive sexuality education* as an essential part of school programming beginning at elementary school ages. GPE works to implement its objectives primarily in developing nations and receives funding from many sources, including George Soros's Open Society Foundations.[44] When the GPE comes forward offering food, education, and medical care to children in developing nations, the draw is very strong for these nations to jump on board. Unfortunately, the help the GPE offers is laced with the seeds of family destruction in many forms including comprehensive sexuality education. The UN's World Health Organization has already used the Incheon Declaration as ammunition for promoting a universal right to comprehensive sexuality education, even though the declaration is not a consensus document ratified by UN member states.[45]

Your Child's School

At last we have come down to the local level—the sixth and final tier on the delivery line from the UN to the classroom. Here are just three US examples of the myriad channels through which UN-aligned objectives are plunging into local schools:

1. **The Collaborating Districts Initiative.** The Collaborative for Academic, Social and Emotional Learning (CASEL) initiated the Collaborating Districts Initiative in 2011.[46] CASEL has ties to UNESCO[47] and is a major player responsible for pushing social and emotional learning (SEL) in today's schools.

CASEL is funded in part by a radical feminist organization called the NoVo Foundation, which says it is "dedicated to catalyzing a transformation in global society," addressing "the root causes of injustice," and "proudly advocating for fundamental social change."[48] These phrases and the bulk of NoVo's tenets invoke the sentiments of Shulamith Firestone and Sophie Lewis and, in barely veiled terms, call for the liberation of girls through the transformation of capitalistic systems and the overthrow of the family, the ultimate genesis of "injustice."[49]

The Collaborating Districts Initiative currently involves eight of the largest school systems in the United States: Anchorage, Austin, Chicago, Cleveland, Nashville, Oakland, Sacramento, and Washoe County, Nevada. CASEL has implemented globally aligned social and emotional learning initiatives in school districts within these areas. Social and emotional learning is "embedded into all aspects of their work" through online pathways.[50] This ensures that the avenues for global assessments and curriculum guidance are firmly secured in schools throughout the United States. The combined population of these school districts includes nearly one million students.

2. **The Consortium for School Networking.** The Consortium for School Networking (CoSN) calls itself "the premier professional association for school system technology leaders," and it "represents over 13 million students in school districts nationwide."[51]

CoSN openly partners with UNESCO, as demonstrated by their joint conference in March 2018 titled "CoSN/UNESCO Symposium: Educating for Digital Citizenship."[52] CoSN has established direct relationships with school districts and other entities across the nation through which it can deliver UN-based curricula.

An example of CoSN in action at the local level is the traditionally conservative state of Utah. A representative from the largest school district in Utah (Alpine School District) serves as a member of the CoSN advisory board,[53] and CoSN has formed a direct relationship with the Utah Technology Coordinator Council.[54] As part of this partnership, CoSN is working with the Millard School District in rural Utah.[55] Millard County is a test case for implementing CoSN's objectives in rural areas.[56] CoSN says this partnership will "enable the success of Millard's 1:1 Chromebook per student program rollout" by "establishing a solid technical infrastructure upon which they can build."[57]

A façade of local control will remain in place in rural and urban areas, but devices and services gifted to schools are provided with strings attached. Schools cooperating with UN partners and adopting their technical infrastructure will increasingly find themselves choosing from carefully crafted options that align with the UN objectives for humanity.[58] Many states, including Utah, are quietly transitioning to the OECD's Global Competency–based framework. The Utah State School Board recently adopted competency-based pilot programs that are based on international competency standards.[59]

3. **Common Core Curriculum.** The Bush administration's No Child Left Behind initiative and the Obama administration's Every Student Succeeds Act/Race to the Top initiatives in concert with the implementation of Common Core standards have enabled UNESCO's objectives for global education.

From its inception in 1945, UNESCO has had its sights set on establishing globally directed education standards.[60] In 1984, UNESCO published *A Methodological Guide to the Application of the Notion of Common Core*, which primed the educational atmosphere for the acceptance of widespread common standards rather than standards established locally according to local needs and desires.[61]

Funding Worldwide Curricula

In 2004, Microsoft signed a twenty-six-page agreement with UNESCO which declares, "Microsoft supports the objectives of UNESCO stipulated in UNESCO's constitution and intends to contribute to UNESCO's programme priorities."[62] After signing the agreement, the UNESCO director-general reportedly said one of its intended goals is "fostering web-based communities of practice including content development and *worldwide curricula reflecting UNESCO values*."[63] This would, of course, include UNESCO's sexual values.

Microsoft founder Bill Gates then went on a promotion blitz for Common Core State Standards, convincing governors to voluntarily climb aboard (since federal entities aren't supposed to dictate local curricula.)[64] The Bill & Melinda Gates Foundation reportedly underwrote the organizations writing the Common Core standards, including the National Governors Association, Student Achievement Partners, the Council of Chief State School Officers, and Achieve, with these organizations receiving a combined $147.9 million from the Gates Foundation.[65] These four organizations represent only a small fraction of the numerous entities Gates allegedly paid in order to further the cause of Common Core and thus pave the way for implementing UNESCO's common global objectives.[66]

It is well known that not only is the Gates Foundation a major funder of UNESCO's global education initiatives, but it is also a longstanding donor to International Planned Parenthood Federation, reportedly giving them over $70 million from before 2009 through 2013.[67] With the Gates

Foundation funding global education *and* the world's largest promoters of children's sexual rights, a perfect storm is brewing for the sexualization of all children—including your child—through UN-guided comprehensive sexuality education in globally directed schools.

UNESCO's vision for worldwide curriculum and ongoing global data collection appears to be ready to ride on the back of blockchain technology which could facilitate not just competency-based school curriculum but a competency- or compliance-based economy that tracks the entirety of a person's digitized interactions and either rewards them when they exhibit "competency" or denies them privileges when they act in non-compliant ways. Microsoft is deeply entwined in facilitating the OECD's expanding blockchain initiatives.[68]

Withdrawal from UNESCO

President Ronald Reagan withdrew the United States from UNESCO in 1984. The administration said the withdrawal came about because "UNESCO has extraneously politicized virtually every subject it deals with, has exhibited hostility toward the basic institutions of a free society, especially a free market and a free press, and has demonstrated unrestrained budgetary expansion."[69] The US also cited "excessive attention given to the so-called New International Economic Order, in which wealthy countries are supposed to transfer resources to the poorer ones" as a reason for the withdrawal.[70] In short, the United States withdrew from UNESCO in large part because of the socialist policies it promotes which stifle basic freedoms and stunt economic prosperity in the name of equality.[71] The convening of the World Government Summit in February 2018, attended heavily by representatives of the United Nations, suggests that the UN's dream of uniting the world under one grand banner remains unchanged and is steaming forward.[72]

In 2003, the US rejoined UNESCO under the direction of President George W. Bush. This may prove to be one of the most perilous decisions of our times.[73] President Trump once again officially withdrew the US from UNESCO at the close of 2018. This could open a crucial window of opportunity to disentangle the US education system from the UN-directed global education system. However, since the OECD is the strong arm pushing UNESCO's agenda forward, the deepest impact on UNES-CO's role in the US education system will occur when the United States not only *defunds UNESCO* but *defunds the OECD*.

But rather than loosening ties with the OECD, in 2019 the US administration officially adopted the OECD's global artificial intelligence (AI) principles which may have significant impact on digital communications worldwide. In the AI principles document, an AI system is defined as "a machine-based system that can . . . make predictions, recommendations, or decisions influencing real or virtual environments."[74] Some outcomes from adopting this agreement may be positive. However, the international AI agreement gives deference to the UN's Sustainable Development Goals and 2030 Agenda, encourages collaboration with UNESCO, and includes many statements that are open to wide interpretation. For instance, it says, "Stakeholders should proactively engage in . . . advancing inclusion of underrepresented populations, reducing economic, social, gender and other inequalities." As you can well perceive by now, in those phrases lie the pernicious seeds of socialism, radical feminism, and sexual radicalism.[75] In addition to distancing ourselves from UNESCO and the OECD, another key action that must be undertaken to regain local control of education is for individual states to cut the financial umbilical cord binding them to federal programs which increasingly feed them infected philosophies stewed in the womb of the United Nations.

Who's at the Top?

Social change can be a good thing. Refining children's attitudes on a host of issues can be a good thing. But a lot depends on who's in charge. If an unfailingly noble, moral, generous, wise being or group of beings who are fundamentally motivated by love rather than money, power, or sex is at the top driving initiatives for children, then enormous good may come of such initiatives. However, if the people at the top are corrupted by ignoble influences, great damage can be done to the world and the children in it. If the people at the top prefer equality over liberty, if they love money more than people, if they promote sexual rights over sexual responsibility, then *catastrophic social change* is most certainly on the horizon.

Unfortunately, it appears the global education ship is run by a crew of socialist, feminist sexual rights activists whose misguided hands are steering the ship—and the children in it—toward disaster. Here is a glimpse of several people at the top of the global education movement:

- The current secretary-general of the United Nations, António Guterres, served as president of Socialist International from 1999–2005.[76]
- The director-general of UNESCO from 2009 to 2017, Irina Bokova, was raised by prominent communist parents, is a former member of the Bulgarian Communist party, and has been a member of the Bulgarian Socialist Party since 1990.[77]
- The UNESCO director-general appointed in 2017, Audrey Azoulay, is a member of the Socialist Party.[78]
- The secretary-general of the OECD from 2006 to present, José Ángel Gurría, is a member of the PRI political party,[79] which is a full member of Socialist International.[80] (Additionally, the OECD, led by Gurría, hosted the global council meeting of Socialist International in Paris in 2010.)[81]

One other individual who has functioned in the upper echelons of the children's sexual education movement for years is Ben Levin, former deputy education minister in Canada. Levin—who has written for both UNESCO and the OECD and presented at global education conferences hosted by them—"pled guilty in 2015 to creating and possessing child pornography and counseling others to commit a sexual assault" against a minor.[82] His online encounters with undercover officers involved language reflecting what might be described as a sickening, deeply ingrained disregard for children's well-being.[83]

Whether or not the heads of UNESCO or the OECD knew of Levin's sexual interest in children or of the presence of other child sexual predators in their midst, UNESCO, UNICEF, UNFPA, WHO, and their partners including IPPF have proven themselves to be tenacious advocates of CSE and/or sexual rights for children. Since this is the case, the global education structure being mounted by them is poised to spread sexual rights ideology like a contagion to children everywhere. UN-directed, tech-based education is the syringe through which comprehensive sexuality education is poised to be administered to the children of the world.[84]

Am I claiming that everyone from UNESCO, UNICEF, OECD, CASEL, GPE, CoSN, and their partners is a children's sexual rights advocate hell-bent on sexualizing and de-gendering the children of the world and establishing a sexually open society? No. Many of the well-meaning people working in these organizations would be appalled at such a prospect. Many who work for UN agencies and their partners are genuinely concerned about the future of the world and the children in it and believe that educational technology can be part of the answer to the world's problems, and they are right. And yet, evidence overwhelmingly suggests that the intent of UN-based educational initiatives is to deliver comprehensive sexuality education—in tandem with a socialist, radical feminist, sexual equalist curriculum—to the children of all nations under the guise of equality, sustainability, and human rights.

You will remember from Part I that the objective of socialist designers from their earliest lessons at the feet of Marx and Engels was nothing short of global annihilation of capitalistic practices, the elimination of private property, the crushing of religion, and the annihilation of the family. They thought this would have to be accomplished through bloody revolution. It turns out it is being accomplished quietly (for now) through the cooperating, capitulating classrooms of the world. This is a perilous course. We must swiftly adjust our trajectory if we do not wish to see the social, emotional, moral, and economic vitality of the world reduced to wreckage through socialized, sexualized global education.

CHAPTER TWENTY

THE ARTIFICIAL MOTHER

It is clear that social and emotional learning (SEL) in today's schools is being used as a feeding tube through which globally prescribed, equalist principles can be shuttled down the throats of the young. But what if there were no nefarious, socialist, sexual rights agenda propelling the social-and-emotional-learning movement on a global level? Is school-based social and emotional instruction a good way to help enhance social and emotional wellness in youth? It can be. There are school-based programs that have proven effective at influencing some elements of social and emotional well-being for at least some students who participate in them.

But is there an even better, more effective way of fostering social and emotional wellness in children and therefore in society at large? Yes. It is this: Let children be raised and taught principally by their mothers and fathers while they are very young.

How Are Social and Emotional Skills Best Taught?

Psychoanalyst Erica Komisar says, "It is indisputable that the first three years [of life] present a crucial, formative window" for children's emotional development.[1] Similarly, psychologist Jordan Peterson says "the research literature is quite clear" that there is a "tight window" in which proper social and emotional behavior must be instilled in children.[2] He writes, "If a child has not been taught to behave properly by the age of four, it will forever be difficult for him or her to make friends" and continue down the path of proper socialization and development.[3] In short, social and emotional skills—to a very large degree—are made or broken by a child's experiences before the age of four. This is chilling when set alongside communist dictator Vladimir Lenin's statement: "Give me four years to teach the children and the seed I have sown will never be uprooted."

Research consistently shows that social and emotional well-being is most effectively instilled in people starting at the earliest ages by primary caregivers. One study cites the long-lasting social and emotional effects of early caregiving on children: "Children's ability to regulate attention, emotion, and arousal develops in the context of their primary caregiving relationships during infancy and appears to be fundamental for the balance of the life span in organizing behavior, social relationships, and adaptive functioning."[4] SEL experts at Economic Policy Institute write that crucial life skills "have their origins in the very earliest years of children's lives. Brain research conducted in recent decades increasingly affirms that the foundations for both types of skills—cognitive and noncognitive—are established starting at birth, and even before."[5] They further cite evidence that "the ability to form strong and trusting relationships with others"—which can have enormous social implications throughout a person's life—has its origins in the caretaking relationships a person experiences at the earliest ages.[6] Thus, the first years of life are "key windows of opportunity for the development of noncognitive [i.e., social and emotional] skills."[7] Studies have further shown that mothers in particular help their children develop social and emotional skills such as having compassion for others,[8] reading social cues, managing their emotions, forming relationships, and developing into socially competent beings.[9] But global education is out to remove any shreds of respect for mothers or motherhood that may remain in the public psyche.

Intervening at Younger and Younger Ages

The OECD is increasing its push for what it calls "Early Childhood Education and Care" (ECEC), which is said to demand "increased labour supply from mothers and massive state-funding for institutionalized daycare," perhaps at the earliest ages.[10] The 2016 UN "Education for Global Citizenship" plan stresses that educational measures must foster the development of the "whole person" by shaping children "emotionally, ethically, intellectually, physically, socially, and spiritually."[11] Seeing the windows of opportunity hanging wide open in infancy and toddlerhood, global education engineers are pushing to intervene in children's lives at earlier and earlier ages so that systems, initiatives, and programs can gain access to children rather than letting parents (i.e., people who actually love them) care for and teach their young children. In line with global trends, the state of Iowa "lowered the compulsory school age to four years old for children enrolled in a statewide preschool program," and the New York City Department of Education outlined a sweeping "birth-to-five system of early care and education" for its youngest citizens.[12]

Further, the UN independent expert on sexual orientation and gender identity discrimination, Vitit Muntarbhorn, reportedly referred to children as "soft entry points" for the advancement of the UN objectives.[13] He said it is "important to start working with the young people, the younger the better, with the politics that amplify empathy for vulnerable populations" and to "advance in education . . . initiatives that integrate sexual diversity." [14]

The Incheon Declaration calls for monitoring the holistic education of "all people." To this end, the UN has implemented the Global Education Monitoring Report (GEM Report), which tracks the world's progress on implementing SDG number 4, "Quality Education," which includes a focus on early childhood education.[15] The GEM Report tracks the numbers of children who are educated outside the home before formal primary education begins, and it reports which countries require or fund public education for toddlers. It promotes at least one year of "free and compulsory" non-parental education for all small children and supports implementation of "compliance monitoring mechanisms" for public and private preschools to ensure equity in what very young children are taught.[16] Interestingly, the Open Society Foundations sired by George Soros is a key funder of the GEM Report, manifesting an intense interest in what the toddlers of the world are learning and from whom.[17]

Social and Emotional Wellness in Sweden and Beyond

Policymakers in Sweden have followed the advice of the UN and the OECD in matters of raising new humans. In Sweden, publicly funded, non-parental care has expanded since the 1970s, and now "over 90 percent of all 18-month to 5-years-olds are in daycare."[18] What has significant separation from their mothers and fathers in the first four years of their lives done for the social and emotional well-being of the children of Sweden? A government inquiry in 2006 found:

> [M]ental health among Swedish 15-year-olds declined faster from 1986 to 2002 than in eleven comparable European countries. *For girls, rates of poor mental health tripled during this period, from nine to 30 percent* . . . The increase happened in all groups of youth regardless of family situation, labour market situation or parental socioeconomic status.[19]

It is not just the emotional well-being of Swedish youth that has faltered. To the shock and dismay of the OECD, scholastic achievement has also plummeted: "Between 2000 and 2012 Sweden's PISA scores dropped more sharply than those of any other participating country, from close to average to significantly below average."[20] Further, PISA assessments themselves show that "Sweden has a high degree of disorder in its classrooms. This includes tardiness, truancy, bad language and disorderly behaviour."[21] While these troubling developments cannot be blamed solely on disassociation from parents, one is left to wonder what impact being removed from the care of their mothers in the early years of their lives has had on the population of Sweden.[22]

Similarly, the Canadian province of Quebec introduced subsidized universal daycare in the late 1990s. Roughly a decade later, a study showed "striking evidence" that children in the program were "worse off in a variety of behavioral and health dimensions, ranging from aggression to motor-social skills to illness."[23] The analysis also indicated that participation in the program "led to more hostile, less consistent parenting, worse parental health, and lower-quality parental relationships."[24] A follow-up study several years later showed many problems were worsening over time and that "boys in day care showed more hyperactivity and aggression, while girls showed more separation anxiety."[25] There was also a sharp increase in criminal behavior among those who participated in the Quebec program.

Additionally, a National Institute of Child Health and Human Development study conducted in the US from 1991 to 2009 found that children placed in center-based, non-parental care "were more likely to engage in risky and impulsive behavior, suffer depression, aggression, anxiety, lack of empathy and behavioral problems proportional to the amount of time spent in the day care." And these negative social and emotional outcomes were long-lasting.[26] To suggest that schools or care centers can do the job of instilling social and emotional wellness in children just as well as mothers and fathers is an overconfident claim.[27]

US president Richard Nixon vetoed a proposal called the Comprehensive Child Development Act in the 1970s on grounds that it would commit "the vast moral authority of the national Government to the side of communal approaches to childrearing over against the family-centered approach."[28] The administration said,

We cannot and will not ignore the challenge to do more for
America's children in their all-important early years, but our
response to this challenge must be . . . consciously designed
to cement the family in its rightful position as the keystone of
our civilization. Good public policy requires that we enhance
rather than diminish both parental authority and parental
involvement with children.[29]

The Artificial Mother

It is becoming clear that the artificial mother Shulamith Firestone
dreamed of is knocking vigorously at the door: It is the state-sponsored,
full-service, globally connected, UN-directed school that will take your
child as early as you will give him up and train him to be a dutiful socialist, radical feminist, and sexual rights activist who eschews family, prizes
pleasure, and demands an endless list of corrupted human rights.

But there is a better way. There is a saner, more sacred, more sustainable way.

It is the way of the family. Mothers and fathers can and do best foster
the social and emotional well-being of the world. Mothers respond in
real time and in unique, personalized ways to the ever-changing needs
of their individual children. They collect endless data points on their
children and respond with the inimitable, incomparable edge of *love*. As
the world comes to grips with how fundamental these functions are to
individuals, communities, and nations, perhaps we will realize—before
it's too late—how crucial mothers, fathers, and families are to the sustainability of the world.

POTENT WEAPON

In concert with the socialist hijacking of education and the expanding sexual equality mentality, comprehensive sexuality education is among the most potent weapons in the arsenal of family destruction. It pulls little children onto its lap and tells them it is their rightful quest to seek and experience sex outside the protective guardrails of committed family living and launches young people into the teeming fray of staggering sexual risks. It speaks little of parenthood and much of pleasure. It speaks much of rights and little of wrongs.

Mothers and fathers are consistently the best gatekeepers of their children's well-being. Sexual rights activists, who have a monetary interest in sexualizing children, are not. While comprehensive sexuality education activists pretend to be concerned gatekeepers of children's well-being, what they do is open the floodgates of sexuality on children and then half-heartedly rescue children from its consuming waters, for a price.

Since parents, especially mothers, are not easily eliminated, those who wish to ideologically devour, exploit, and sexually mentor a mother's children have learned that they must deftly sidestep her. They tell the mother she has more important and liberating things to do. They convince the mother to surrender her child—her most valuable asset—into their gnarled hands without a fight. They chuckle deviously because they intend to turn the child not only against her mother, but against motherhood itself and against the ingenious design of the child's own anatomy. They intend to disabuse the child of any notions that she should unite with a member of humanity from the other side of the sexual aisle, create life, experience parenthood, and become a masterful steward of that which she possesses.

Get Her to Do It Herself

In the end, since motherhood is virtually indestructible, if you want to destroy motherhood and its commanding force over the youngest citizens of the world, there is really only one way to do it: Get mothers to relinquish their children voluntarily. This is the fourth and final tactic for unseating the woman I promised we would come to, and we have finally arrived. In truth, we have been striking at this point all along, as you will likely have perceived. Virtually every problematic ideology discussed in this book promotes, encourages, or demands the relinquishment of the child by the mother.[1]

One Russian communist said:

> Children, like soft wax, are very malleable and they should be molded into good Communists. We must rescue children from the harmful influence of the family . . . We must nationalize them. From the earliest days of their little lives, they must find themselves under the beneficent influence of Communist schools . . . To oblige the mother to give her child to the Soviet state—that is our task.[2]

So how do you get a woman to fully or partially relinquish stewardship of her own child? Here is a list of strategies used by the three major paradigms we have examined:

Socialism

- Convince women and society that mothers can be replaced by paid caretakers. Promote the philosophy that unpaid mothering is mindless drudgery and socially unproductive work.
- Conversely, convince people that child-rearing is so crucial that it is best done by trained professionals, not by mothers.
- Convince people that raising money is more important than raising children.
- Present sex as a recreational activity everyone is entitled to, not as the means of forming and sustaining permanent relationships.
- Foster an entitlement or equality mentality in society, which produces people who are too self-focused and emotionally unskilled to act as successful parents.
- Require women to leave their children in the care of non-parents.
- Provide full-service, state-funded care facilities for children in order to entice the woman to "free" herself from the drudgery of caring for her children.
- Teach children socialistic principles, including sexual freedom, at the earliest ages possible through education initiatives including *comprehensive sexuality education.*
- Promote abortion in order to ideologically and literally sever familial bonds and gain control of the production of human beings.

Radical Feminism

- Convince women (and all of society) that work done for money is more important than work done in the name of love.

- Portray pregnancy as an unnatural, dangerous injustice to women.
- Portray abortion as a safe practice that brings justice and empowerment to women.
- Present children as burdens rather than assets.
- Honor and celebrate women only when they are acting in non-motherhood roles.
- Denigrate family-based living and exalt career-focused living.
- Present the public sphere as being more important than the private sphere.
- Present men as unnecessary to families and societies at large.
- Deride and demean masculinity in men; encourage masculinity in women.
- Present sexual pleasure as a right unrelated to risks, permanent relationships, or childbearing.
- Promote as rights the products and services that limit a woman's ability to conceive and bear life.
- Teach children the principles of gender equality, sexual rights, and sexual freedom at the earliest ages possible through education initiatives including *comprehensive sexuality education.*

Sexual Radicalism

- Convince people that children do not need mothers or fathers.
- Convince people that any person or group of people can raise any child as successfully as any other entity and to say otherwise is hateful, bigoted, and a violation of equality.

- Present sex and marriage as recreational activities to which everyone is entitled, but not as the means of forming families, tethering men to their children, and organizing society into autonomous biological groupings.
- Negate the validity of a child's connection to its mother.
- Negate the validity of a child's connection to its father.
- Legalize and expand surrogacy (and with it, the buying and selling of children's rights) on the basis of men's rights to have children.
- Teach equalistic principles, sexual rights principles, and gender fluidity ideology to children at the earliest possible ages through education initiatives including *comprehensive sexuality education.*

Discard, Eradicate, and Eliminate

The endgame of all these tactics is to convince the woman and society that children do not need their mothers or fathers. The goal is to convince women and men that raising their own children is a waste of their time, their money, and ultimately—their lives. When the woman begins to be persuaded to this position, her guiding grip on the destiny of her children—and therefore the world—goes slack. The reins are snatched up by less worthy stewards, she is unseated in the name of her own rights, and a behemoth state settles its rotting rump into her chair bellowing about equality while crushing the life, prosperity, and vitality out of the world.

But what's even better than getting a child away from its mother is getting the mother to teach her child exactly what you want it to hear. As misguided tolerance, love, and equality seep their way into a mother's mind, she then pours corrupted versions of these doctrines dutifully into her child's mind as any good, politically correct parent would do.[3] A mother most likely prizes her role in the life of her child, and yet she almost unknowingly teaches her child to disavow motherhood, to discredit biological tethering, and to spurn the inherent family and heteronormativity in the name of tolerance, equality, women's rights, and love.

You will remember that Shulamith Firestone's feminist goal was to "dismantle," "uproot," "annihilate," "totally discard," and "truly eradicate," the biological family as the fundamental unit of society and to "eliminate the sex distinction itself." You will observe that Firestone's objectives are being enacted on a global scale through the operations of the United Nations and beyond.

The erasure of men and women as physical classes of people is advancing at a rapid pace. As gender equality and gender fluidity are taught to children all over the globe through comprehensive sexuality education, the pace will increase exponentially. Such efforts lead toward the obliteration of two-pronged biological sex as a defensible designation on a global scale and instead favors and legally empowers a sliding scale of self-proclaimed, non-bodily gender.

When the machinations of the United Nations as driven by socialism, radical feminism, and sexual radicalism combine with forces in modern culture including political movements, social media, Hollywood, the music industry, the judicial system, and the education system, there emerges a global onslaught against the family and principally against the woman as the core of that anatomically ordered institution. This war against women and the family is cunningly waged in the name of the woman, and the woman often climbs aboard the movement unawares. She thinks she is being paraded down the street in honor—an honor she has long deserved— but she is really being carted out of the way in order to clear the path for her usurpers to seize the reins of property, privacy, and life itself.

Coming Full Circle

Earlier, I posed these questions:

- What laws or practices are working to disavow biological relationships and "sever blood ties" between parents and their children?

- What laws or initiatives seek to loosen long-standing sexual norms?
- Who is suggesting or legislating that mothers are unnecessary to families?
- Who is suggesting or legislating that fathers are detrimental to families or, at best, optional?
- What social movements promote the concept that not knowing one's biological mother or father is normal and even a manifestation of human rights?
- What efforts are setting the stage for the state to become the gatekeeper for the creation and distribution of children?
- Which initiatives are working to erase the differences between men and women?
- Who is working to make the care of young children a government-run endeavor?
- What entities are trying to infuse socialist, feminist, and sexually radical philosophies into the education systems of the world?
- What entities are working to advance "sexual freedom" and "sexual rights" for children?
- Who is trying to enact education programs for children that normalize a wide range of sexual behaviors including child sex?
- Who is trying to enact education programs for youth that de-normalize families in which parents claim their own children?

The prime answers to these questions are: 1) the expansion of socialist and feminist influences, 2) the LGBT movement which legitimizes the commodification of children and obliterates distinctions between men and women through the codification of transgenderism, and 3) the UN's globalization and sexualization of education.

Of course, it must be noted that not all proponents of same-sex marriage are socialists. Nor are all socialists in favor of all tenets of the LGBT movement. Nor are all feminist-minded people cheering for same-sex marriage or for the induction of a global socialist regime. But these movements are inextricably intertwined, and the pursuit of one enables the others. In their own way, each of them undermines the inherent sovereignty of the family and enthrones equality as the pinnacle of all virtues. These combined movements, together with the crushing of religion (Marx's intention was to "dethrone God"[4]), contribute to a social environment conducive to socialist/communist encroachment.[5] All these elements are cooperating heads on a massive hydra which is charging forward to overthrow the social and political structures of the world in the name of equality and world peace. Through all of this, the family finds itself in grave danger.

Any social movements, laws, initiatives, programs, or ideologies that hack at the root of women's private, inherent bond to their children—as socialism, radical feminism, and sexual equalism all do—serve the purpose of a global regime. Throughout history, raw socialist-communism and other forms of tyranny have barreled forward, ripping people's freedoms and families from their bosoms, which has often resulted in defiance, bloodshed, and eventual revolution against them. But as other movements now come penitently strolling in wearing the robes of love, inclusion, and equality, the intoxication of such gentle invasions persuades people to loosen their grip on the very things they hold most dear. And as the grip of families and patriots loses its tenacity, iron fists sit flexing their eager muscles.

This Global Course of Action Is Doomed to Failure Because of Mothers

Since there is an immense socialist-communist presence in the upper echelons of global education and since the success of socialist systems hinges upon the annihilation of the biological family,[6] the goal of those at the helm is to unhinge the family unit, and they are making fantastic headway. Sophie Lewis observes, "World legislation around biological filiation, property and heredity has never looked closer to buckling."[7] In other words, the legal recognition of biological relationships appears to be teetering on the edge of collapse.

If the family *is* dismembered and abandoned, if mothers are severed from (or sever themselves from) their children and global rule by "equality" is enacted, the chaos and mayhem of a world biologically unhinged will be far worse than any possible alternative.

I assert, however, that a significant portion of mothers will refuse to give their children over to the state—either literally or ideologically—even under the most severe circumstances. Mothers and fathers will ferociously contend for the minds and bodies and souls of their children.

The battle for the babies of the world is fierce because those in power know that babies always end up ruining the evil plans of socialist villains and bloody tyrants. Babies eventually win because there is always a mother somewhere raising up a valorous, moral, liberty-loving, intelligent, intrepid girl or boy who grows up to detonate a rebellion—either by the pen or by the sword—that ruptures the foul tethers by which his countrymen are bound. E. T. Sullivan put it this way:

> When God wants a great work done in the world or a great wrong righted, he goes about it in a very unusual way. He doesn't stir up his earthquakes or send forth his thunderbolts. Instead, he has a helpless baby born, perhaps in a simple home and of some obscure mother. And then God puts the idea into the mother's heart, and she puts it into the baby's mind. And then God waits. The greatest forces in the world are not the earthquakes and the thunderbolts. The greatest forces in the world are babies.[8]

Woman, in her role as mother, *will* exert her invincible power and will determine the fate of nations and the world. In the most ultimate sense, the love of mothers will decide the destiny of humanity as mothers decide one by one to cast the ballot of their very lives in favor of their children. And in the end, it will be said, "LOVE WINS." The family will persist as it always has and will reemerge as the strongest, most enduring entity in society, even as the mass wreckage of socialist equality passes like a horrible nightmare on the tides of time.

I laughed out loud when I read this statement by Simone de Beauvoir: "Gestation . . . offers woman no benefit as an individual." On the contrary, bearing one's own child is the greatest benefit the world has to offer. The advantages of privately creating, claiming, and commanding life itself are overwhelming in their scope and staggering in their magnitude. And that is why a global army is hunting the woman, eager to strip her of the precious, living cargo she carries.

PART V

THE SOLUTION

CHAPTER TWENTY-TWO

IN THE CELLAR

U nfortunately, the UN's well-orchestrated intrusion into your child's classroom is not the only way comprehensive sexuality education with all its socialist-feminist warts is barreling gruesomely through society. State legislatures are adopting CSE by force of law;[1] state school boards are adopting CSE health curricula; sexual rights activists are flooding magazines, newspapers, blogs, vlogs, and YouTube channels with pro-CSE messages;[2] and cartoons, apps, and other programs are being rolled out to comprehensively educate people of all ages about a wide range of sexual practices and gender fluidity.[3] Ridiculing the idea that marriage is the place where sex should occur is commonplace, and the message that sex is meaningless entertainment that children have a right to engage in is emerging almost at every corner.

But there is hope.

We can influence legislatures, and we must. We can defund organizations that seek to undermine children's well-being. We can influence school boards. We can exercise the right affirmed by the UN's own Universal Declaration of Human Rights: "Parents have a prior right to choose the kind of education that shall be given to their children."[4] We can support organizations that work to protect the family as the fundamental unit of society. We can support laws and initiatives that encourage public decency.[5] We can remove gender identity curriculum from schools. We can resist and reject socialist solutions to local and global problems at all costs. We can regain local control of education by cutting ourselves loose from national and international education initiatives and organizations (such as the Every Student Succeeds Act, the OECD, PISA testing, and UNESCO) . . . *and we must.*

But there is something else we must do, or else all other efforts will be in vain. It has been done in Romania, Albania, Russia, Germany, and virtually every other nation that has been infiltrated and dominated by corrupt regimes. But perhaps nowhere has this thing been so eloquently done and documented as in Hungary, which is where we will end our journey.

Communist Takeover of Education in Hungary

For decades, the nation of Hungary lived under the blackened, brutal boot of communism.[6] The platitudes of Marx and Engels had intoxicated the Soviet Union, and in 1945 the Soviets, with the help of Germany, extended their claws towards Hungary and secured it as a satellite state. Promises of prosperity and equality rang everywhere, but the once-proud Hungarians saw economic devastation, political corruption, and staggering social oppression bring their country to its knees. Widespread suffering, Soviet propaganda, and even sadistic torture marred the lives of Hungarians.

Once, in 1956, the patriots of Hungary rose intrepidly to their feet. They toppled Stalin's statue in the public square, disarmed tanks with raw ingenuity born of desperation, and sent Soviet officers scurrying through the streets of Budapest. The people hungered for freedom and fought courageously for it. But the freedom they won was short-lived. Within days, Soviet tanks and soldiers invaded in massive numbers, crushing Hungarian freedom for another thirty-three years.

The Soviets occupying Hungary believed the secret to their success was the children. If they secured the minds of the children, they would secure a communist future for the nation and perhaps the world. Therefore, "communism made great efforts to ingratiate itself with children. More effort was spent on them than upon on any other segment of the population."[7] Young boys joined the communist youth program where they were taught not only tactical battle skills but also to hate America and the basic tenets for which it stood. Children were taught "the principles of socialist patriotism, of devotion and love toward the Hungarian communist party, and of boundless loyalty toward the great Soviet Union."[8]

Writer James Michener explains the social pressures that weighed upon the people of Hungary under communist rule:

> It was in school that the pressure of the communist propaganda became intense. In every class a boy's teachers were required to indoctrinate him in communism. They gave lectures about the glory of Russia and instruction in the communist history of Hungary. They took their students to march in communist parades, to see propaganda movies and to protest against American imperialism. The teachers praised what communism said should be praised and damned its supposed enemies. From the first grade through the last, no child could escape this pressure.[9]

Some teachers resisted the hostile takeover of Hungarian education, but because of a few well-placed communist loyalists positioned in each school, "a teacher who might in his heart hate communism was nevertheless required by fear of these perpetual spies to indoctrinate his pupils with hatred of Britain and America and an unreasoning trust in Russia." Teachers were required to hang three giant pictures of communist leaders on the walls, which became known to the children as "the Holy Trinity."[10]

A climate of distrust and suspicion permeated communist Hungarian society. Schoolchildren were required to become informants on each other. If they observed any behavior or speech that "might be harmful to the communist state," they were to report their schoolmates to the authorities.[11] Perhaps more insidious was that "the school became a potential trap for every household." A child would "gain approval by informing upon his parents' love for religion or persistence in old-fashioned ideas." Teachers might ask their students things like, "Does your father keep a picture of Comrade Stalin in your home? What radio station does your mother like best? Does your father think that Comrade Rakosi is always right? Does your mother ever take you to religious meetings at night?"[12] These probing questions (like the ones poised to be asked on UN-centric OECD assessments) served to fracture social and religious loyalties and to pit family members against each other. Distrust, suspicion, and fear ran rampant.

A Hungarian citizen could only get ahead in society if he adhered to and openly professed the ideals the reigning socialist regime required. Participation in sports, acceptance to college, job advancement, and escaping arrest all hinged upon celebrating the publicly required but privately loathed principles of socialist communism. Thus, parents and teachers were forced to endorse the "total fraud" of communism to their children or suffer severe repercussions.[13]

Private Rebellion

For the proud and tenacious people of Hungary, this was a bitter pill to take. To see their children manhandled by a perverse regime, to hear the history of their country corrupted in their children's ears through communist history lessons, to witness their young sons and daughters parroting the poisonous propaganda of pretended "equality" at school was almost more than Hungarian parents could endure. Under threat of estrangement, unemployment, punishment, and even death, parents stood by biting their tongues and wringing their hands as their children were educated by communist tyrants. But there came a point where tongue-biting and hand-wringing became unbearable.

And so the parents rebelled.

It is said that "the time always came when the mother would cry, 'I won't see my child perverted any longer. Tonight we will tell him the truth.'"[14] But since grave consequences could come to the child and the whole family if the child blurted out in an unguarded moment what his parents told him, the father might insist that the boy was too young. And so the parents waited, carefully weighing the time when they could salvage their children's souls from the disguised horrors of communism without imperiling the entire family. Then, it is said, "the mother would be the one who pleaded for the family to take a bold chance and save this child."[15]

And on that very night, the family would descend to the cellar to tell their child the truth. They might begin by asking their child what he learned in school that day, whereupon the child would recite shreds of injurious nonsense about the glories of communism and the sure promises of Stalin. "And the father would say simply, 'That's all a lie, son.'" The son stared in astonished wonder as the seriousness of the matter settled over the small room. And then the parents would begin to tell their child the truth. And so began the countereducation of an entire generation.

A Family

Two Hungarian children educated by their parents in the secrecy of their cellar were Vera and Johan Hadjok. They were thirteen and nine when they escaped over the Austrian border with their parents, Janos and Irene Hadjok. They fled hurriedly, braving grave dangers and lived to tell the tale of their beloved Hungary awash in cruelty, scarcity, and socialist insanity.

At an informal meeting with interested foreigners soon after the family's escape from Hungary and communism, the children bubbled over with information and passionate recitations about the history of their motherland. They told the true story of their country, complete with heroes and martyrs and passages of poetry and pivotal moments in the saga of truth versus error that had played out on their soil. To the wonder of many who listened, these children had not been swayed or seduced by the incessant lies, promises, and propaganda the communist state had rammed down their throats. Despite the bitter and almost unbearable atmosphere in which they lived, Vera's and Johan's faces shone with patriotism and the power of having heard and embraced the truth. Many in the assembled group wanted to know, "How is this possible? How could your family have endured the crushing pressures of communism?"[16] Mrs. Hadjok provided the answer:

> At night after we had put out the lights upstairs we would gather in the cellar, and I would teach the children the true history of Hungary. We would discuss morality and the Catholic religion and the lessons of Cardinal Mindszenty. We never allowed the children to go to sleep until we had washed away the evil things they might have heard that day.[17]

She suspected most families did the same thing without ever discussing it openly with anyone.

When asked later how she knew enough to teach her children, she replied, "Books." She had secretly obtained one book in particular that told the stories of Hungary's greatest patriots. "I made my children memorize it," Mrs. Hadjok said. "They considered this book almost sacred, since it was the only place in their world where they could find the truth." In the cellar, she also taught them "the fiery old poetry of Hungary" which Johan recited with relish.[18] Vera said of her schoolteachers who peddled communism, "Neither Russia nor the communists in Hungary could ever make us believe the lies they told us."[19]

As in any truly socialist state, "The battle between school and parents never relaxed an instant."[20] Mrs. Hadjok explained,

They had everything on their side. Candy, fruit, games, terror. We had only one thing, the lessons at night . . . We taught them above everything else to trust in God. But almost as strongly we told them to hold together as a family . . . The more communists tried to destroy our family life, the more we taught family loyalty. It was like their pressing us down all day, in every way you could think of, but at night we grew up strongly again.[21]

The result of Mr. and Mrs. Hadjok's nightly teaching in the cellar was captured in a brother-in-law's assessment of young Vera: "At six she disliked the Russians. At nine she hated them. At ten she understood the evil of communism. At thirteen she is a holy patriot."[22] "Against such children," said her father, "what could communism do?"[23]

Why did the children of Hungary believe their parents more than they believed anyone else? Because parents love their children more than regimes love children, and children can tell the difference.

In the cellars and attics and kitchens and closets of the world is where wars against all great evils in the world will be won. Such battles will be won at the feet of mothers and fathers. That is the hallowed place where holy patriots will grow and where all corrupt and soulless schemes will meet their demise, penetrated and slain by the sword of truth. The final thing we can do—we *must* do—is go to the cellar. And in that holy, private place speak the truth, and in so doing plant seeds that will bear shining, incorruptible fruit.

Remember, Mrs. Hadjok said, "We had only one thing, the lessons at night."

And that was enough.

CHAPTER TWENTY-THREE

STAND

We now descend on the roof of a home. In this home there is a family. And in this family there is a mother, a father, and a child. Perhaps two children. Perhaps ten. In this home exists the cosmos in miniature. This home is its inhabitants' private piece of the world. In this home exists anatomically inherent diversity, opposition, and complementarity. In this home exists tolerance, patience, rage, and power. In this home exists creation, possession, jealousy, and joy. This home is where its inhabitants practice for every other setting in life. This home, and millions like it, is where the world learns to walk, talk, think, eat, laugh, fight, forgive, serve, sacrifice, reason, deliberate, cooperate, labor, take turns, negotiate, dream, and love.

In this house resides the ancient institution that has produced and sustained civilization for millennia. This unassuming institution occurs naturally without the leverage of lobbyists, sweeping mandates of courts, passionate cries of activists, or endorsements of celebrities. This archaic organization, *the family*, arises from the anatomy of ordinary people and claims the distinction of being the most enduring and influential institution on earth.

Dictators may denounce, congresses may crush, and governments may attempt to gut the family, but as long as families persist, humanity has a fighting chance. If the family falters, either by mandate or by choice, civilization will not remain civil for long; it will decline into a mass of unconnected people who hardly know how to love anymore. As we increasingly dismantle and redefine the family, denigrate biological connections, and separate children from their parents, we will foster a generation with neither root nor branch, with no connection to generations past and no place on the family tree of humanity. How well will the children of the upcoming world tolerate liberation from their families?

We should not be surprised when the throngs of solitary souls we are creating—who claim neither gender nor family—are unhappy, violent, reckless, diseased, and dying both body and soul. We should not be surprised if, after we have destroyed it, we find ourselves hungering for the family and trying to reconstruct it from the tatters of humanity we have deliberately, tolerantly torn to pieces.

The Coming Days

In the coming days, as families are being systematically disassembled around us, people will turn to look at the family and finally see it for what it is. It is not merely a nice way of organizing earthlings, or a nifty reason to buy matching shirts, or a byproduct of evolutionary mistakes. Families are a wonder of sociological architecture. Families are the vehicle for sustaining individual people as well as societies at large. The family has long been and will always be the most reliable source of food, clothing, shelter, education, protection, dignity, and love for members of the human family. Families are the reason we have survived for thousands of years without killing each other off or perishing before we could. Imperfect as they can be, families are the prime elements that have made life both possible and desirable.

If we want to provide the essentials of life, freedom, love, property, and prosperity to the greatest number of people, we must maintain the system of small, regenerative groups forged by two unique yet united individuals. If we want to ensure the *most human rights* for the *most people*, we must maintain the system initiated and perpetuated by the anatomy of human bodies themselves: *the family.*

Home

The most socially productive work that happens on earth does not occur in a factory, or in a mine, or in a cubicle. The most socially productive work in society happens at home. The highest quality environment for new humans has consistently been and will remain within the arms of a mother and father who know and love their own child.[1] The best possible system already exists. It is here. It is *us*. It is families. A family may live in a high-rise apartment above the glitz of city lights; they may live in a sweaty bungalow with one dangling bulb to light their faces; they may live in a tin hut, or a remote cottage, a mansion, or a cookie-cutter house in suburbia. But if there is a father who loves a mother, and a mother who loves a child, and a child who knows and loves his parents, this is the highest quality environment available on earth. This is *family*. This is the ideal for which we must stand. If we give up the fight for the family, there will be little left to fight for.

The Time Will Come

If woman is the secret weapon of humanity and stealth is part of the genius of her power as I have asserted in this book, then why am I blowing her cover now? Why am I exposing the woman as the origin of private property, the keystone of the family, the master of the private sphere, the architect of society, and the genesis of the most powerful force in the world—love itself?

Because the gig is up. Her hungry opponents know where she is. They have isolated her position, they want it, and they are coming after her en masse with a barely veiled vengeance. Everyone who cares must stand and must act. Most of all, she herself must stand. She is up to the challenge. In fact, she was born for such a time and such a task as this. It has been said, "The time will come when only those who believe deeply and actively in the family will be able to preserve their families in the midst of the gathering [forces] around us."[2]

That time is now.

Take heart. The family cannot be destroyed. It can only be abandoned. Mothers, fathers, stand fast. Do not step aside. Your child is uniquely yours and no one else's. Do not be dissuaded. Do not abandon your post. Do not surrender your greatest treasure.

Guard it with your life.

WHAT YOU CAN DO

- **Teach what you believe** about family, marriage, gender, sex, and parenthood to your family.
- **Become informed** on family issues. Sign up for regular communications from organizations whose message and approach resonates with you.
- **Start an organization or initiative**—large or small—that does what you think needs to be done to support the family as the fundamental unit of society in your area.
- **Start or expand your collection of books** that tell the stories, recount the moments, uphold the heroes, explain the philosophies, and teach the principles you want your family to know and cherish. Include fiction and non-fiction in your collection.
- **Study the history of socialism.** Read the stories of nations, families, and people oppressed by socialist principles. Fortify your family against the follies of the past and the indoctrination of the present.

- **Study the history of freedom**, representative government, and free markets.
- **Donate time and resources** to organizations that protect and strengthen the family, fight pornography, preserve freedom, and advocate for responsible sex education.
- **Attend pro-family events** such as conferences, webinars, cottage meetings, and forums.
- **Seek out a social community** (such as a church or other gathering place) that aligns with your basic views and supports the family as the fundamental unit of society.
- **Oppose abortion.** Join or start a movement in your area to cherish life and support pregnant mothers. Work for legislation that supports the rights of the unborn and protects women from the risks of abortion.
- **Watch** *The War on Children* at StopCSE.org.
- **Become involved in the fight against comprehensive sexual education** in your area and invite others to join you. Go to StopCSE.org to get started.
- **Expose and oppose the children's sexual rights campaign** spearheaded by International Planned Parenthood Federation and United Nations agencies.
- **Support the narrative that mothers and fathers matter** and are vital to their children's well-being through social media, blogging, articles, conversation, and other means.
- **Influence policymakers** at all levels on the issues in this book you find most compelling.
- **Never lose heart.** The family is invincible in its design, irreplaceable in its effects, and everlasting in its position. Keep up the fight in the public square and at home.
- **Share** this book with others.

Visit InvincibleFamily.com

ACKNOWLEDGMENTS

Without Marji Ross's good-heartedness and penchant for risk-taking, this book would not be in your hands today. I am grateful for her vision in bringing this project to the fore. Tom Spence treated me with generosity from our first meeting onward and has been an advocate every step of the way. His professionalism paired with true humility makes him a gem among publishers.

The editing prowess of Erica Rogers, Kathleen Curran, and Crystal Ferguson brought the manuscript to a shine and their encouragement urged me over numerous hurdles along the way. John Caruso's talent for insightful cover design is unrivaled, and Grant Soderberg has been a savvy publicist. Regnery's entire team is a joy to work with as well as a creative and technological force to be reckoned with.

Bill Nixon provided a crucial introduction into the publishing world that changed the course of this book and the course of my life. His timing proved to be impeccable.

I am indebted to a few key friends (you know who you are) who read early drafts of the manuscript, offered listening ears, gave crucial input, and kicked in with cheerleading when I needed it most. Thank you.

My husband and children have given unceasing support to me and to this project over the course of years and celebrated with me every time I "finished" the book. Their sacrifices and contributions are impossible to enumerate.

And finally, I'm grateful to my parents for believing not just in this book, but for believing in me for as long as I can remember.

BIBLIOGRAPHY

"2018 Report on Planned Parenthood CEO Compensation." STOPP
International. Stafford, VA: American Life League, 2018. https://
www.stopp.org/pdfs/2018_PP_CEO_Report.pdf.

ABC. "Consequences, Citizenship and Climate." Q + A. September 11,
2017. https://www.abc.net.au/qanda/
consequences-citizenship-and-climate/10650354#.

Abbamonte, Jonathan. "25-Year-Old Mom Has Toes Amputated and
Hysterectomy after IUD Migrates to Her Stomach." Population
Research Institute. August 1, 2018. https://www.pop.
org/25-year-old-mom-has-toes-amputated-and-hysterectomy-
after-iud-migrates-to-her-stomach/.

AccessMatters. "AccessMatters Knows Planned Parenthood Matters to
Pennsylvania." https://www.accessmatters.org/
accessmatters-knows-planned-parenthood-matters-to-pennsylvania/.

Adams, Barbara and Karen Judd. "Data Is the New Gold—Development Players Mine a New Seam." *Global Policy Watch* 19
(November 28, 2017). https://www.globalpolicywatch.org/wp-con-
tent/uploads/2017/11/GPW19_2017_11_28.pdf.

Akbar, Arifa. "Mao's Great Leap Forward 'Killed 45 Million in Four Years.'" *Independent.* September 17, 2010. https://www.independent. co.uk/arts-entertainment/books/news/maos-great-leap-forward-killed-45-million-in-four-years-2081630.html.

"AMAZE Brings Sex Education Online to End Sexual Assault Epidemic." NowThis Her Facebook page. May 27, 2018. https:// www.facebook.com/NowThisHer/videos/1280543175409888/ UzpfSTEwMDAwMDA5NzI2OTM1NDoxOTk1OTg2MzE3M-DgxMjU4ymju4.

AMAZE Org. "Gender Identity: Being Female, Male, Transgender or Genderfluid." YouTube. October 20, 2016. https://www.youtube. com/watch?v=W9YwOE8ndnc.

American Psychiatric Association. *Diagnostic and Statistical Manual of Mental Disorders (DSM-5).* 5th ed. New Delhi: CBS Publishers and Distributors, 2017.

Ancient History Encyclopedia, s.v. "Yin and Yang." Last updated May 16, 2018. https://www.ancient.eu/Yin_and_Yang.

Anderson, Ryan T. "Biology Isn't Bigotry: Why Sex Matters in the Age of Gender Identity." Heritage Foundation Commentary. February 16, 2017. http://www.https://www.heritage.org/ marriage-and-family/event/ biology-isnt-bigotry-why-sex-matters-the-age-gender-identity.

———. *When Harry Became Sally: Responding to the Transgender Movement.* New York: Encounter Books, 2018.

———. "*The New York Times* Reveals Painful Truths about Transgender Lives." Public Discourse. November 25, 2018. https://www. thepublicdiscourse.com/2018/11/47220.

Andrews, Robin George. "To Stop Climate Change, Educate Girls and Give Them Birth Control." Wired. February 18, 2018. https:// www.wired.com/story/ to-stop-climate-change-educate-girls-and-give-them-birth-control.

Aristotle. "Aristotle > Quotes > Quotable Quote." GoodReads. https:// www.goodreads.com/

quotes/814532-all-who-have-meditated-upon-the-art-of-gover-
ning-mankind.

———. "Motherhood." Tendernest. http://www.tendernest.com.au/
motherhood.

Arter, Melanie. "Planned Parenthood Got $528M in Tax Dollars, Paid
Cecile Richards $523,000." CNSNews. September 29, 2015.
http://www.cnsnews.com/news/article/melanie-hunter/
maloney-admonishes-chaffetz-beating-woman-making-good-sal-
ary.

The Austin Institute. "The Economics of Sex." YouTube. February 14,
2014. https://www.youtube.com/watch?v=cO1ifNaNABY.

Bachofen, Joseph. *Mutterrecht* (*Mother Right*). 1861.

Bachiochi, Erika. "Embodied Equality: Debunking Equal Protection
Arguments for Abortion Rights." *Harvard Journal of Law and
Public Policy* 34, no. 3 (Summer 2011). https://papers.ssrn.com/
sol3/papers.cfm?abstract_id=1873485.

———. "The Cost of Choice: Women Evaluate the Impact of Abortion." *Journal of Psychology and Clinical Psychiatry* 1, no. 6
(June 2016): 339. http://medcraveonline.com/JPCPY/JPCPY-06-
00339.pdf.

Bachiochi, Erika, ed. *The Cost of Choice: Women Evaluate the Impact of
Abortion.* San Francisco: Encounter Books, 2004.

Bailey, J. Michael and Ray Blanchard. "Suicide or Transition: The Only
Options for Gender Dysphoric Kids?" 4thWaveNow. September 8,
2017. https://4thwavenow.com/2017/09/08/
suicide-or-transition-the-only-options-for-gender-dysphoric-kids/.

Baillargeon, Jean-Patrice, Donna K. McClish, Paulina A Essah, and
John E. Neslter. "Association between the Current Use of Low-
Dose Oral Contraceptives and Cardiovascular Arterial Disease: A
Meta-Analysis." *Journal of Clinical Endocrinology & Metabo-
lism* 90, no. 7 (July 1, 2005): 3863–70. https://academic.oup.com/
jcem/articleabstract/90/7/3863/2837207?redirectedFrom=fulltext.

Baker, Michael et al. "Universal Childcare, Maternal Labor Supply, and
Family Well-Being." NBER Working Paper 11832. National Bureau

of Economic Research. December 2005. https://www.nber.org/
papers/w11832.

Banbury, Anthony. "I Love the UN, But It Is Failing." *New York
Times*. March 18, 2016. https://www.nytimes.com/2016/03/20/
opinion/sunday/i-love-the-un-but-it-is-failing.html.

Barclay, Dolores. "The Family: It's Surviving and Healthy." *Tulsa
World*. August 21, 1977. Quoted in William Grigg. "Nationalizing
Children." LewRockwell.com. April 8, 2013. https://www.lewrock-
well.com/2013/04/william-norman-grigg/
to-whom-do-children-belong.

Batty, David. "Sex Changes Are Not Effective, Say Researchers." *The
Guardian*. July 30, 2004. https://www.theguardian.com/soci-
ety/2004/jul/30/health.mentalhealth.

Beauvoir, Simone de. *The Second Sex*. Translated by H. M. Parshley.
New York: Vintage Books, 1989.

"Ben Levin Defends Child Porn." *The Interim*. December 5, 2017.
http://www.theinterim.com/issues/society-culture/
ben-levin-defends-child-porn.

Berry, Susan. "Trump Administration Proposes Merging Education
and Labor Departments." Breitbart. June 22, 2018. http://www.
breitbart.com/big-government/2018/06/22/
trump-administration-proposes-merging-education-labor-depart-
ments.

Beyond Marriage: Unrecognized Family Relationships. City and
County of San Francisco, Human Rights Commission. Panel dis-
cussion October 29, 2009. Report adopted March 10, 2011.
Uploaded to Scribd by Cecilia C Chung at https://www.scribd.
com/document/54614840/
Beyond-Marriage-Unrecognized-Family-Relationships.

Bilefsky, Dan. "Bulgarian Who Is to Lead UNESCO Advocates Political
Pluralism." *New York Times*. September 23, 2009. https://www.
nytimes.com/2009/09/24/world/europe/24unesco.html.

Bilek, Jennifer. "Who Are the Rich, White Men Institutionalizing
Transgender Ideology?" The Federalist. February 20, 2018. http://

thefederalist.com/2018/02/20/
rich-white-men-institutionalizing-transgender-ideology.
———. "The Billionaires behind the LGBT Movement." *First Things.*
January 21, 2020. https://www.firstthings.com/web-exclu-
sives/2020/01/the-billionaires-behind-the-lgbt-movement.
Bill & Melinda Gates Foundation. "How We Work: Grant." https://
www.gatesfoundation.org/How-We-Work/Quick-Links/Grants-
Database/Grants/2013/11/OPP1095783.
"Birthstory." Radiolab WNYC Studios. June 7, 2018. https://www.wnyc-
studios.org/podcasts/radiolab/articles/birthstory2018.
Black, Tori. "The Equality Act—an Atrocity against Women." United
Families International. April 11, 2019. https://unitedfamilies.org/
womens-rights/the-equality-act-an-atrocity-against-women.
Blaine, K. "The Dangerous Effects of Surrogacy: How Big Fertility
Exploits Poor Women." MercatorNet. November 16, 2018. https://
www.mercatornet.com/mobile/view/
the-dangerous-effects-of-surrogacy-how-big-fertility-exploits-poor-
women.
Bloomberg News. "Melinda Gates Will Step In to Help Trudeau Push
Gender Equality at G7." *Montreal Gazette.* June 5, 2018. https://
montrealgazette.com/news/quebec/
melinda-gates-to-step-in-to-help-trudeau-push-gender-equality-at-g7.
Bomberger, Ryan. "Abortion Is Systemic Racism: Truth vs Lies in
Dueling Ohio Billboard Campaigns." Townhall. January 29,
2018, https://townhall.com/columnists/ryanbomb-
erger/2018/01/29/
abortion-is-systemic-racism-truth-vs-lies-in-dueling-ohio-bill-
board-campaigns-n2441068.
Bornstein, Marc H., Joan T. D. Suwalsky, and Dana A. Breakstone.
"Emotional Relationships between Mothers and Infants: Knowns,
Unknowns, and Unknown Unknowns." *Development and Psy-
chopathology* 24, no. 1 (February 2012).
British Pathe. "One Minute News (1947)." YouTube. https://www.you-
tube.com/watch?v=_BG11OHrCDk.

Bronfenbrenner, Urie. Quoted in Hunt, Nancy and Kathleen Marshall. *Exceptional Children and Youth*, 5th ed. Belmont: Wadsworth, 2012.

Brown, Belinda. "We Like Heteronormativity and We Don't Want You to Smash It." MercatorNet. September 17, 2019. https://www.mercatornet.com/conjugality/view/we-like-heteronormativity-and-we-dont-want-you-to-smash-it/22871.

Brown, Susanne. "Innovating Rural School Districts—CoSN to Improve Student Success through New Technology Initiative." CoSN. July 31, 2017. https://cosn.org/about/news/innovating-rural-school-districts—cosn-improve-student-success-through-new-technology.

Bruce, Tammy. "Rape, Sex Trafficking and the Spread of Disease on the UN's Watch." *Washington Times*. December 27, 2017. https://www.washingtontimes.com/news/2017/dec/27/united-nations-problems-bigger-than-inefficiency-o.

Butts, Charlie. "PA School Mulls Planned Parenthood Clinic." NE News Now. June 30, 2017. https://www.onenewsnow.com/education/2017/06/30/pa-school-mulls-planned-parenthood-clinic.

Carcillo, Stéphane and Marie-Anne Valfort. "LGBT Inclusivity: A Priority for the OECD." OECD Insights. November 16, 2016. http://oecdinsights.org/2016/11/16/lgbt-inclusivity-a-priority-for-the-oecd.

CASEL. *Key Insights from the Collaborating Districts Initiative*. Chicago: CASEL, 2017. https://www.casel.org/wp-content/uploads/2017/03/Final-CDI-Report-3-17-17.pdf.

———. "What is SEL?" https://casel.org/what-is-sel.

Charen, Mona. "Unwarranted: Elizabeth Warren's Flawed Idea." Townhall. February 21, 2019. https://townhall.com/columnists/monacharen/2019/02/21/unwarranted-elizabeth-warrens-flawed-idea-n2541970?utm_source=thdaily&utm_medium=email&utm_campaign=nl&newsletterad=02/21/2019&bcid=2f42f9885cc2b30c3453b1ebbc133733&recip=18362275.

Chretien, Claire. "Breast Cancer Risk Skyrockets with Longtime Hormonal Contraception Use: New Study." LifeSite News. December 8, 2017. https://www.lifesitenews.com/news/new-study-hormonal-contraception-increases-breast-cancer-risk-by-20.

———. "Liberal Feminist: Hookup Culture Hurts Women, and We Hate It. So Why Do We Join in Anyway?" LifeSite News. June 3, 2016. https://www.lifesitenews.com/news/liberal-feminist-hookup-culture-hurts-women-and-we-hate-it.-so-why-do-we-jo.

Christensen, Bryce. "Dispelling Utopian Illusion, Building Real World Families." MercatorNet. August 16, 2017. https://www.mercatornet.com/features/view/dispelling- utopian-illusions-building-real-world-families/20260.

Christie, Gracie Pozo. "Let's Compare Studies to See If Abortion Really Harms Women's Mental Health." The Federalist. April 24, 2017. http://thefederalist.com/2017/04/24/lets-compare-studies-see-abortion-really-harms-womens-mental-health.

Christofferson, D. Todd. "The Moral Force of Women." *Ensign*. November 2013.

Cleveland, Margot. "LGBT Activists Teaching Judges to Yank Kids from Parents Who Won't Transgender Them." The Federalist. February 12, 2019. http://thefederalist.com/2019/02/12/lgbt-activists-teaching-judges-yank-kids-parents-wont-transgender/.

Code Blue Campaign. "Primer: Privileges and Immunities of the United Nations." http://www.codebluecampaign.com/primer-privileges-and-immunities-of-the-united-nations.

———. "The Problem." http://www.codebluecampaign.com/the-problem.

———. "The UN's Dirty Secret: The Untold Story of Anders Kompass and Peacekeeper Sex Abuse in the Central African Republic." May 29, 2015. http://www.codebluecampaign.com/carstatement.

"Collaborative for Academic, Social, and Emotional Learning, CASEL."
Education for Safety, Resilience and Social Cohesion. http://educa-
tion4resilience.iiep.unesco.org/en/taxonomy/term/735.

Cole, Brendan. "Former Senior United Nations Official Faces Pedophilia Charges in Nepal." *Newsweek.* April 9, 2018. http://www.
newsweek.com/
former-senior-united-nations-official-facing-pedophilia-charges-
nepal-876783.

Coleman, Priscilla K. "Abortion and Mental Health: Quantitative Synthesis and Analysis of Research Published 1995–2009." *The British Journal of Psychiatry* 199, no. 3 (September 2011): 180–86.
https://doi.org/10.1192/bjp.bp.110.077230.

"Comprehensive Sex Ed Is Now the Law." Health Connected. November 12, 2015. https://www.health-connected.org/single-
post/2015/11/12/Comprehensive-Sex-Ed-is-Now-the-Law.

Confucius. "Confucius > Quotes > Quotable Quote." GoodReads.
https://www.goodreads.com/.
quotes/79127-if-your-plan-is-for-one-year-plant-rice-if.

"Convention on the Elimination of All Forms of Discrimination against
Women." UN Women. https://www.un.org/womenwatch/daw/
cedaw/cedaw.htm.

Cook, Michael. "Do Transgender Women Have a Right to Gestation?" MercatorNet. September 12, 2018. https://www.mercator-
net.com/conjugality/view/
do-transgender-women-have-a-right-to-gestation/21709.

———. "Ectogenesis Keeps Chugging Along." MercatorNet. October
21, 2019. https://mercatornet.com/
ectogenesis-keeps-chugging-along/24832/.

———. "Is It Immoral to Love Your Kids Because They Are Related to
You? Some Bioethicists Think It Is." MercatorNet. June 7, 2018.
https://www.mercatornet.com/features/view/
is-it-immoral-to-love-your-kids-because-they-are-related-to-
you/21406.

———."Is There Really No Difference between Straight and Gay Parenting?" MercatorNet. September 20, 2016. https://www.mercatornet.com/conjugality/view/is-there-really-no-difference-between-straight-and-gay-parenting/18693.

———. "Utilitarianism Goes On a Charm Offensive." MercatorNet. January 29, 2018. https://www.mercatornet.com/features/view/utilitarianism-goes-on-a-charm-offensive/20946.

Cleveland, Margot. "LGBT Activists Teaching Judges to Yank Kids from Parents Who Won't Transgender Them." The Federalist. February 12, 2019. http://thefederalist.com/2019/02/12/lgbt-activists-teaching-judges-yank-kids-parents-wont-transgender/.

CoSN. "About CoSN." https://cosn.org/about-cosn.

———. "Driving K–12 Innovation Advisory Board." https://cosn.org/driving-k-12-innovation-advisory-board.

———. "Innovating Rural School Districts—CoSN to Improve Student Success through New Technology Collaboration." https://cosn.org/about/news/innovating-rural-school-districts%E2%80%94cosn-improve-student-success-through-new-technology.

———. "Rapid Technological Changes, Exponential Implications—COSN 2018 Conference to Design Learning in the Fourth Industrial Revolution." March 2, 2018. https://cosn.org/about/news/rapid-technological-changes-exponential-implications%E2%80%94cosn-2018-conference-design-learning.

Cretella, Michelle. "Gender Ideology Harms Children." American College of Pediatricians. Last updated September 2017. http://www.acpeds.org/the-college-speaks/position-statements/gender-ideology-harms-children.

———. "I'm a Pediatrician. Here's What I Did When a Little Boy Patient Said He Was a Girl." The Daily Signal. December 11, 2017. https://www.dailysignal.com/2017/12/11/cretella-transcript.

"Chosen Family." Queer Queries (blog). https://complicatingqueertheory.wordpress.com/queer-families/chosen-family/.

Christakis, Nicholas. "The Hidden Influence of Social Networks."
    TED. February 2010. https://www.ted.com/talks/nicholas_christa-
    kis_the_hidden_influence_of_social_networks/
    details?language=en.
Crittenden, Ann. *The Price of Motherhood*. New York: Picador, 2010.
"CSW61 Agreed Conclusions Revision 1." UN Commission on the
    Status of Women. New York: UN Women, 2017. https://www.
    ngocsw.org/wp-content/uploads/2017/03/CSW61-Rev1-
    13March-2017.pdf.
Dhejne, Cecelia, Paul Lichtenstein, Marcus Boman, Anna L. V.
    Johansson, Niklas Langstrom, and Mikael Landen. "Long-Term
    Follow-Up of Transsexual Persons Undergoing Sex Reassignment
    Surgery: Cohort Study in Sweden." *PLoS One* 6, no. 2 (February
    22, 2011). https://doi.org/10.1371/journal.pone.0016885.
Dodds, Paisley. "AP Exclusive: UN Child Sex Ring Left Victims but
    No Arrests." AP News. April 12, 2017. https://apnews.com/e6ebc
    331460345c5abd4f57d77f535c1?utm_
    campaign=SocialFlow&utm_source=Twitter&utm_medium=AP.
———. "UN Peacekeepers in Haiti Implicated in Child Sex Ring."
    Independent. April 14, 2017. https://www.independent.co.uk/
    news/world/americas/un-haiti-peacekeepers-child-sex-ring-sri-
    lankan-underage-girls-boys-teenage-a7681966.html.
Donati, Pierpaolo, and Paul Sullins. *The Conjugal Family: An Irre-
    placeable Resource for Society*. Rome: Libreria Editrice Vaticana,
    2015.
"Drag Queen Story Hour at NYC Library." CBS News. https://www.
    cbsnews.com/pictures/drag-queen-story-hour-at-nyc-library/4.
Edwards, Lee. "The Legacy of Mao Zedong Is Mass Murder." Heritage
    Foundation. February 2, 2010. https://www.heritage.org/asia/com-
    mentary/the-legacy-of-mao-zedong-mass-murder.
"Effective Altruism Is Changing the Way We Do Good." https://www.
    effectivealtruism.org.
Einbinder, Nicole. "French Police to Investigate New Abuse Claims
    against Former UN Peacekeeper." Frontline. July 24, 2018. https://

www.pbs.org/wgbh/frontline/article/
french-police-to-investigate-new-abuse-claims-against-former-un-
peacekeeper.

Engels, Friedrich. *The Origin of the Family, Private Property, and the State*. London: Penguin Books, 2010.

Erickson, Jenet. "Fathers Don't Mother and Mothers Don't Father: What Social Science Research Indicates about the Distinctive Contributions of Mothers and Fathers to Children's Development." April 18, 2015. https://ssrn.com/abstract=2519862.

Fagan, Patrick. "The Real Root Causes of Violent Crime: The Breakdown of Marriage, Family, and Community." Heritage Foundation. March 17, 1995. https://www.heritage.org/crime-and-justice/report/ the-real-root-causes-violent-crime-the-breakdown-marriage-family- and.

Fagan, Patrick, Kirk Johnson, and Robert Rector. "Marriage: Still the Safest Place for Women and Children." Heritage Foundation. March 9, 2004. https://www.heritage.org/marriage-and-family/report/ marriage-still-the-safest-place-women-and-children.

Family Scholars. *Why Marriage Matters: Thirty Conclusions from the Social Sciences*. 3rd edition. New York: Institute for American Values, 2011. http://www.americanvalues.org/search/item. php?id=81.

Family Watch International. "Deceptive UN Transgender Resolution Must Be Stopped." March 12, 2019. https://familywatch.org/ resources/newsletters/alert-deceptive-un-transgender-resolution- must-be-stopped/#.XoJcc9NKi6s.

———. "Policy Brief: International Planned Parenthood Federation and Children's 'Right' to Sex." Gilbert, AZ: Family Watch International, 2014. http://familywatch.org/wp-content/uploads/ sites/5/2017/10/fwipolicybriefIPPFupdated7-15.pdf.

Feller, Madison. "5 Women on Deciding Not to Have Children Because of Climate Change." *Elle*. October 19, 2018. https:// www.elle.com/life-love/sex-relationships/a23837085/ women-not-having-children-climate-change.

Fielding, James. "Top UNICEF Children's Rights Campaigner—Who Led UK's Anti-Smacking Campaign—Is Jailed for Rape of Boy, 13, in Latest Charity Sex Scandal." *Daily Mail*. February 16, 2018. http://www.dailymail.co.uk/news/article-5399247/UNICEF-kids-rights-campaigner-jailed-rape-boy-13.html.

Figes, Orlando. *The Whisperers: Private Life in Stalin's Russia*. New York: Picador, 2007.

"Figueres: First Time the World Economy Is Transformed Intentionally." UNRIC archive. February 3, 2015. https://archive.unric.org/en/latest-un-buzz/29623-figueres-first-time-the-world-economy-is-transformed-intentionally.

Firestone, Shulamith. *The Dialectic of Sex*. New York: Farrar, Straus and Giroux, 1970.

Gandhi, Mahatma. *Young India*. 1931.

Garcia, Emma, and Elaine Weiss. *Making Whole-Child Education the Norm*. Washington, D.C.: Economic Policy Institute, 2016. https://www.epi.org/files/pdf/107051.pdf.

Gates, Bill. "Bill Gates—National Conference of State Legislatures." Bill & Melinda Gates Foundation. Prepared speech given July 21, 2009. https://www.gatesfoundation.org/media-center/speeches/2009/07/bill-gates-national-conference-of-state-legislatures-ncsl.

Gay Star News. "Elly Barnes—Educate and Celebrate." YouTube. April 29, 2017. https://www.youtube.com/watch?v=nt2bSF2xOVg.

Gebbard, Paul H. "In Memoriam: Wardell B. Pomeroy." *Archive of Sexual Behavior* 31, no. 2 (April 2002). https://search.proquest.com/openview/48edff3c0441e7a4200807daceb13b64/1?pq-origsite=gscholar&cbl=48144.

Geiger, H. Kent. *The Family in Soviet Russia*. Cambridge: Harvard University Press, 1968.

"Gender Dysphoria in Children: Summary Points." American College of Pediatricians. 2016. https://www.acpeds.org/gender-dysphoria-in-children-summary-points.

Gennarini, Stefano. "Saint Lucia/Africans Put Parental Rights Back in UN Sex Ed Policy." *St. Lucia Times*. December 7, 2017. https://

stluciatimes.com/
saint-lucia-africans-put-parental-rights-back-un-sex-ed-policy/.
———. "UN Agency Defies General Assembly, Promotes "Comprehensive Sexuality Education." Center for Family & Human Rights. January 19, 2018. https://c-fam.org/friday_fax/un-agency-defies-general-assembly-promotes-comprehensive-sexuality-education-part-1.
———. "UNESCO Pushes Controversial Sex-Ed Rejected by General Assembly." Center for Family and Human Rights. March 8, 2018. https://c-fam.org/friday_fax/unesco-pushes-controversial-sex-ed-rejected-general-assembly.
Gessen, Masha. "Why Get Married When You Can Be Happy?" Sydney Writer's Conference. May 2012. Audio MP3. http://mpegmedia.abc.net.au/rn/podcast/2012/06/lms_20120611_0905.mp3.
Givas, Nick. "California State Senate Committee Bans the Use of 'He' and 'She' during Hearings, Then Breaks Its Own Rule." The Daily Caller. January 22, 2019. https://dailycaller.com/2019/01/22/california-state-senate-gender-pronouns.
Global Partnership for Education. "About GPE." https://www.globalpartnership.org/about-us.
———. "How to Improve Health and Learning in School-Age Children." April 7, 2018. www.globalpartnership.org/multimedia/infographic/how-improve-health-and-learning-school-age-children.
Gomes, Patricia. "How PISA Is Changing to Reflect 21st Century Workforce Needs and Skills." EdSurge. April 6, 2016. https://www.edsurge.com/news/2016-04-26-how-pisa-is-changing-to-reflect-21st-century-workforce-needs-and-skills.
Gordon, Linda. *The Moral Property of Women*. Urbana and Chicago: University of Illinois Press, 2002. Originally published as *Woman's Body, Woman's Right*, 1976.
Grossman, Miriam. *Unprotected*. New York: Sentinel, 2007.
———. "A Brief History of Sex Ed: How We Reached Today's Madness—Part II." MiriamGrossmanMD. June 6, 2013. https://www.

miriamgrossmanmd.
com/a-brief-history-of-sex-ed-how-we-reached-todays-madness-part-ii/.

Guttmacher Institute. "The History of the Guttmacher Institute." https://www.guttmacher.org/about/history.

Gwertzman, Bernard. "U.S. Is Quitting UNESCO, Affirms Backing for U.N." *New York Times*. December 30, 1983. https://www.nytimes.com/1983/12/30/world/us-is-quitting-unesco-affirms-backing-for-un.html.

"Gyeongju Action Plan." Education for Global Citizenship. 66th United Nations NPI/NGO. 2016. https://outreach.un.org/sites/outreach.un.org/files/ngorelations_legacy/2016/08/ActionPlan-EN.pdf.

Harrod, Horatia. "The Tragic True Story behind the Danish Girl." *The Telegraph*. February 28, 2016. https://www.telegraph.co.uk/films/2016/04/14/the-tragic-true-story-behind-the-danish-girl/.

Hellyer, Paul. "U.N. Documents in U.S. Case Law." *Library Staff Publications* 14 (2007). https://scholarship.law.wm.edu/libpubs/14/.

Himmelstrand, Jonas. "Swedish Daycare: International Example or Cautionary Tale?" MercatorNet. September 16, 2015. https://www.mercatornet.com/articles/view/swedish-daycare-international-example-or-cautionary-tale/16830.

———. "Swedish Daycare II: Weak Parenting, Big Problems." MercatorNet. September 17, 2015. https://www.mercatornet.com/articles/view/swedish-daycare-ii-weak-parenting-big-problems/16844.

Hinckley, Gordon B. "First Presidency Message: These, Our Little Ones." *Liahona* 31 no. 12 (December 2007). Church of Jesus Christ of Latter-Day Saints.

Hoffman, Matthew. "Planned Parenthood Seeking to Lower Age of Sexual Consent to 14 in Peru." LifeSite News. November 19, 2010, https://www.lifesitenews.com/news/planned-parenthood-seeking-to-lower-age-of-sexual-consent-to-14-in-peru.

Holland, Josiah G. *The Life of Abraham Lincoln*. (Springfield, MA: G. Bill, 1866). http://www.bartleby.com/73/1225.html.

Hopper, Bruce. *What Russia Intends: The Peoples, Plans and Policy of Soviet Russia.* London: Cape, 1931.

Houeix, Romain. "Hollande's Protégé Azoulay Wins UNESCO's Top Job." France 24. October 13, 2017. https://www.france24.com/en/20171013-clone-french-qatari-candidates-face-off-final-vote-top-unesco-job.

Huxley, Julian. *UNESCO: Its Purpose and Its Philosophy.* Preparatory Commission of UNESCO. 1946. http://unesdoc.unesco.org/images/0006/000681/068197eo.pdf.

ID2020. "ID2020 Alliance." https://id2020.org/alliance.

International Planned Parenthood Federation. *Exclaim! Young People's Guide to 'Sexual Rights: An IPPF Declaration.'* London: April 2011. https://www.ippf.org/sites/default/files/ippf_exclaim_lores.pdf.

———. "Inside and Out: Comprehensive Sexuality Education (CSE) Assessment Tool." https://www.ippf.org/resource/inside-and-out-comprehensive-sexuality-education-cse-assessment-tool.

———. "IPPF and Youth," https://www.ippf.org/resource/ippf-and-youth.

———. "Love, Sex and Young People: Learning from Our Peer Educators." https://www.ippf.org/resource/love-sex-and-young-people-learning-our-peer-educators.

———. "Member Associations." https://www.ippf.org/about-us/member-associations.

———. *Sexual Rights: An IPPF Declaration.* London. October 2008.

———. *The Truth about Men, Boys and Sex.* June 2009. https://www.ippf.org/sites/default/files/truth_about_men_boys_sex.pdf.

International Sexuality and HIV Curriculum Working Group. *It's All One Curriculum,* volumes 1 and 2. Nicole Haberland and Deborah Rogow, eds. New York: Population Council, 2009. https://www.popcouncil.org/uploads/pdfs/2011PGY_ItsAllOneGuidelines_en.pdf; https://www.popcouncil.org/uploads/pdfs/2011PGY_ItsAllOneActivities_en.pdf.

"Investigative Footage." Center for Medical Progress. May 15, 2018. http://www.centerformedicalprogress.org/cmp/investigative-footage.

Iscan, Candan. "Hitler Youth: The Indoctrination of a Population." Wiener Holocaust Library Blog. October 5, 2016. https://www.wienerlibrary.co.uk/Blog?item=200&returnoffset=40.

"It All Depends on the Definition of 'Sex.'" Eagle Forum. April 6, 2018. https://eagleforum.org/topics/era/why-era-would-be-bad-for-women.html.

Jasper, William F. "The United Nations: On the Brink of Becoming a World Government." *New American*. October 11, 2012. https://www.thenewamerican.com/world-news/item/13126-the-united-nations-on-the-brink-of-becoming-a-world-government.

Jean Paul (Johann Paul Friedrich Richter). "Jean Paul Quotes." BrainyQuote. https://www.brainyquote.com/quotes/jean_paul_147431.

Jenkins, Wesley. "Is Blockchain the Future of Academic Credentials?" The Chronicle of Higher Education. December 3, 2019. https://www.chronicle.com/article/Is-Blockchain-the-Future-of/247647.

Jones, David. "The Designer Baby Factory: Eggs from Beautiful Eastern Europeans, Sperm from Wealthy Westerners and Embryos Implanted in Desperate Women." *Daily Mail*. May 4, 2012. http://www.dailymail.co.uk/news/article-2139708/The-designer-baby-factory-Eggs-beautiful-Eastern-Europeans-Sperm-wealthy-Westerners-And-embryos-implanted-desperate-women.html#ixzz5B4K4Q3Yd.

Junying, Piao. "Students in China Are Forced to Sign Away Their Religious Commitments." MercatorNet. February 13, 2019. https://www.mercatornet.com/above/view/students-in-china-are-forced-to-sign-away-their-religious-beliefs/22175.

"Just Figured Out My Uncle Is Actually My Father, and My Mother Is My Aunt." Anonymous Us. February 15, 2015. https://anonymousus.org/

just-figured-out-my-uncle-is-actually-my-father-and-my-mother-is-my-aunt/.

Kankaras, Milo, and Javier Suarez-Alvarez. "OECD's New International Study on Social and Emotional Skills." Measuring SEL. December 6, 2017. https://measuringsel.casel.org/oecds-new-international-study-social-emotional-skills.

Karlsson, Jonas, and Marie Brenner. "Danger in the Ring." *Vanity Fair.* December 13, 2013. https://www.vanityfair.com/news/politics/2014/01/nuvaring-lethal-contraceptive-trial.

Kennedy, John F. "Re: United States Committee for UNICEF July 25, 1963." John F. Kennedy Presidential Library and Museum. https://www.jfklibrary.org/Research/Research-Aids/Ready-Reference/JFK-Fast-Facts/Appeal-UNICEF.aspx.

Kew, Ben. "Socialism: Venezuelans Scavenging, Selling Garbage for Survival." Breitbart. January 19, 2018. http://www.breitbart.com/national-security/2018/01/19/socialism-venezuelans-turn-to-selling-garbage-for-survival/.

Kimball, Spencer W. "Families Can Be Eternal." *Ensign.* Church of Jesus Christ of Latter-Day Saints: October 1980.

Komisar, Erica. *Being There: Why Prioritizing Motherhood in the First Three Years Matters.* New York: Tarcher Perigee, 2017.

Krason, Stephen M. "Same-Sex Parenting: The Child Maltreatment No One Mentions." *Crisis Magazine.* May 2, 2018. https://www.crisismagazine.com/2018/sex-parenting-child-maltreatment-no-one-mentions.

Kyllonen, Patrick. "Social-Emotional and School Climate Assessment in Latin America." Measuring SEL. July 26, 2017. https://measuringsel.casel.org/social-emotional-school-climate-assessment-latin-america/.

LaFollette, Hugh. "Licensing Parents." *Philosophy and Public Affairs* (Winter 1980). http://www.hughlafollette.com/papers/lic-par.htm.

Laidlaw, Michael K. "Gender Dysphoria and Children: An Endocrinologist's Evaluation of *I Am Jazz*." Public Discourse. April 5, 2018. http://www.thepublicdiscourse.com/2018/04/21220.

———. "The Gender Identity Phantom." MercatorNet. November 12, 2018. https://www.mercatornet.com/conjugality/view/the-gender-identity-phantom/21915.

Landau, Elizabeth. "Mothers' Talk Is Key to Kids' Social Skills, Study Says." CNN. May 15, 2009. http://www.cnn.com/2009/HEALTH/05/15/mother.children.social.skills/index.html.

Landsmann, Carolina. "Opinion: The Nuclear Family Threat." HAARETZ. October 19, 2017. https://www.haaretz.com/opinion/premium-opinion-the-nuclear-family-threat-1.5459170.

Langhart, Karen. "NuvaRing Caused My Daughter's Death. Like So Many Women, She Had No Idea of the Risks." *The Guardian.* June 22, 2015. https://www.theguardian.com/commentis-free/2015/jun/22/nuvaring-merck-daughter- death-women-risks.

Laurence, Lianne. "Ontario Conservatives Will 'Restore' Sex-Ed to Pre-Wynne Days, but When?" LifeSite News. July 6, 2018. https://www.lifesitenews.com/news/ontario-conservatives-will-restore-sex-ed-to-pre-wynne-days-but-when.

Laville, Sandra. "Child Sex Abuse Whistleblower Resigns from UN." *The Guardian.* June 7, 2016. https://www.theguardian.com/world/2016/jun/07/child-sex-abuse-whistleblower-resigns-from-un.

Lewis, Paul. "Child Sex Scandal Roils UNICEF Unit." *New York Times.* June 25, 1987. https://www.nytimes.com/1987/06/25/world/child-sex-scandal-roils-unicef-unit.html.

Lewis, Sophie. *Full Surrogacy Now: Feminism Against Family.* London: Verso, 2019.

Liberate Prometheus. "Hjernevask-Brainwashing (Eng Sub): The Gender Equality Paradox." YouTube. March 26, 2014. https://www.youtube.com/watch?v=cVaTc15plVs&app=desktop.

Lydersen, Kari. "Make Room For Daddies: Surrogate Demand Grows." Chicago Business. February 2, 2013. http://www.chicagobusiness.com/article/20130202/ISSUE03/302029981/make-room-for-daddies-surrogate-demand-grows.

Malkin, Michelle. "How to Protect Your Kids from Google Predators." Townhall. March 13, 2019. https://townhall.com/columnists/michellemalkin/2019/03/13/how-to-protect-your-kids-from-google-predators-n2543030.

Mandela, Nelson. "Address by President Nelson Mandela at National Men's March, Pretoria." November 22, 1997. www.mandela.gov.za/mandela_speeches/1997/971122_mensmarch.htm.

"Mark Zuckerberg's Commencement Address at Harvard." Harvard Gazette. May 25, 2017. http://news.harvard.edu/gazette/story/2017/05/mark-zuckerbergs-speech-as-written-for-harvards-class-of-2017/.

Marx, Karl, and Friedrich Engels. "Chapter II. Proletarians and Communists." The Communist Manifesto. 1848. https://www.marxists.org/archive/marx/works/1848/communist-manifesto/ch02.htm.

McCarthy, Margaret. "Gender Ideology and the Humanum." Communio 43 (Summer 2016). https://www.communio-icr.com/files/43.2_McCarthy.pdf.

McCormack, Chris. "The Real Cost of Institutionalised Care." News Weekly. May 19, 2018. http://newsweekly.com.au/article.php?id=58076.

McDonald, Kerry. "Harvard Study Shows the Dangers of Early School Enrollment." MercatorNet. December 3, 2018. https://www.mercatornet.com/features/view/harvard-study-shows-the-dangers-of-early-school-enrolment/21993.

McLanahan, Sara, and Gary Sandefur. Growing Up with a Single Parent: What Hurts, What Helps. Cambridge: Harvard University Press, 1994.

McLerran, Barry, and Rick Stout, executive producers. "Demographic Winter: The Decline of the Human Family." YouTube. July 28, 2011. https://www.youtube.com/watch?v=lZeyYIsGdAA.

Mero, Paul T. Vouchers, Vows, and Vexations: The Historic Dilemma over Utah's Education Identity. Sutherland Institute: 2007. http://sutherlandinstitute.org/uploaded_files/sdmc/vouchersvows.pdf.

Merriam-Webster, s.v. "social construct (*n.*)." https://www.merriam-webster.com/dictionary/social%20construct.

Michener, James. *The Bridge at Andau: The Compelling True Story of a Brave, Embattled People*. New York: Fawcett, 1957.

Millett, Kate. *Sexual Politics*. New York: Ballantine, 1983.

Milloy, Christian S. "Don't Let the Doctor Do This to Your Newborn." Slate. June 26, 2014. http://www.slate.com/blogs/outward/2014/06/26/infant_gender_assignment_unnecessary_and_potentially_harmful.html.

Mises, Ludwig von. *Human Action*. 1949. Digital book available at https://mises.org/library/human-action-0/html/pp/746.

Mitchelson, Alana. "Merav Michaeli's Marriage Feud with Liberal Senator Seselja on *Q&A*." September 11, 2017. https://thenewdaily.com.au/entertainment/tv/2017/09/11/merav-michaeli-zed-seselja-q-a/.

Montesquieu Institute. "I.G. (Irina) Bokova." https://www.montesquieu-institute.eu/id/vk1lgubr2bza/i_g_irina_bokova#p3.

Morch, Lina S., C. W. Skovlund, P. C. Hannaford, L. Iversen, S. Fielding, and O. Lidegaard. "Hormonal Contraception and the Risk of Breast Cancer." *New England Journal of Medicine* (December 7, 2017): 2228–39. doi: 10.1056/NEJMoa1700732.

Moriarty, Cassie. "Miscontraceptions." YouTube. February 23, 2015. https://www.youtube.com/watch?v=-IEf73_l7Yo.

Mosher, Steven W. *A Mother's Ordeal*. Washington, D.C.: Park Press, 1993.

Mount, Ferdinand. *The Subversive Family*. New York: Free Press, 1992.

Moynihan, Carolyn. "Why Should Respect for Nature Stop at the Human Being?" MercatorNet. September 7, 2017. https://mercatornet.com/why-should-respect-for-nature-stop-at-the-human-being/22244/.

Nash, Elizabeth et al. "State and Federal Lawmakers Promote Sexual Consent, LGBTQ+ Inclusivity in Sex Education." Guttmacher Institute. May 13, 2019. https://www.guttmacher.org/article/2019/05/

state-and-federal-lawmakers-promote-sexual-consent-lgbtq-inclusiv-ity-sex-education?utm_source=Guttmacher+Email+Alerts& utm_campaign=9c03067b42-EMAIL_CAM-PAIGN_2019_02_05_06_40_COPY_01&utm_ medium=email&utm_term=0_9ac83dc920-9c03067b42-260720841.

National Fatherhood Initiative. "Just the Facts" postcard. https://cdn2. hubspot.net/hubfs/135704/Father-Facts-8/sharable_images/FF8_ infant_mortality_700px.jpg.

National Institute of Child Health and Human Development. "Study of Early Child Care and Youth Development." December 30, 2017. U.S. Department of Health and Human Services. https:// www.nichd.nih.gov/research/supported/seccyd/overview.

National Telecommunications and Information Administration. "U.S. Joins with OECD in Adopting Global AI Policies." May 22, 2019. https://www.ntia.doc.gov/blog/2019/ us-joins-oecd-adopting-global-ai-principles.

Natural Womanhood. "The Fertility Diaries Episode 1." YouTube. July 23, 2016. https://www.youtube.com/watch?v=BXb0_IhOB2w.

Navai, Ramita, and Sam Collyns. "UN Sex Abuse Scandal." *Front-line.* July 24, 2018. https://www.pbs.org/wgbh/frontline/film/ un-sex-abuse-scandal.

Newman, Alana S., ed. *The Anonymous Us Project.* New York: Broadway Publications, 2013.

Newman, Alex. "Creepy 'World Government Summit' Targets Amer-ica, Freedom." *New American.* February 21, 2018. https://www. thenewamerican.com/world-news/asia/ item/28339-creepy-world-government-summit-targets-america-freedom.

———. "UN Exposed as Haven for Child Rapists; More Scandals Coming." *New American.* February 19, 2018. https://www.the-newamerican.com/world-news/europe/ item/28313-un-exposed-as-haven-for-child-rapists-More-scan-dals-coming.

———. "UN LGBT Czar on Indoctrinating Children: 'The Younger the Better.'" *New American*. April 4, 2017. https://www.the-newamerican.com/culture/faith-and-morals/item/25742-un-pushing-homosexuality-gender-confusion-on-children.

Nicholls, Peter. "I Don't Know How Many Children I Raped While Working for the UN." *The Times*. July 29, 2018. https://www.thetimes.co.uk/article/i-dont-know-how-many-children-i-raped-while-working-for-the-un-c99qx5mzn.

NoVo Foundation. "About Us." https://novofoundation.org/about-us.

Nossiter, Bernard. "Population Prizes from UN Assailed." *New York Times*. July 24, 1983. https://www.nytimes.com/1983/07/24/world/population-prizes-from-un-assailed.html.

OECD. *The Future of Education and Skills: Education 2030*. 2018. http://www.oecd.org/education/2030/E2030%20Position%20Paper%20(05.04.2018).pdf.

———. *Global Competency for an Inclusive World*. Paris: OECD, 2016. http://globalcitizen.nctu.edu.tw/wp-content/uploads/2016/12/2.-Global-competency-for-an-inclusive-world.pdf.

———. "Global Relations." http://www.oecd.org/global-relations/oecdpartnershipswithinternationalorganisations/.

———. "Inclusive Growth." http://www.oecd.org/inclusive-growth/about/partners/.

———. "LGBTI Inclusiveness." http://www.oecd.org/social/soc/lgbti.htm.

———. "OECD Global Blockhain Policy Forum Agenda." Paris: OECD, September 2019. https://www.oecd.org/finance/OECD-Global-Blockchain-Policy-Forum-2019-Agenda.pdf.

———. *Preparing Our Youth for an Inclusive and Sustainable World: The OECD PISA Global Competence Framework*. Paris: OECD, 2018. http://www.oecd.org/pisa/Handbook-PISA-2018-Global-Competence.pdf.

———. "Recommendation of the Council on Artificial Intelligence." May 21, 2019. https://legalinstruments.oecd.org/en/instruments/OECD-LEGAL-0449.

———. *Social and Emotional Skills: Well-Being, Connectedness and Success.* http://www.oecd.org/education/school/UPDATED%20Social%20and%20Emotional%20Skills%20-%20Well-being,%20connectedness%20and%20success.pdf%20(website).pdf.

———. "Using Educational Research and Innovation to Address Inequality and Achievement Gaps in Education." December 2017. http://www.oecd.org/officialdocuments/publicdisplaydocumentpdf/?cote=EDU/CERI/CD(2018)11&docLanguage=En.

"Organizations That Support the Decriminalization of Prostitution." Decriminalize Sex Work. https://decriminalizesex.work/news/endorsement/.

Osher, David, Lawrence B. Friedman, and Kimberly Kindziora. *CASEL/NoVo Collaborating Disctricts Initiative Evalution Executive Summary.* American Institutes for Research. November 2012. https://casel.org/wp-content/uploads/2016/09/THURS-8-AIR-OSHER-Exec-Summary.pdf.

Panné, Jean-Louis et al. *The Black Book of Communism: Crimes, Terror, Repression.* Cambridge: Harvard University Press, 1999.

Parker, Luke. "ID2020, Held at the United Nations, Features 'Lots and Lots of Blockchain.'" Brave New Coin. May 21, 2016. https://brave-newcoin.com/insights/id2020-held-at-the-united-nations-features-lots-and-lots-of-blockchain.

Pauvert, Jean Claude. *A Methodological Guide to the Application of Various Categories of Educational Personnel.* UNESCO. 1984. http://unesdoc.unesco.org/images/0008/000836/083649eb.pdf.

Peterson, Jordan B., *12 Rules for Life: An Antidote to Chaos.* Toronto: Random House Canada, 2018.

Pike, Molly Rose. "Parents Hail 'Drag Queen Story Time' in Primary Schools as a 'Really Brilliant Idea' to Teach Children about Gender Identity—But What Do You Think?" *Daily Mail.* March 14,

2018. http://www.dailymail.co.uk/femail/article-5499553/Parents-praise-drag-queen-story-time-Morning.html.

Pirog, Maureen, and Edward D. Vargas. "Cohabiting Violence" in Jackson, Nicky Ali, ed. *Encyclopedia of Domestic Violence*. New York, NY: Routledge, 2007. http://edwardvargas.com/wp-content/uploads/2016/04/Encyclopedia-of-Domestic-Violence-1.pdf.

Pizan, Christine de. *The Book of the City of Ladies*, revised edition. Translated by Earl Jeffrey Richards. New York: Persea Books, 1998.

Planned Parenthood. "How Safe Is NuvaRing?" https://www.planned-parenthood.org/learn/birth-control/birth-control-vaginal-ring-nuvaring/how-safe-nuvaring.

———. "Planned Parenthood Global Congratulates Carmen Barroso on Winning the Prestigious 2016 United Nations Population Award." April 28, 2016. https://www.plannedparenthood.org/about-us/newsroom/press-releases/planned-parenthood-global-congratulates-carmen-barroso-on-winning-the-prestigious-2016-united-nations-population-award.

———. "What Are STDs and How Are They Transmitted." YouTube. January 4, 2016. https://www.youtube.com/watch?v=pBMhfIHUP8M&feature=youtu.be.

———. "When Someone Definitely Wants to Have Sex." YouTube. September 21, 2015. https://www.youtube.com/watch?v=VmcGigHzpK0.

———. "When Someone Doesn't Want to Have Sex." YouTube. September 21, 2015. https://www.youtube.com/watch?annotation_id=annotation_3410390393&feature=iv&src_vid=D-8isMT2u9A&v=QSDjSetlGiw.

———. "When Someone Isn't Quite Sure If They Want to Have Sex: What Is Consent?" YouTube. September 21, 2015. https://www.youtube.com/watch?v=D-8isMT2u9A.

Planned Parenthood Mar Monte. "Transgender Hormone Services." https://www.plannedparenthood.org/planned-parenthood-mar-monte/patient-resources/transgender-services.

Population Research Institute. "Natural Family Planning: The Best Worst Thing Ever." YouTube. October 18, 2014. https://www.youtube.com/watch?v=wixyH9LoJP8.

———. "Keep U.S. Tax Dollars from Funding Population Control in China." https://www.pop.org/project/stop-tax-dollars-funding-population-control-china.

Powell, Gary. "Why the Gay and Lesbian Equality Movement Must Oppose Surrogacy." MercatorNet. June 28, 2019. https://www.mercatornet.com/conjugality/view/why-the-gay-and-lesbian-equality-movement-must-oppose-surrogacy/22602.

Poy, Petrina Lee, María Faget Montero, and Martha Murdock. *You, Your Life, Your Dreams: A Book for Caribbean Adolescents*, vols. 1–3. New York: Family Care International, Inc., 2008.

"Problems with Contraceptives." *Natural Womanhood*. Accessed July 10, 2018. https://naturalwomanhood.org/learn/problems-with-contraceptives.

Rarick, Tim. "Fathers Be Good to Your Daughters: The Powerful Connection between Fatherlessness and Sexual Exploitation." Presentation. November 2017. Facebook Page for the National Center on Sexual Exploitation. https://www.facebook.com/centeronexploitation/videos/1632297383496034.

Ravitch, Diane. "Mercedes Schneider Explains: Who Paid for the Common Core Standards." HuffPost. December 10, 2013. https://www.huffingtonpost.com/diane-ravitch/bill-gates-common-core_b_4079447.html.

Read, Herbert. Preface to Ashton-Warner, Sylvia. *Teacher*. New York: Simon and Schuster, 1963.

Regnerus, Mark. *Cheap Sex: The Transformation of Men, Marriage, and Monogamy.* New York: Oxford University Press, 2017.

Ribar, David C., "Why Marriage Matters for Child Wellbeing." *The Future of Children* 25, no. 2 (Fall 2015). https://futureofchildren.princeton.edu/sites/futureofchildren/files/media/marriage_and_child_wellbeing_revisited_25_2_full_journal.pdf.

Roberts, David. "This Book Ranks the Top 100 Solutions to Climate Change. The Results Are Surprising." Vox. April 22, 2019. https://www.vox.com/energy-and-environment/2017/5/10/15589038/top-100-solutions-climate-change-ranked.

Rockwell Jr., Llewellyn H. "The Horrors of Communist China." Mises Institute. May 1, 2017. https://mises.org/wire/horrors-communist-china.

Rosenthal, Jack. "President Vetoes Child Care Plan as Irresponsible." *New York Times*. December 10, 1971. https://www.nytimes.com/1971/12/10/archives/president-vetoes-child-care-plan-as-irresponsible-he-terms-bill.html.

Ruth Institute. "Dr J Show—Brandon Showalter Interview." YouTube. September 6, 2019. https://www.youtube.com/watch?v=Kxy2mGPQ8z4.

Ruse, Austin. "Your Children 'Soft Entry Points' for Homosexual Agenda." Center for Family and Human Rights. February 7, 2017. https://c-fam.org/children-soft-entry-points-homosexual-agenda.

Rutz, David. "MSNBC Calls Republican's Belief in Only Two Genders 'Incendiary.'" The Washington Free Beacon. August 23, 2019. https://freebeacon.com/politics/msnbc-calls-republicans-belief-in-only-two-genders-incendiary/?fbclid=IwAR2Cp-6VIPKytHL5JZOjojH3_BODm1ss9Yh-UCr-wxiT-Xzd5O6kaQf2jXk.

Sadeleski, Vanessa. "Legal Minimum Ages and the Realization of Adolescents' Rights." UNICEF: 2015. https://www.comprehensivesexualityeducation.org/wp-content/uploads/20160406_UNICEF_Edades_Minima_Eng1.pdf.

Sanger, Margaret. *The Pivot of Civilization*. San Bernardino, 2015.

Schlafly, Phyllis. "Microsoft Founder Bill Gates Teams Up with UNESCO." Townhall. November 28, 2005. https://townhall.com/columnists/phyllisschlafly/2005/11/28/microsoft-founder-bill-gates-teams-up-with-unesco-n1027756.

Schleicher, Andreas. "Use Data to Build Better Schools." TED. July 2012. https://www.ted.com/talks/andreas_schleicher_use_data_to_build_better_schools.

"School-Based Health Centers—a Bad Idea?" Clallam County Republican Party. February 18, 2017. https://clallamrepublicans.org/sbhc/.

Schroeder, Elizabeth, Eva S. Goldforb, and Nora Gelperin. 3 R's: *Rights, Respect, and Responsibility: A K-12 Sexuality Curriculum.* Advocates for Youth, 2015.

Schrupp, Antjie. *A Brief History of Feminism.* Translated by Sophie Lewis. Cambridge: MIT Press, 2017.

Schultz, Kai, and Rajneesh Bhandari. "Noted Humanitarian Charged with Child Rape in Nepal, Stunning a Village." *New York Times.* May 11, 2018. https://www.nytimes.com/2018/05/11/world/asia/nepal-peter-dalglish-aid-pedophilia.html.

Sedletzki, Vanessa. *Legal Minimum Ages and the Realization of Adolescents' Rights.* UNICEF. January 2016. https://www.comprehensivesexualityeducation.org/wp-content/uploads/20160406_UNICEF_Edades_Minima_Engl.pdf.

"SETDA Launches Updated Digital Instructional Materials Acquisition Policies for States (DMAPS) Portal." EconoTimes. April 12, 2018. https://www.econotimes.com/SETDA-Launches-Updated-Digital-Instructional-Materials-Acquisition-Policies-for-States-DMAPS-Portal-1251715.

"Sexes: Attacking the Last Taboo." *Time.* April 14, 1980. http://content.time.com/time/magazine/article/0,9171,923966,00.html.

Shahi, Pragati. "In Nepal, Child Abuse Trial Highlights Shortcomings in Sector." Devex. June 8, 2018. https://www.devex.com/news/in-nepal-child-abuse-trial-highlights-shortcomings-in-sector-92855.

Showalter, Brandon. "Feminists Activists Expose Abuse, Horrors of Girls Harmed by Transgender Medicalization." *Christian Post.* January 30, 2019. https://www.christianpost.com/us/feminist-activists-expose-abuse-horrors-of-girls-harmed-by-transgender-medicalization.html.

SIECUS. "About Us." https://siecus.org/about-siecus/.

———. *Guidelines for Comprehensive Sexuality Education.* 3rd edition. (New York and Washington, D.C.: Fulton Press, 2004).

https://siecus.org/wp-content/uploads/2018/07/Guidelines-CSE.
pdf.

———. "News & Updates." https://siecus.org/
sex-ed-is-a-vehicle-for-social-change/.

———. "Our History." https://siecus.org/about-siecus/our-history/.

Siggins, Dustin. "Using Contraception Increases Breast Cancer by
50%, New Study Finds." LifeSite News. August 4, 2014. https://
www.lifesitenews.com/news/
using-contraception-increases-breast-cancer-by-50-new-study-
finds.

Silver, Lee. "Can a Man Really Get Pregnant? Sure, but It Might Kill
Him." *Science20* (blog). April 7, 2008. https://www.science20.
com/
challenging_nature/a_real_pregnant_man_almost_certainly_pos-
sible_but_it_might_kill_him.

Singer, Peter. *The Life You Can Save: Acting Now to End World Poverty.* New York: Random House, 2009.

Skousen, W. Cleon. *The Naked Communist.* Salt Lake City: Ensign
Publishing, 1958.

Skovlund, C. W., L. S. Morch, L.V . Kessing, T. Lange, and O. Lide-
gaard. "Association of Hormonal Contraception with Suicide
Attempts and Suicide." *American Journal of Psychiatry* 175, no. 4
(April 1, 2018). https://www.ncbi.nlm.nih.gov/pubmed/29145752.

Slater, Sharon. *Stand for the Family: Alarming Evidence and Firsthand
Accounts from the Frontlines of the Battle for the Family.* Mesa, Ari-
zona: Inglestone Publishing, 2016.

Socialist International. "About Us: Full List of Member Parties and
Organisations." https://www.socialistinternational.org/about-us/
members/.

———. "Councils: Paris Council: Global Economy—Climate
Change—Resolution of Conflicts." https://www.socialistinterna-
tional.org/councils/paris-2010/.

———. "Progressive Politics for a Fairer World." https://www.socialistint-
ernational.org/about-us/.

Stanton, Glenn T. "CDC Study Says Teen Virgins Are Healthier." The Federalist. November 29, 2016. https://thefederalist.com/2016/11/29/cdc-study-says-teen-virgins-healthier/.

Steward, Melissa. "The Father Factor." National Fatherhood Initiative. November 12, 2013. https://www.fatherhood.org/the-father-absence-crisis-in-america.

Strahan, Thomas W., ed. *Detrimental Effects of Abortion: An Annotated Bibliography with Commentary.* Springfield, IL: Acorn Books, 2002.

Strudwick, Patrick. "This Trans Woman Kept Her Beard And Couldn't Be Happier." BuzzFeed. July 16, 2015, https://www.buzzfeed.com/patrickstrudwick/this-transgender-woman-has-a-full-beard-and-she-couldnt-be-h?utm_term=.qhx8O4ejw#.sy9YwBWlE.

Sullins, Paul. "The Gay Gene Myth Has Been Exploded." MercatorNet. September 3, 2019. https://www.mercatornet.com/conjugality/view/the-gay-gene-myth-has-been-exploded/22824.

Sullivan, JaKell. "2018 Utah Eagle Forum Convention Jakell Sullivan 'K-12 Assessments.'" YouTube. January 20, 2018. https://www.youtube.com/watch?v=FrOYWz148VQ&feature=youtu.be&app=desktop.

Sutherland, Anna. "How Strong Families Help Create Prosperous States." Institute for Family Studies. October 21, 2015. https://ifstudies.org/blog/how-strong-families-help-create-prosperous-states.

Tacopino, Joe. "Not Using Transgender Pronouns Could Get You Fined." *New York Post.* May 19, 2016. http://nypost.com/2016/05/19/city-issues-new-guidelines-on-transgender-pronouns.

Tapson, Mark. "My Sister Kate: The Destructive Feminist Legacy of Kate Millet." FrontPage Magazine. February 7, 2018. https://www.frontpagemag.com/fpm/269251/my-sister-kate-destructive-feminist-legacy-kate-mark-tapson.

Tayag, Yasmin. "Population Control Is the Climate Change Fix Nobody Wants to Talk About: But Scientists Insist It's Not as Bad

as It Sounds." *Inverse*. August 31, 2018. https://www.inverse.com/
article/48236-population-control-can-help-climate-change.

———. "The Voluntary Human Extinction Movement Is Both Anti-
Republican and Anti-Death." *Inverse*. April 11, 2016. https://
www.inverse.com/
article/14056-the-voluntary-human-extinction-movement-is-
both-anti-republican-and-anti-death.

TEDx Talks. "Cancel Marriage: Merav Michaeli at TEDxJaffa." You-
Tube. November 10, 2012. https://www.youtube.com/
watch?v=tTf8jKMGsGE.

———. "Reimagining Learning: Richard Culatta at TEDxBeaconStreet."
YouTube. January 10, 2013. https://www.youtube.com/
watch?v=Z0uAuonMXrg.

Teresi, Dick. "How to Get a Man Pregnant." *New York Times*.
November 27, 1994. https://www.nytimes.com/1994/11/27/maga-
zine/how-to-get-a-man-pregnant.html.

Thomas, Cal. "Slaughter of the Innocents Reaches New Depths."
Townhall. February 5, 2019. https://townhall.com/columnists/
calthomas/2019/02/05/slaughter-of-the-innocents-reaches-new-
depths-n2540767?utm_source=thdaily&utm_
medium=email&utm_campaign=nl&newsletterad=02/05/2019&
bcid=2f42f9885cc2b30c3453b1ebbc133733&recip=18362275.

Tracy, Matt. "New York State Legalizes Gestational Surrogacy." Gay
City News. April 2, 2020. https://www.gaycitynews.com/
new-york-state-legalizes-gestational-surrogacy/.

Treacher, Jim. "Flashback: Melissa-Harris Perry Says Children Belong
to the Government." The Daily Caller. February 29, 2016. http://
dailycaller.com/2016/02/29/
flashback-melissa-harris-perry-says-children-belong-to-the-gov-
ernment.

"The UN Sex-for-Food Scandal." *Washington Times*. May 9, 2006.
https://www.washingtontimes.com/news/2006/
may/9/20060509-090826-9806r.

United Nations. Convention on the Privileges and Immunities of the United Nations. February 13, 1946. http://www.un.org/en/ethics/pdf/convention.pdf.

———. "Sustainable Development Goals." https://sustainabledevelopment.un.org/sdgs.

———. Universal Declaration of Human Rights. December 10, 1948. http://www.un.org/en/universal-declaration-human-rights.

United Nations Educational, Scientific and Cultural Organisation (UNESCO). "Cooperation Agreement between UNESCO and Microsoft Corporation." November 17, 2004. http://www.unesco.org/new/fileadmin/MULTIMEDIA/HQ/CI/CI/pdf/strategy_microsoft_agreement.pdf.

———. "Funders." GEM Report. https://en.unesco.org/gem-report/funders.

———. "Target 4.2—Early Childhood." Global Education Monitoring Report. http://gem-report-2017.unesco.org/en/chapter/target-4-2-early-childhood-2.

———. "About Us." Global Education Monitoring Report. https://en.unesco.org/gem-report/about.

———. Incheon Declaration and Framework for Action, Education 2030. 2016. https://unesdoc.unesco.org/ark:/48223/pf0000245656.

———. International Technical Guidance on Sexuality Education: An Evidence-Informed Approach. Revised edition. 2018. http://www.unaids.org/en/resources/documents/2018/international-technical-guidance-on-sexuality-education.

———. International Guidelines on Sexuality Education: An Evidence Informed Approach to Effective Sex, Relationships and HIV/STI Education. June 2009. ED-2009/WS/36 (CLD 1983.9). http://www.refworld.org/docid/4a69b8902.html.

———. "New International Guidelines Spell Out What Sexuality Education Needs to Teach." October 2009. http://portal.unesco.org/education/en/ev.php-URL_ID=59504&URL_DO=DO_TOPIC&URL_SECTION=201.html.

————. *UNESCO ICT Competency Framework for Teachers.* Paris: UNESCO, 2011. https://unesdoc.unesco.org/ark:/48223/pf0000213475.

United Nations Global Compact. "Who We Are." https://www.unglobalcompact.org/what-is-gc/mission.

United Nations International Children's Emergency Fund (UNICEF). *All In to End the Adolescent AIDS Epidemic.* December 2016. https://www.unaids.org/sites/default/files/media_asset/ALLIN2016ProgressReport_en.pdf.

————. *Implementation Handbook for the Convention on the Rights of the Child,* 3rd edition. Geneva: United Nations Children's Fund, 2007. https://www.unicef.org/publications/files/Implementation_Handbook_for_the_Convention_on_the_Rights_of_the_Child.pdfpdf.

United Nations Population Fund (UNFPA). *The Evaluation of Comprehensive Sexuality Education Programmes: A Focus on the Gender and Empowerment Outcomes.* New York: UNPFA, 2015. https://www.unfpa.org/sites/default/files/pub-pdf/UNFPAEvaluationWEB4.pdf.

————. "Press Release: Physician, Two NGOs Win 2018 UN Population Award." March 29, 2018. https://www.unfpa.org/press/physician-two-ngos-win-2018-un-population-award.

United Nations Secretary-General. "Secretary-General's Address to High Level Meeting on the United Nations Response to Sexual Exploitation and Abuse [as delivered]." September 18, 2017. https://www.un.org/sg/en/content/sg/statement/2017-09-18/secretary-generals-address-high-level-meeting-united-nations.

USBE Media. "March 19, 2020 Utah State Board of Education Board Meeting." YouTube. March 29, 2020. https://www.youtube.com/watch?v=apbV3Oik8GM.

Utah TCC. "Utah CoSN Chapter." http://utcc.us/cosn.

Vespa, Matt. "Venezuela: 21st Century Socialism Is so Great That Doctors and Teachers Are Now Hooking for Food." Townhall. September 26, 2017. https://townhall.com/tipsheet/mattvespa/2017/09/26/

venezuela-21st-century-socialism-is-so-great-that-doctors-and-teach-ers-are-now-h-n2386208.

Ward, Helen. "Defamilialisation: An Ideology That Shapes Our Lives." MercatorNet. December 8, 2015. https://www.mercator-net.com/articles/view/defamilialisation-an-ideology-that-shapes-our-lives/17310.

Warmington, Joe. "Ex-Deputy Education Minister, Jailed for Child Porn Charges, Out on Parole." *Toronto Sun.* October 7, 2017. https://torontosun.com/2017/10/07/ex-deputy-education-minister-jailed-for-child-porn-charges-out-on-parole/wcm/0d5fc1be-152e-49d2-9f2f-5e4966ad3dbe.

Washington, George. "George Washington > Quotes > Quotable Quote." GoodReads. https://www.goodreads.com/quotes/24983-my-mother-was-The-most-Beautiful-woman-i-ever-saw.

Weale, Sally. "'It's a Political Failure:' How Sweden's Celebrated Schools System Fell into Crisis." *The Guardian.* June 10, 2015. https://www.theguardian.com/world/2015/jun/10/sweden-schools-crisis-political-failure-education.

Weed, Stan E., and Irene H. Ericksen. *Re-Examining the Evidence for Comprehensive Sex Education in Schools, Part One: Research Findings in the United States.* Salt Lake City: Institute for Research and Evaluation, 2018. https://www.comprehensivesexu-alityeducation.org/wp-content/uploads/Reexamining_the_Evi-dence-CSE_in_USA_6-1-18FINAL.pdf.

Welcoming Schools. "'Yes, They Are a family!': Kids' Questions with Sample Responses about Family." Welcoming Schools. Human Rights Campaign Foundation. http://www.welcomingschools.org/pages/yes-they-are-a-family.

Western, John. "'Why Did You Let Us Do This?' As a Teen I Had My Breasts Removed Because I Wanted to Be a Boy—but It Was a Mistake so I'm Transitioning Back." *The Sun.* December 19, 2018. https://www.thesun.co.uk/news/7997226/teenager-breasts-removed-transgender-male.

Wikipedia, s.v. "Audrey Azoulay." Last modified February 16, 2020, 23:24. https://en.wikipedia.org/wiki/Audrey_Azoulay. https://en.wikipedia.org/wiki/Audrey_Azoulay.

———. "Irina Bokova." Last modified February 17, 2020, 05:25. https://en.wikipedia.org/wiki/Irina_Bokova. https://en.wikipedia.org/wiki/Irina_Bokova.

———. "Jose Angel Gurria." Last modified February 9, 2020, 09:36. https://en.wikipedia.org/wiki/José_Ángel_Gurría. https://en.wikipedia.org/wiki/Jos%C3%A9_%C3%81ngel_Gurr%C3%ADa.

———. "International Planned Parenthood Federation." Last modified January 4, 2020, 20:34. https://en.wikipedia.org/wiki/International_Planned_Parenthood_Federation.

———. "Yin and Yang." Last modified February 19, 2020, 05:29. https://en.wikipedia.org/wiki/Yin_and_yang.

White, Hilary. "Age of Consent at 14 Makes Canada Favoured Sex Tourism Destination." LifeSite News. December 19, 2006. https://www.lifesitenews.com/news/age-of-consent-at-14-makes-canada-favoured-sex-tourism-destination.

World Health Organization (WHO). *Sexual Health, Human Rights and the Law*. Geneva: World Health Organization, 2015. https://apps.who.int/iris/bitstream/handle/10665/175556/9789241564984_eng.pdf;jsessionid=48C01ACCF9E9DC2B1E657D97A9798D23?sequence=1.

WHO Regional Office for Europe and BZgA. *Training Matters: A Framework for Core Competencies of Sexuality Educators*. Cologne: BZgA, 2017. http://www.euro.who.int/__data/assets/pdf_file/0003/337593/BZgA-training-framework.pdf.

Wilcox, Bradford W. "Suffer the Little Children: Cohabitation and the Abuse of America's Children." Public Discourse. Witherspoon Institute. April 22, 2011. http://www.thepublicdiscourse.com/2011/04/3181.

———. "The Nuclear Family Is Still Indispensable." *The Atlantic*. February 21, 2020. https://www.theatlantic.com/ideas/archive/2020/02/nuclear-family-still-indispensable/606841/.

Wilcox, Bradford W. et al. *Why Marriage Matters, Third Edition: Thirty Conclusions from the Social Sciences*. New York: Institute for American Values, 2011. https://irp-cdn.multiscreensite.com/64484987/files/uploaded/Why-Marriage-Matters-Third-Edition-FINAL.pdf

Williams, Abigail. "Trump Admin Expands Ban on Foreign Aid for Abortion Services." NBC News. March 26, 2019. https://www.nbcnews.com/politics/politics-news/trump-admin-expands-ban-foreign-aid-abortion-services-n987546.

"Women Have Gone to the Labour Front," in *The Socialist Upsurge in China's Countryside*. Chinese ed., vol. II.

Wyld, Adrian. "Melinda Gates Will Step In to Help Trudeau Push Gender Equality at G7." *Montreal Gazette*. June 5, 2018. https://montrealgazette.com/news/quebec/melinda-gates-to-step-in-to-help-trudeau-push-gender-equality-at-g7.

Yenor, Scott. "Sex, Gender, and the Origin of the Culture Wars: An Intellectual History." Heritage Foundation. June 30, 2017. http://report.heritage.org/fp63.

Yoshihara, Susan. "UN Women to Replace 'Women' with 'Gender.'" Center for Family & Human Rights. July 25, 2019. https://c-fam.org/friday_fax/un-women-to-replace-women-with-gender/?inf_contact_key=f91f00628a045abb2c5253b5c7563190f651f238aa2edbb9c8b7cff03e0b16a0.

Zedong, Mao. Introductory note to "A Youth Shock Brigade of the No. 9 Agricultural Producers' Co-operative in Hsinping Township, Chungshan County." *The Socialist Upsurge in China's Countryside*. Chinese ed., vol III. 1955.

NOTES

Chapter Two: True Power

1. Firestone, *The Dialectic of Sex*, 65.
2. Ibid., 66.
3. Millett, *Sexual Politics*, 178.
4. Gordon, *The Moral Property of Women*.
5. McCarthy, "Gender Ideology and the Humanum," 280.
6. Aristotle, "Aristotle > Quotes > Quotable Quote."
7. Gandhi, *Young India*, 361.
8. Zedong, "A Youth Shock Brigade."
9. Mandela, "Address by President Nelson Mandela at the National Men's March."
10. Confucius, "Confucius > Quotes > Quotable Quote."
11. Kennedy, "Re: United States Committee for UNICEF July 25, 1963." Interestingly, this quotation is from Kennedy's plea to support the children of the world through the efforts of the United Nations agency UNICEF. We will discuss the unfortunate corruption of UNICEF in Part IV.
12. Read, Preface to *Teacher*.
13. Hopper, *What Russia Intends*, 83.
14. Iscan, "Hitler Youth: The Indoctrination of a Population."
15. Firestone, *The Dialectic of Sex*, 180–81.

16.   Washington, "George Washington > Quotes > Quotable Quote."
17.   Holland, *The Life of Abraham Lincoln*, 23.
18.   Erickson, "Fathers Don't Mother and Mothers Don't Father," 7.
19.   Jean Paul, "Jean Paul Quotes."

Chapter Three: Freeing Women and Socialism

1.   See Panné et al., *The Black Book of Communism: Crimes, Terror, Repression.*
2.   Marx and Engels, "Chapter II. Proletarians and Communists."
3.   Engels, *The Origin of the Family, Private Property, and the State*, 17.
4.   Ferdinand Mount wrote a book refuting Engels's premises called *The Subversive Family*. It's fascinating that even though Engels's premises have been shown to be grossly incorrect, his conclusions based on those premises have been widely embraced. The preface to the 2010 edition of *The Origin of the Family* says it is "among the more important and politically applicable texts in the Marxist canon, influencing gender equality legislation in much of the twentieth-century communist world—not least, divorce and family planning policy in Maoist China—and providing the ideological underpinnings for socialist feminism in the West." The widespread influence of Engels's misguided, discredited, grossly incorrect ideas is nothing short of stunning.
5.   Engels, *The Origin of the Family*, 80.
6.   Ibid., 105.
7.   Ibid., 106.
8.   Ibid., 86–87.
9.   Ibid., 114.
10.   Ibid., 107.
11.   Ibid.
12.   Engels's socialist doctrine of diffusing parenthood in the name of equality has persisted and garnered eager disciples. For example, political commentator Melissa Harris-Perry famously said in 2013: "We have to break through our . . . private idea that kids belong to their parents or kids belong to their families and recognize that kids belong to whole communities. Once it is everybody's responsibility and not just the household's, then we start to make better investments." See Treacher, "Flashback: Melissa-Harris Perry Says Children Belong to the Government."
13.   Engels, *The Origin of the Family*, 105.

14. Mao Zedong was an avowed communist/socialist whose reign in China was one of the bloodiest and most destructive eras in history. We will delve into the horrific details of Mao's socialist policies that victimized women and undercut the family in Part II. See these articles for a brief overview of the horrors of Maoist socialism: 1) Edwards, "The Legacy of Mao Zedong Is Mass Murder"; 2) Akbar, "Mao's Great Leap Forward"; and 3) Rockwell Jr., "The Horrors of Communist China." See also the memoirs *Wild Swans* by Jung Chang and *Socialism Is Great!* by Lijia Zhang.

15. Introductory note to "Women Have Gone to the Labour Front," in *The Socialist Upsurge in China's Countryside*.

16. Engels, *The Origin of the Family*, 105; Geiger, *The Family in Soviet Russia*, 47–48.

17. Geiger, *The Family in Soviet Russia*, 47–48.

18. Ibid., 68.

19. Engels, *The Origin of the Family*, 106.

20. Skousen, *The Naked Communist*, 72.

21. Ibid., 73.

22. Ibid.

23. Marx and Engels, "Chapter II. Proletarians and Communists."

24. Engels, *The Origin of the Family*, 106.

25. Engels's idea that monogamous marriage is a recent invention has been soundly debunked by modern scholars who insist "there is little evidence . . . for the prevalence of group marriage and extensive promiscuity." Engels, *The Origin of the Family*, 17.

26. See Engels, *The Origin of the Family*, 39. Bachofen's original work was called *Das Mutterrecht*.

27. Ibid., 71–72.

28. Ibid., 86.

29. Ibid., 87.

30. Ibid., 82.

Chapter Four: Freeing Women and Feminism

1. Skousen, *The Naked Communist*, 17.

2. Ibid., 56.

3. Ibid., 18, 51, 55.

4. Gordon, *The Moral Property of Women*.

5. Millett, *Sexual Politics*.

6. Schrupp, *A Brief History of Feminism*, vi.

7. I readily acknowledge that socialist and feminist ideas have circulated for millennia, dating back to at least the time of Plato, and that Engels and Firestone are by no means the only ones who have held the views they promote in their writings. I have chosen to focus on these two figures because they are considered iconic, representative figures in the socialist and feminist traditions.

8. Firestone, *The Dialectic of Sex*, 197.

9. Socialist experiments have been tried with large and small groups throughout history. Entire countries have been or are currently mired in the bog of Engels-style socialism that promises utopia but delivers destruction. Russia, Cuba, and Hungary are well-known instances of socialist catastrophe. Currently, the most alarming instance of epic socialist failure is Venezuela, a formerly prosperous country with rich natural resources and an educated populace, where former doctors now work as prostitutes and the masses scavenge for garbage to sell to stay alive. This is the ongoing legacy of socialism. Some countries who have adopted some socialist-leaning policies have not yet succumbed to socialist devastation. But time will take its toll on all countries that forfeit freedom and personal accountability in the name of "equality." See Vespa, "Venezuela: 21st Century Socialism Is So Great"; Kew, "Socialism: Venezuelans Scavenging."

10. Firestone, *The Dialectic of Sex*, 198.

11. Ibid., 185.

12. Ibid., 208.

13. Ibid., 11.

14. Ibid., 209.

15. Ibid., 94.

16. Ibid., 175.

17. Ibid., 180.

18. Ibid., 209.

19. Ibid., 186.

20. Ibid., 187.

21. Ibid., 209.

22. Ibid., 211.

23. For more on the power of intergenerational teaching, see Christensen, "Dispelling Utopian Illusions."

24. Mark Zuckerberg, founder and CEO of Facebook who achieved billionaire status in the free market capitalist system based on private ownership, made a proposal in 2016 that would make Shulamith

Firestone's Marxist-feminist heart beat proudly. In a commencement speech at Harvard, Zuckerberg said, "Every generation expands its definition of equality . . . Now it's our time to define a new social contract for our generation . . . We should explore ideas like universal basic income to give everyone a cushion to try new things." Firestone proposed a "guaranteed annual income from the state." Zuckerberg proposed a "universal basic income." These proposals are drawn from the same diseased well of socialism which employs the tactic of taking someone's private property and giving it to somebody else in order to achieve manufactured equality. See "Mark Zuckerberg's Commencement Address at Harvard."

25. Firestone, *Dialectic of Sex*, 82.
26. Ibid., 213.
27. Ibid., 187.
28. Ibid., 55.
29. Ibid., 93.
30. Ibid., 215.
31. Ibid., 187.
32. See Planned Parenthood, "What Are STDs and How Are They Transmitted" as an example of normalizing sexual disease.
33. The current implementation of massive, state-imposed sexuality instruction is a core focus of Part IV.
34. Lewis, *Full Surrogacy Now*, 27.
35. Ibid., 16.
36. Ibid., 26.
37. Ibid., 2.
38. Ibid., 140.
39. Ibid., 150.
40. Ibid., 28.
41. Ibid., 21.
42. Ibid., 60.
43. Ibid., 16.
44. Ibid., 119.
45. Ibid., 17.
46. Ibid., 19.
47. Ibid., 26.
48. Ibid., 29.
49. Ibid., 119.
50. Ibid., 47.

51.   Ibid., 153.
52.   Ibid., 130.
53.   Ibid., 18.
54.   Ibid., 156.
55.   Ibid., 167.
56.   Ibid., 118.
57.   Ibid., 119.
58.   Ibid., 117.

Chapter Five: Insanity

1.   All references to Chi An's story are from *A Mother's Ordeal* by Steven Mosher.
2.   Ibid., 240.
3.   Ibid., 274.
4.   Ibid., 218.
5.   Ibid., 177.
6.   Ibid., 333.
7.   Ibid., 145.
8.   We will extensively explore the key role International Planned Parenthood Federation plays in accomplishing global socialist aims through partnerships with the United Nations in Part IV.
9.   See the infamous videos of undercover encounters with Planned Parenthood Federation of America doctors and employees at the Center for Medical Progress website http://www. centerformedicalprogress.org/cmp/investigative-footage. Even after these videos—in which Planned Parenthood workers appear to offer information about the selling of fetal body parts to interested buyers— were brought to light, a massive campaign to "stand with Planned Parenthood" was enacted and Congress failed to defund the abortion giant. Some states that have tried to direct funding away from Planned Parenthood have been barred from doing so by court actions. Why? Because "planned parenthood" must persist if socialist aims are to be fully achieved.
10.   Mosher, *A Mother's Ordeal*, 213. Emphasis added.
11.   Research indicates that nearly two-thirds of abortions in America occur under situations of coercion wherein sexual partners, family members, or sexual abusers pressure the mother to abort her child. See TheUnChoice.com for more information, research, statistics, and resources on abortion.

12. Mosher, *A Mother's Ordeal*, 148.
13. Ibid., 216.
14. We will address abortion as a tenet of the women's rights movement in greater depth in Chapter Sixteen.
15. Mosher, *A Mother's Ordeal*, 243.
16. Ibid., 250.

Chapter Six: The Sanity of Anatomy

1. For information on non-uterus gestation and to see an artificial womb model, see Cook, "Ectogenesis Keeps Chugging Along." Sophie Lewis is an advocate for cyborg ecology, which seeks to mesh man and machine especially in matters of reproduction. Some believe artificial gestation will be a possibility in a few short years.
2. Lewis vehemently disagrees. She says the "substance of parents gets scrambled" in their children and "their source code doesn't 'live on' in kids after they die any more than that of nonparents." She calls a child "a randomly reassembled genetic package" that has no meaningful connection to its biological parents. On the other hand, one bioethicist argues that genetic inheritance is so robust that "having the newborn infant in the world that carries the genetic material of the genetic parents violates their right to genetic privacy." See Thomas, "Slaughter of the Innocents." This line of reasoning is used to defend the rights of parents "to kill (or leave to die) their newborn infant" or to abort it before birth, all of which violate the child's rights on every level.

Chapter Seven: Perfection, Freedom, and Parenthood

1. Mount, *The Subversive Family*, 218.
2. Barclay, "The Family: It's Surviving and Healthy."
3. In a 1947 interview for *One Minute News*, Margaret Sanger argued that there should be "no more babies" in "starving" countries for the next ten years. Her books *The Pivot of Civilization* and *Woman and the New Race* are peppered with references to "those who should never have been born," "human junk," "surplus children," and the "wickedness of creating large families."
4. LaFollette, "Licensing Parents," 182–97.
5. Peterson, *12 Rules for Life*, 41.

6. Women's influence in regulating the ongoing quality of human life has been called "the moral force of women." See Christofferson, "The Moral Force of Women."

7. Mero, *Vouchers, Vows, and Vexations,* 30.

8. An example of a state bill that seeks to implement regulation of young children by way of an appointed committee can be found at https://le.utah.gov/~2018/bills/static/HB0319.html. If interpreted to encompass home settings, this bill and others like it could pave the way for government regulation of parents' teaching of their own children in the home.

Chapter Eight: Love or Money

1. Firestone, *The Dialectic of Sex,* 114.

2. Engels, *The Origin of the Family,* 14.

3. Tapson, "My Sister Kate."

4. Ibid.

5. Crittenden, *The Price of Motherhood,* 34.

6. For discussion on the anatomical smallness of women, see Pizan, *The Book of the City of Ladies,* 36–37. Christine de Pizan was a brilliant fifteenth-century woman who wrote in defense of womanhood and is regarded as one of the earliest feminists.

7. Wikipedia, s.v. "Yin and Yang."

8. Mount, *The Subversive Family,* 43.

9. See "Effective Altruism Is Changing the Way We Do Good."

10. Singer, *The Life You Can Save,* 134.

11. Cook, "Utilitarianism Goes On a Charm Offensive."

12. Family Watch International, familywatch.org.

13. Cook, "Is It Immoral to Love Your Kids Because They Are Related to You?"

14. Ibid.

15. Gordon, *The Moral Property of Women.*

Chapter Nine: The Goodness of Men

1. Firestone, *The Dialectic of Sex,* 177.

2. Mount, *The Subversive Family,* 192.

3. ABC, "Consequences, Citizenship and Climate."

4. Steward, "The Father Factor."

5. Rarick, "Fathers, Be Good to Your Daughters."

6. For more information about the importance of fathers, see the National Fatherhood Initiative at fatherhood.org.
7. Mount, *The Subversive Family*, 130.
8. Ibid., 221.
9. The Austin Institute, "The Economics of Sex." See also Regnerus, *Cheap Sex*.
10. Fagan, "The Real Root Causes of Violent Crime."
11. Wilcox et al., *Why Marriage Matters*.
12. Pirog and Vargas, "Cohabiting Violence," 174.
13. Wilcox et al., *Why Marriage Matters*.
14. Fagan, Johnson, and Rector, "Marriage: Still the Safest Place for Women and Children."
15. National Fatherhood Initiative, "Just the Facts."

Chapter Ten: Sexual Equality and a New Right

1. Firestone, *The Dialectic of Sex*, 11.
2. The Beijing Declaration is a non-binding UN document. The Convention on the Rights of Persons with Disabilities and the Convention on the Rights of the Child (CRC) are binding documents, but neither has been ratified by the United States by the required two-thirds Senate vote.
3. The exceptions to this, of course, are cases where a child is orphaned or in other extreme circumstances where it is considered in the best interest of the child to transfer legal stewardship of an existing child to a nonbiologically connected entity.
4. Sophie Lewis cuts to the quick on this question, insisting that there is no right to parenthood over one's offspring, nor is there any right for children to claim their own parents.
5. The Welcoming Schools program promoted by the Human Rights Campaign coaches teachers on how to respond to children's questions such as, "Don't you need a woman and a man to have a baby?" The teacher is instructed to say: "Children come into families in many different ways, and the families that love the children may have a mom and a dad, some a mom, some a dad, and some have two moms or two dads." The suggested answer to the question above negates the medically accurate fact that it does indeed take a woman and a man to have a baby regardless of how the reproductive cells of their bodies get together. The proposed answer de-normalizes the possessing of one's own biological children and parents.

6. See Brown, "We Like Heteronormativity and We Don't Want You to Smash It."
7. Gay Star News, "Elly Barnes—Educate and Celebrate."
8. UNESCO, *International Guidelines on Sexuality Education*, 51.

Chapter Eleven: Commercializing Parenthood

1. Hear the story of two homosexual American men who commission a baby through a surrogate in India in "Birthstory," Radiolab WNYC Studios.
2. For women who wish to exercise their "right" to parenthood without coupling with a man, finding a sperm donor is often easier and less expensive than finding a woman who will act as a surrogate since the time, inconvenience, emotional investment, pain, health risks, and physical consequences of donating sperm is less significant than donating eggs. For an in-depth look at egg donation, see the documentary *Eggsploitation* and other documentaries from the Center for Bioethics and Culture at   cbc-network.org.
3. Jones, "The Designer Baby Factory."
4. See a review of *A Transnational Feminist View of Surrogacy Biomarkets in India* at Blaine, "The Dangerous Effects of Surrogacy."
5. Tracy, "New York State Legalizes Gestational Surrogacy."
6. Jones, "The Designer Baby Factory."
7. Powell, "Why the Gay and Lesbian Equality Movement Must Oppose Surrogacy."
8. Ibid.
9. Ibid.
10. Ibid.
11. Newman, ed., *The Anonymous Us Project*, 33.
12. Ibid., 85.
13. Ibid., 78.
14. Ibid., 79.
15. Ibid., 92.
16. Ibid., 62.
17. "Just Figured Out My Uncle Is Actually My Father, and My Mother Is My Aunt."
18. For more stories from donor-conceived people and more information on children's rights and third-party reproduction, see ThemBeforeUs. com.

19. Of course, a percentage of heterosexual marriage partners do not or cannot have biological children either. Should they abandon sexual exclusivity? Is there any reason for opposite-sex, non-childbearing couples to pledge monogamy to each other since no one's biological identity is on the line in consequence of their sexual interactions? They could certainly make vows of sexual exclusivity and then bend those vows, as is increasingly occurring. But that would undercut three other purposes of marriage: 1) binding the husband and the wife specifically to each other, 2) increasing self-mastery through committing to a cause beyond one's self, and 3) publicly accepting someone from the other half of humanity into your bosom, which requires a certain humility and a fundamental respect for sexual diversity as the wellspring of existence even if you do not or cannot participate in it directly.

20. Longtime gay activist Dennis Altman says, "Commitment should not be measured primarily by monogamy." (Gessen, "Why Get Married When You Can Be Happy?") In the panel cited here, Altman and other activists encourage the expansion and acceptance of non-monogamy. They express the desire to get past the whole family structure debate that same-sex marriage is couched in and talk about more important things, "like sex." This underscores the point that sexually non-diverse marriage is primarily about the desires of adults, not the well-being of children. Of course, this view is more defensible in the context of same-sex marriage since the creation of children is not connected to sexual intercourse in same-sex marriage as it is in opposite-sex marriage.

Chapter Twelve: Trans-Forming the Argument

1. It is not my purpose to refute the born-that-way argument as applied to sexual orientation. There may be biological factors that influence sexual orientation. However, the American Psychiatric Society (APA), widely known as a left-leaning organization, does not claim that people are "born that way." Their official position on the genesis of sexual orientation is as follows: "There is no consensus among scientists about the exact reasons that an individual develops a heterosexual, bisexual, gay, or lesbian orientation. Although much research has examined the possible genetic, hormonal, developmental, social, and cultural influences on sexual orientation, no findings have emerged that permit scientists to conclude that sexual orientation is determined by any particular factor or factors. Many think that nature

and nurture both play complex roles." (See "Sexual Orientation & Homosexuality," American Psychological Association, http://www. apa.org/topics/lgbt/orientation.aspx.) This position was supported by a major study released in 2019 which found that a host of factors may affect sexual orientation and concluded, "It will be basically impossible to predict one's sexual activity or orientation just from genetics." See Sullins, "The Gay Gene Myth Has Been Exploded."

2.   See Rutz, "MSNBC Calls Republican's Belief in Only Two Genders 'Incendiary.'"
3.   Tacopino, "Not Using Transgender Pronouns Could Get You Fined."
4.   Milloy, "Don't Let the Doctor Do This to Your Newborn."
5.   The exceptions to this, of course, are very rare intersex individuals—sadly exploited by the LGBT movement—who are born with a condition that gives them physical manifestations of both sexes. This condition is not transgenderism. Transgenderism and intersexism are entirely different conditions. Intersexism is a set of recognized disorders of the body and does not represent a "third sex."
6.   Beauvoir, *The Second Sex*, ixx, 267.
7.   Yenor, "Sex, Gender, and the Origin of the Culture Wars."
8.   Beauvoir, *The Second Sex*, 697.
9.   For discussion on the possible harms of hormone therapy in children, see the position statement by the American College of Pediatrics at acpeds.org.
10. Showalter, "Feminist Activists Expose Abuse."
11. Ibid.
12. To see images of gender reassignment surgery, see Ruth Institute, "Dr J Show—Brandon Showalter Interview." Images begin at about 38:40. Images may be disturbing.
13. Showalter, "Feminist Activists Expose Abuse." Notice that state-encouraged transgenderism in children unseats the mother as an authority on her own child. When laws enforce the affirmation of certain behaviors in children, the mother and father's wisdom regarding the well-being of their own children is discarded. Some parents are now losing custody of their gender dysphoric children because they maintain that biological sex is a valuable and indestructible designation. See also Cleveland, "LGBT Activists Teaching Judges to Yank Kids."
14. See Cretella, "I'm a Pediatrician. Here's What I Did When a Little Boy Patient Said He Was a Girl," for a five-minute video on child

transgenderism by the president of the American College of Pediatricians.

15. American Psychiatric Association, *Diagnostic and Statistical Manual of Mental Disorders*, 455. For further discussion on this data, see Cretella, "Gender Ideology Harms Children." See Christina Buttons, "England's National Health Service Abandons Gender-Affirming Model of Care," The Daily Wire, October 24, 2022, https://www.dailywire.com/news/englands-national-health-service-abandons-gender-affirming-model-of-care.

16. A common argument for starting children down the path of transgender medical interventions is that doing so will reduce the high suicide rates among transgender people. While this is an emotionally moving claim, there is scant evidence for it. Sadly, research instead shows that even after undergoing gender-masking surgeries, suicide rates among transgender people remain high. Some even report feelings of increased suicidality after taking cross-sex hormones. See Western, "'Why Did You Let Us Do This?'" See also Anderson, "The *New York Times* Reveals Painful Truths." One major study in Sweden, where transgenderism has been generally accepted for many years, shows that the suicide rate for post-surgical transgender people was 19 times higher than that of the general population. See Dhejne et al., "Long-Term Follow-Up of Transsexual Persons Undergoing Sex Reassignment Surgery." Further, a University of Birmingham study reviewing more than 100 international medical studies of post-operative transsexuals "found no robust scientific evidence that gender reassignment surgery is clinically effective." One researcher said, "There is no conclusive evidence that sex change operations improve the lives of transsexuals, with many people remaining severely distressed and even suicidal after the operation." See Batty, "Sex Changes Are Not Effective." See also Bailey and Blanchard, "Suicide or Transition: The Only Options for Gender Dysphoric Kids?"

17. Dhejne et al., "Long-Term Follow-Up of Transsexual Persons."

18. See the work of Walt Heyer and Rene Jax for extensive information on transition regret.

19. Physician Michael K. Laidlaw documents some of the health risks associated with transgender hormone treatments: "Males taking female hormones are at high risk for blood clots, which may be fatal if lodged in the lungs. They are also at increased risk for breast cancer, coronary artery disease, cerebrovascular disease, gallstones, and high

levels of the lactation hormone prolactin. Females taking male
hormones are at high risk for erythrocytosis (having a higher than
normal number of red blood cells). They are also at increased risk for
severe liver dysfunction, coronary artery disease, cerebrovascular
disease, hypertension, and breast or uterine cancer. Furthermore, the
use of puberty-blocking drugs in adolescents has been associated with
incomplete mineralization of bone, meaning these children may be at
future risk for osteoporosis. There is very little information on the use
of these blockers on brain development, but the studies we do have
show potential for cognitive impairment." See Laidlaw, "Gender
Dysphoria and Children." Laidlaw also writes, "Children begun on
puberty blockers and continuing to cross sex hormones are infertile . . .
Another important human function that will be altered, diminished
and impaired when blocking puberty at a young age is sexual function,
because the sex organs will never develop and therefore will remain
stunted." See Laidlaw, "The Gender Identity Phantom."
20. *Merriam-Webster*, s.v. "social construct (*n.*)."
21. For a complete treatment of transgenderism, see Ryan Anderson's
     book *When Harry Became Sally.*
22. Anderson, "Biology Isn't Bigotry."
23. Ibid.
24. Ibid.
25. Ibid.
26. Ibid.
27. Ibid.
28. Ibid.
29. Ibid.
30. Sophie Lewis says the fear of female erasure is perpetuated by
     "paranoid, ultra-pessimist" second-wave feminists who have yet to get
     with the times. She also says she feels no need to use the words
     "women and girls" (25) and refers to gender as a form of "violence"
     (118).
31. Danielle (formerly Dave) Muscato's Facebook page says, "If you think
     I am 'less' of a woman, or NOT a woman, because I don't fit your
     mental picture of what a woman 'should' look like, or what body parts
     women 'should' or 'shouldn't' have, newsflash: Your mental
     description of women is not only inaccurately narrow, but anti-
     feminist and bigoted as well."

32. See the writings of Judith Butler for a full exploration of gender as a "performance."

33. Cartwright, "Yin and Yang."

34. See "Gender Dysphoria in Children," American College of Pediatricians.

35. Ibid.

36. The long and calculated effort (led in part by Justice Ruth Bader Ginsberg) to legally disavow the biological differences between men and women by activating the Equal Protection Clause is reviewed in Bachiochi, "Embodied Equality." To activate this clause in the context of the abortion debate, it must be shown that "men and women are similarly situated." This has not yet been accepted or ratified in legal terms because men and women are not similarly situated in regard to reproduction. Their bodies themselves situate them differently. However, increasing acceptance and codification of transgenderism, which disavows the physical body, is likely to fast-track efforts to "eliminate the sex distinction" in law. If enacted, the Equal Rights Amendment would also help accomplish this.

37. Firestone, *The Dialectic of Sex*, 54.

Chapter Thirteen: Socialist Feminism and Same-Sex Marriage

1. Bilek, "Who Are the Rich, White Men Institutionalizing Transgender Ideology?" See also Bilek, "The Billionaires behind the LGBT Movement."

2. ABC, "Consequences, Citizenship, and Climate."

3. Ibid.

4. Ibid.

5. Ibid.

6. Ibid.

7. Ibid.

8. One same-sex marriage advocate said, "Fighting for gay marriage generally involves lying about what we're going to do with marriage when we get there because we lie that the institution of marriage is not going to change, and that is a lie. The institution of marriage is going to change, and it should change, and again, I don't think it should exist." See Gessen, "Why Get Married When You Can Be Happy?" This statement is from the segment spanning 6:10 to 9:05. The entire fifty-minute panel is instructive and addresses the implosion of monogamous marriage in part through the mechanism of same-sex

marriage. Most people argue that same-sex marriage is simply "expanding" marriage so it can enrich more people's lives. They argue this because that is what most people really believe. And yet, at least some gay activists openly admit—as they do on this panel—that the end goal is not to extend marriage to everyone. The goal is to eliminate sexually exclusive marriage and biologically organized families as the basis of civilized living.

9.   The Human Rights Campaign report "Beyond Marriage: Unrecognized Family Relationships" outlines strategies intended to allow legal creation of nonfamilial families out of virtually any combination of people. These relationships are called "relationships of choice" (as opposed to biological relationships, which are considered relationships of chance or force since one does not choose his or her own biological parents or siblings.) The goal is to legally equalize virtually all relationships so as not to discriminate against those who do not wish to claim their biological connections. This movement is being legally propelled by non-discrimination efforts and could allow a person to legally choose his own siblings, parents, grandparents, etc., regardless of biological realities. See also "Chosen Family," *Queer Queries*.

10. Mises, *Human Action*, 264.

11. Mitchelson, "Merav Michaeli's Marriage Feud."

Chapter Fourteen: The Sanity of Family

1.   TEDx Talks, "Cancel Marriage."

2.   Donati and Sullins, *The Conjugal Family*, 73. Emphasis added.

3.   Ibid.

4.   Ribar, "Why Marriage Matters for Child Wellbeing," 12.

5.   Donati and Sullins, *The Conjugal Family*, 73.

6.   Rates of abuse are often relatively low in adoptive families, as they are in biologically inherent families. Rates of abuse and neglect in stepparent and foster families, however, are often notably higher. As the biologically inherent family model is increasingly disfigured and debased, instances of abuse, social and emotional instability, and mistreatment of children are likely to increase, not decrease.

7.   Donati and Sullins, *The Conjugal Family*, 76.

8.   Wilcox, "Suffer the Little Children." Emphasis added.

9.   Ibid.

10. Family Scholars, *Why Marriage Matters*.

11. McLanahan and Sandefur, *Growing Up with a Single Parent,* 1.
12. Ibid., 38.
13. Krason, "Same-Sex Parenting: The Child Maltreatment No One Mentions."
14. For more on the documented benefits associated with biological families, see Chapter Fourteen.
15. For a wealth of social science information on marriage, family structure, sustainable societies, and child thriving, see the Institute for Family Studies at https://ifstudies.org/. See also the Marriage and Religion Research Initiative (MARRI) at https://marri.us/.
16. Christakis, "The Hidden Influence of Social Networks."

Chapter Fifteen: Taking It to the Top

1.   The following are five key ways the UN's influence penetrates society: 1) The US Senate can approve UN treaties for ratification by a two-thirds vote; 2) UN treaties can be adopted on a city-by-city basis; 3) UN agencies partner with NGOs and other entities to influence cultural movements, attitudes, and initiatives; 4) Courts of various nations cite international documents to support their rulings on domestic matters [See Hellyer, "U.N. Documents in U.S. Case Law" for a full explanation of how elements from "non-binding" UN documents make their way into court rulings]; and 5) UN agencies collaborate with educational institutions to implement their objectives in schools throughout the world.
2.   "CSW61 Agreed Conclusions Revision 1," UN Commission on the Status of Women, 14.
3.   Landsmann, "Opinion: The Nuclear Family Threat."
4.   This is one way the phrase "the reconciliation of work and family life" can be interpreted. Other interpretations of this phrase may be more positive and can include certain allowances for women (or men) that give them flexibility in accommodating for their individual family situations. However, when considering the language proposed in UN documents, one must consider what the most problematic interpretations and applications of any phrase could be, and what outcomes those interpretations could bring about.

Chapter Sixteen: Sexual Rights and Gender Equality

1. International Planned Parenthood Federation, "Member Associations." As one example of IPPF partnering with UN agencies, see https://www.who.int/reproductivehealth/about_us/hrp/partners/en/, where IPPF is listed as a permanent partner in the World Health Organization's Human Reproduction Programme.

2. International Planned Parenthood Federation, *Sexual Rights: An IPPF Declaration*, i.

3. One of the few sexual boundaries (and perhaps the only sexual boundary) maintained by the Sexuality Information and Education Council of the United States (SIECUS) and other sexual rights organizations is obtaining consent from the party you wish to gain sexual pleasure from. If there is consent, SIECUS and other sexual rights organizations see virtually all sexual practices as being equal and assert that freely participating in any consensual sexual practices constitutes an important expression of a person's sexual rights.

4. Attempts to stitch ovaries and wombs into the bodies of men have thus far ended in death rather than life, and the theoretically possible avenue of injecting a fertilized egg into a man's abdomen—while it could induce pregnancy if accompanied by a specific cocktail of hormones—would constitute a "life-threatening condition for the man." See Silver, "Can a Man Really Get Pregnant?" See also Teresi, "How to Get a Man Pregnant." To hear arguments for the new frontier of biological men's "right" to become pregnant, see Cook, "Do Transgender Men Have a Right to Gestation?" To read about the tragic consequences of trying to give wombs to men, see Harrod, "The Tragic True Story behind the Danish Girl."

5. Daphne Clair de Jong says, "For women to get what they need to combine childbearing, education, and careers, society has to recognize that female bodies come with wombs." Quoted in Bachiochi, *The Cost of Choice*, 921.

6. Firestone, *The Dialectic of Sex*, 11.

7. An analysis of this resolution by Family Watch International appears in the bibliography.

8. Interestingly, the resolution says that "women and girl athletes" (i.e., intersex athletes and presumably men and boy athletes who do not identify as male) should not be "forced," "coerced," or "pressured" into "undergoing unnecessary, irreversible and harmful medical procedures in order to participate as women in competitive sport" and

should not be forced to "undergo humiliating medical treatment and interventions that negate their right to bodily autonomy and integrity." This appears to be a 180-degree turnaround in the pursuit of transgender rights. On one hand, there is raucous demand for insurance companies and taxpayers to pay for "affirming" and "life-saving" transition procedures that instate and respect one's bodily autonomy and integrity, while on the other hand this resolution labels at least some gender-related medical interventions as "unnecessary, irreversible, harmful, and humiliating." The whiplashing of transgender philosophy is inconsistent and nearly impossible to legally or socially keep pace with. And it is accomplishing exactly what it is meant to: the unhinging of biological sex and the mass sacrifice of bodily gender on the altar of transgender rights.

9.   Yoshihara, "UN Women to Replace 'Women' with 'Gender.'"
10.   Ibid.
11.   Moynihan, "Why Should Respect for Nature Stop at the Human Being?"
12.   Givas, "California State Senate Committee Bans the Use of 'He' and 'She' during Hearings."
13.   Another example of gender abolition in high places in the name of gender equality is the G7 (consisting of Canada, France, Germany, Italy, Japan, the United Kingdom, and the United States). The G7 was advised by a gender equality advisory council in advance of its 2018 summit. The council advised G7 leaders to: "Set binding dates to 'mandate' gender parity on boards and in leadership positions by 2030; incentivize the private sector to achieve pay equality for men and women by 2030; fight gender-based violence and sexual harassment; provide comprehensive sexual and reproductive health services, including safe abortion services; support developing nations in offering a minimum of 12 years of free, safe, quality and gender-responsive education; and recognize and redistribute unpaid domestic work that falls overwhelmingly to women." Elements of this agenda could be interpreted to demand transgender parity in leadership positions, gender-fluid education in schools, and other forced promotions of transgenderism. Furthermore, the bulk of these phrases require an alarming dose of manufactured equality, socialistic economic control, expansion of abortion, and the fracturing of the private family unit in favor of public control in the name of gender equality. See Bloomberg News, "Melinda Gates Will Step In."

14.   Black, "The Equality Act."

15.   Ibid.

16.   See "It All Depends on the Definition of 'Sex'" and other Eagle Forum resources on the ERA.

17.   See "Convention on the Elimination of All Forms of Discrimination against Women." At present, the United States has not ratified CEDAW, but some individual U.S. cities have done so.

18.   Coleman, "Abortion and Mental Health."

19.   Strahan, ed. *Detrimental Effects of Abortion.*

20.   The average compensation for a CEO at a Planned Parenthood affiliate in 2017 was $255,523. (See "2018 Report on Planned Parenthood CEO Compensation" compiled by STOPP.) Planned Parenthood Federation of America president Cecile Richards received a salary of $523,000 in 2014. See Arter, "Planned Parenthood Got $528M in Tax Dollars."

21.   One company called Ipas manufactures a portable, handheld abortion device. Its instruction manual acknowledges the risks for women undergoing abortions, saying, "One or more of the following complications may occur during or after procedures: uterine or cervical injury or perforation, pelvic infection, vagal reaction, incomplete evacuation or acute hematometra. Some of these conditions can lead to secondary infertility, other serious injury or death." Not surprisingly, Ipas is an enthusiastic supporter of comprehensive sexuality education for children and hosted an event at the Commission on the Status of Women at the UN in 2018 titled, "Without Abortion, It's Not Comprehensive Sexuality Education for Rural Youth."

22.   The risks involved in using some forms of contraception are well-documented, but many women are unaware of them. Some forms of hormonal contraception increase women's risk of breast cancer (See Morch et al., "Hormonal Contraception and the Risk of Breast Cancer"; Chretien, "Breast Cancer Risk Skyrockets"; Siggins, "Using Contraception Increases Breast Cancer by 50%") and lethal blood clots (See Baillargeon et al., "Association between the Current Use of Low-Dose Oral Contraceptives and Cardiovascular Arterial Disease"). Hormonal contraception can also lead to liver malfunction, mood swings, weight changes, acne, vaginitis, vitamin deficiencies, vision impairment (see naturalwomanhood.org), increased suicidality (Skovlund et al., "Association of Hormonal Contraception with

Suicide Attempts and Suicides"), and, in some cases, death (see Langhart, "NuvaRing Caused My Daughter's Death"; Karlsson and Brenner, "Danger in the Ring"). Even Planned Parenthood admits that hormonal birth control can cause death (See Planned Parenthood, "How Safe Is NuvaRing?"). Intrauterine devices (IUDs) can increase the risk of ectopic pregnancy, pelvic inflammatory disease, abnormal bleeding, infection, and can cause severe complications from displacement of the device (See Abbamonte, "25-Year-Old Mom Has Toes Amputated"). Women are also more susceptible to sexually transmitted diseases than men. For an entire treatment of the effects of sex on women, see Miriam Grossman's eye-opening book, *Unprotected*.

23. Though some women feel compelled to "shout their abortions" (see shoutyourabortion.com), the reality of many women's difficult and sometimes devastating post-abortive experiences—at times even decades later—cannot be ignored.

24. Bachiochi, *The Cost of Choice*.

25. See TheUnChoice.com for extensive information, research, statistics, and resources on coerced abortion.

26. The UN created the Intergovernmental Panel on Climate Change (IPCC) to assess climate issues and solutions. One supporter of the IPCC's mission says their current initiatives to combat climate change "clearly are not enough" and that "[o]nly time will tell whether the IPCC will seriously consider population control to mitigate the worsening effects of climate change." Tayag, "Population Control Is the Climate Change Fix."

27. Roberts, "This Book Ranks the Top 100 Solutions to Climate Change."

28. Notice that this solution—the elimination of human beings—is being promoted in the face of a world population decline so significant that it is threatening the economic prosperity of nations and may bring about the demise of entire national identities. This exposes the fact that the climate change agenda is about saving the world, not necessarily saving the people in the world. Les Knight, leader of the Voluntary Human Extinction Movement, says, "Planet Earth's biosphere would be far better off if Homo sapiens weren't a part of it." See Tayag, "The Voluntary Human Extinction Movement Is Both Anti-Republican and Anti-Death." Those who cherish human life may argue that if humans are eliminated in the name of saving the world, there is little reason to

save it. For more on population decline, see the documentary *Demographic Winter* by Barry McLerran and Rick Stout, available on YouTube at https://www.youtube.com/watch?v=lZeyYIsGdAA.

29. Andrews, "To Stop Climate Change, Educate Girls."
30. Feller, "5 Women on Deciding Not to Have Children."
31. See unfpa.org.
32. UNFPA, "Physician, Two NGOs Win 2018 UN Population Award."
33. Planned Parenthood, "Planned Parenthood Global Congratulates Carmen Barroso."
34. Nossiter, "Population Prizes from UN Assailed."
35. For more on UNFPA's involvement with Chinese population efforts, see Population Research Institute, "Keep U.S. Tax Dollars from Funding Population Control in China."
36. Williams, "Trump Admin Expands Ban on Foreign Aid."
37. There are alternatives to coercing women to risk the consequences of abortion and contraception and to enriching those who seek to exploit them. They are two-fold: 1) Revere the creation of new people instead of revering the cessation and decimation of new people, and 2) Promote birth planning methods that do not disrupt or impair the natural functioning of the woman's body. These alternatives can be either low-cost or free. Further, women (and men) can benefit from jointly building a culture in which the woman's right to decide when and under what conditions sex will occur is rigorously valued and defended. (See these three videos for an introduction to woman-conscious family-planning methods: Natural Womanhood, "The Fertility Diaries Episode 1"; Moriarty, "Miscontraceptions"; and Population Research Institute, "Natural Family Planning." Find additional resources at naturalwomanhood.org.)
38. Psychologist Sidney Callahan states, "A culturally dominant demand for monogamy, self-control, and emotionally bonded and committed sex works well for women in every stage of their sexual life cycles. When love, chastity, fidelity, and commitment for better or for worse are the ascendant cultural prerequisites for sexual functioning, young girls [are protected], adult women justifiably demand male support in childrearing, and older women are more protected from abandonment as their biological attractions wane." See Bachiochi, *The Cost of Choice*, 948. When the majority of women in a society demand sexual fidelity, this best protects women's, men's, and children's best interests

and serves to strengthen society at large. See the Austin Institute, "The Economics of Sex."

Chapter Seventeen: Children's Sexual Rights

1. This link at StopCSE.org shows IPPF listed as an official partner to UNDP, UNFPA, UNICEF, and WHO on sexual and reproductive health initiatives: https://www.comprehensivesexualityeducation.org/wp-content/uploads/UNICEF-IPPF-HRP-Screen-Shot-marked.pdf?inf_contact_key=1b71552a4079fab5a9f3529753acea7202eb10f6868670a063e1911461b4b1ad. As two other examples of IPPF partnering with UNESCO, see International Planned Parenthood, "Inside and Out" and UNICEF, *All In to End the Adolescent AIDS Epidemic*, 11.

2. See the full document at International Planned Parenthood Federation, *Exlaim!* For a full analysis of the document see this link at StopCSE.org: https://www.comprehensivesexualityeducation.org/curriculum/international-technical-guidance-on-sexuality-education-unesco-2018/.

3. International Planned Parenthood Federation, *Exclaim!*, 4.

4. Ibid., 37.

5. Ibid., 9.

6. Ibid., 37.

7. This document can be found on the websites of UNAIDS, UNFPA, UNESCO, UNWOMEN, WHO, IPPF, and elsewhere.

8. UNESCO, *International Technical Guidance on Sexuality Education: An Evidence-Informed Approach*, 35.

9. Ibid., 71. Emphasis added.

10. Ibid., 18.

11. Ibid., 17.

12. For the full text of the Convention on the Rights of the Child see https://www.ohchr.org/en/professionalinterest/pages/crc.aspx.

13. Notice that the words "sexual" and "rights" both appear in the phrase, but not adjacent to each other. This is purposeful, so that the intent to advance sexual rights, especially children's sexual rights, will not be as obvious. Using SRHR to call for children's sexual rights is one intent of this carefully crafted phrase.

14. WHO Regional Office for Europe and BZgA, *Training Matters*, 26.

15. Ibid., 25.

16. Sedletzki, *Legal Minimum Ages and the Realization of Adolescents' Rights*, 32. Emphasis added.

17. Ibid., 28. Emphasis added.

18. Ibid. Emphasis added.

19. World Health Organization, *Sexual Health, Human Rights and the Law*.

20. Fielding, "Exclusive: Top UNICEF Children's Rights Campaigner."

21. Ibid.

22. See Peter Newell and Rachel Hodgkin listed as co-authors at UNICEF, *Implementation Handbook for the Convention on the Rights of the Child*.

23. Shahi, "In Nepal, Child Abuse Trial."

24. Cole, "Former Senior United Nations Official."

25. Shahi, "In Nepal, Child Abuse Trial."

26. Schultz and Bhandari, "Noted Humanitarian Charged with Child Rape."

27. Code Blue Campaign, "The UN's Dirty Secret."

28. Ibid.

29. Ibid.

30. Ibid.

31. Ibid.

32. Laville, "Child Sex Abuse Whistleblower Resigns." Anders Kompass and Miranda Brown, both UN officials, sought to expose sexual abuses perpetrated against children in the Central African Republic. Both were disciplined by the UN system. Brown eventually lost her post at the UN and Kompass resigned. This highlights the troubling atmosphere at the UN, which appears to discourage whistleblowing and reward silence even at the grave expense of children.

33. Quoted from a private interview with the author, March 1, 2019.

34. Dodds, "AP Exclusive: UN Child Sex Ring Left Victims."

35. Ibid.

36. "The UN Sex-for-Food Scandal," *Washington Times*.

37. Bruce, "Rape, Sex Trafficking and the Spread of Disease."

38. Ibid.

39. Einbinder, "French Police to Investigate New Abuse Claims."

40. Ibid.

41. Ibid.

42. Lewis, "Child Sex Scandal Roils UNICEF Unit."

43. For a full explanation of this estimate see http://www.heartheircries. org/2018/07/ just-how-many-victims-of-aid-industry-sex-abuse-are-there.

44. Banbury, "I Love the UN, but It Is Failing."

45. Code Blue Campaign, "The Probem."

46. Quoted from a private interview with the author, March 1, 2019.

47. See http://www.heartheircries.org. HearTheirCries.org is committed to stopping the sexual abuse of children by peacekeeping troops, civilian staff, and other aid industry workers.

48. This convention also exempts UN personnel from paying taxes and performing national service obligations and states, "The premises of the United Nations shall be inviolable. The property and assets of the United Nations . . . shall be immune from search, requisition, confiscation, expropriation and any other form of interference, whether by executive, administrative, judicial or legislative action."

49. Quoted from a private interview with the author, March 1, 2019. Additionally, the stance of the UN is that participating in sexual misconduct is never part of executing one's official UN duties, and therefore such actions are not protected under the Convention on the Privileges and Immunities of the United Nations. (See Code Blue Campaign, "Primer: Privileges and Immunities of the United Nations.") However, in most cases immunity must be waived in order for actions to be pursued against alleged offenders. Often this process is so mired in what Gallo calls "unbelievable inefficiency" and a "truly shocking lack of accountability" that both victims and sexual offenders are lost in a vast sea of bureaucratic mismanagement, and justice can go unserved for months, years, or may never be served at all.

50. United Nations Secretary-General, "Secretary-General's Address to High-Level Meeting."

51. From a personal communication with the author on March 26, 2019.

52. Code Blue Campaign, "The Problem."

Chapter Eighteen: Comprehensive Sexuality Education

1. See Annex C in the Access, Services and Knowledge (ASK) Programme Essential Packages Manual as one example of partnering between UN agencies and sexual rights–based NGOs at http://www. stopaidsnow.org/sites/ stopaidsnow.org/files/0151-opmaak%20 EP%20manual_web.pdf.

2. For UNESCO's explanation of CSE, see UNESCO, *International Technical Guidance on Sexuality Education*, 16.

3. Be aware that some CSE quotations included in this chapter are graphic in nature. Go to Chapter Nineteen to see how comprehensive sexuality education is being implemented in schools all over the globe. Go to Chapter Twenty-Two to learn how to protect your family from harmful ideologies, including those taught in CSE programs.

4. See StopCSE.org for content rubrics of many major CSE programs.

5. Gennarini, "UNESCO Pushes Controversial Sex-Ed."

6. UNESCO, *International Guidelines on Sexuality Education*, 43, 48.

7. Ibid., 51. This statement invalidates the love of literal mothers and fathers, rejects parents' biological connections to their children, and rejects children's inherent belonging to their parents.

8. Ibid., 48.

9. Ibid., 44, 49.

10. Ibid., 51.

11. Ibid.

12. Ibid., 48.

13. Ibid., 52.

14. Ibid., 50.

15. Ibid. Although abstinence is not prominently promoted in the guidelines and there is a pervasive expectation of sexual activity among youth, the section on sexual disease reduction for twelve- to fifteen-year-olds does include this statement: "Not having sexual intercourse is the most effective protection against STIs, HIV and unintended pregnancy." (UNESCO, *International Guidelines on Sexuality Education*, 54.) The inclusion of this statement allows for the claim that the guidelines support "abstinence."

16. UNESCO, "New International Guidelines Spell Out What Sexuality Education Needs to Teach."

17. SIECUS, "Our History." Note that SIECUS is not a government entity but rather a private group of sexual rights advocates that has given itself an official-sounding name.

18. Gebbard, "In Memoriam: Wardell B. Pomeroy," 155–56.

19. See *Sexual Sabotage* and other works by Judith Reisman.

20. "Sexes: Attacking the Last Taboo," *Time*.

21. See Grossman, "A Brief History of Sex Ed."

22. See the full document at http://www.comprehensivesexualityeducation. org/wp-content/uploads/Utah_CSE_Summary_final.pdf.

23. These consent videos were formerly found on the Planned Parenthood site for teens but have since been moved to YouTube.

24. If you do not wish to read through these potentially troubling examples, go to Chapter Nineteen, which explains how CSE is on track to be implemented in schools worldwide through the workings of the United Nations in cooperation with national education systems and what can be done about it.

25. For a complete overview of the *It's All One* curriculum, see https://www.comprehensivesexualityeducation.org/wp-content/uploads/15-CSE-Harmful-Elements-Analysis_Its-All-One_updated-8_22_for-posting.pdf.

26. International Sexuality and HIV Curriculum Working Group, *It's All One Curriculum* vol. 1, 2.

27. Ibid., 166.

28. Ibid., vol. 2, 80.

29. Ibid., 152. I have declined to include the actual curriculum content here because of its graphic nature.

30. Ibid., vol. 1, 99. There are numerous graphic, positive discussions of self-stimulation throughout the curriculum.

31. Ibid., 98. I have declined to include the actual curriculum content here because of its graphic nature.

32. Ibid., 99.

33. Gennarini, "UNESCO Pushes Controversial Sex Ed."

34. Ibid.

35. Ibid.

36. UNESCO, *International Technical Guidance on Sexuality Education*, 31. Emphasis added.

37. International Planned Parenthood Federation, "Love, Sex and Young People."

38. International Planned Parenthood Federation, *The Truth about Men, Boys and Sex.*

39. International Planned Parenthood Federation, "IPPF and Youth." Emphasis added.

40. For a review of IPPF's position in relation to children's sexual rights. see Family Watch International, "Policy Brief: International Planned Parenthood Federation and Children's 'Right' to Sex." Family Watch International is a global leader in combating CSE at the United Nations and throughout the world.

41. See Planned Parenthood Mar Monte, "Transgender Hormone Services" as one example. See also Showalter, "Feminist Activists Expose Abuse."

42. Poy et al., *You, Your Life, Your Dreams*, 85.

43. Ibid., 3.

44. Ibid., 79.

45. Ibid., 120.

46. Ibid., 19, 26, 28, 86, 104.

47. Ibid., 84.

48. Ibid., 6.

49. Ibid., 95.

50. Schroeder et al., *Rights, Respect, and Responsibility*, 30. Referenced hereafter as 3Rs.

51. Ibid., 6th grade book, 2.

52. Ibid., high school book, 31.

53. Ibid., 18.

54. United Nations Population Fund, *The Evaluation of Comprehensive Sexuality Education Programmes*, 12.

55. SIECUS, "About Us."

56. SIECUS, "News & Updates." The official name of the organization is now SIECUS: Sex Ed for Social Change, which underscores their intent to transform society through sex education initiatives. See https://siecus.org/siecus-rebrand-announcement/.

57. SIECUS, "News & Updates."

58. Ibid.

59. See "Organizations That Support the Decriminalization of Prostitution," Decriminalize Sex Work.

60. See Hoffman, "Planned Parenthood Seeking to Lower Age"; White, "Age of Consent at 14."

61. United Nations Population Fund, *The Evaluation of Comprehensive Sexuality Education Programmes*, 11.

62. It is a common strategy to use citations from nonbinding UN documents as ammunition to push forward certain agenda points, even though such documents have no real binding power or authority. Often just saying something comes from a UN document is enough to convince some people of its validity. For this reason, the UN creates numerous declarations, resolutions, and other documents and then rallies entities from around the world to support them. This provides a façade of authority and jurisdiction where none really exists. However,

these nonbinding documents are increasingly cited by courts around the world and used to support domestic laws and court rulings. This is one way the UN pushes its objectives (including its sexual objectives) forward without the consensus of its member states, and this is how non-negotiated documents become soft law.

63. United Nations Population Fund, *The Evaluation of Comprehensive Sexuality Education Programme*, 12.

64. Ibid.

65. Weed and Ericksen, *Re-Examining the Evidence for Comprehensive Sex Education in Schools*.

66. Ibid., 3.

67. UNESCO, *International Technical Guidance on Sexuality Education*, 128.

68. Ibid., 127–28.

69. Ibid., 28. See also Gennarini, "UN Agency Defies General Assembly."

70. This is true of Norway. In December 2017 a UN delegate from Norway, distraught that an amendment allowing for "appropriate direction and guidance from parents" in matters of sexual education was added to a document, said his country could not accept the amendment because "children should decide freely and autonomously" on matters of sexual education and services. See Gennarini, "Saint Lucia/Africans Put Parental Rights Back."

71. For an in-depth look at the United Nations' push for children's sexual rights and comprehensive sexuality education—and how to push back against it—see Slater, *Stand for the Family*.

72. See Stanton, "CDC Study Says Teen Virgins Are Healthier."

Chapter Nineteen: The Global Hijacking of Education

1. For simplicity, I have arranged the graphic above from top to bottom, but in some cases a more tangled and interweaving representation would be appropriate.

2. UNESCO's 2018 *International Technical Guidance on Sexuality Education*, published in cooperation with UNICEF, UNFPA, WHO, and UNAIDS, is entirely CSE-based.

3. For an interactive graphic outlining the SDGs, see United Nations, "Sustainable Development Goals."

4. United Nations, "Sustainable Development Goal 3," https://sustainabledevelopment.un.org/sdg3.

5.   United Nations, "Sustainable Development Goal 4," https://
      sustainabledevelopment.un.org/sdg4.

6.   The word "inclusive"—which can be interpreted to mean that girls,
      disabled people, or other groups must be included in education
      efforts—is often interpreted to mean that sexuality education must
      include instruction on virtually any and all sexual behaviors in which
      people wish to engage. It is interpreted to mean that school-based CSE
      instruction should address diverse issues related to sexuality including
      the teaching of gender fluidity theory, transgenderism, and a growing
      list of sexual orientations such as pansexual, metrosexual, omnisexual,
      etc.

7.   United Nations Global Compact, "Who We Are."

8.   For a list of OECD partners, see OECD, "Global Relations."

9.   Wikipedia, s.v. "International Planned Parenthood Federation."

10.   OECD, "Inclusive Growth."

11.   Bill & Melinda Gates Foundation, "How We Work: Grant."

12.   OECD, *The Future of Education and Skills: Education 2030*.

13.   Environmentalism and economic change are overlapping initiatives.
      Christiana Figueres, the executive secretary of the UN's Framework
      Convention on Climate Change, said in anticipation of the Paris
      Agreement in 2015, "This is the first time in the history of mankind
      that we are setting ourselves the task of intentionally, within a defined
      period of time to change the economic development model that has
      been reigning for at least 150 years, since the industrial revolution."
      (See "Figueres: First Time the World Economy Is Transformed
      Intentionally.") This statement shows that the goal of climate change
      initiatives is to have a compelling reason to change the "reigning
      economic model," i.e., capitalism, to another economic model. And
      what economic model could that be? The darling of the UN and
      virtually all its highest-ranking officials: socialism. The underlying
      goal of climate change hysteria is to send citizens running in panic to
      the welcoming arms of socialist planners who will save the world, even
      though all they have been able to do in the past is cripple, demoralize,
      and destroy it.

14.   OECD, *The Future of Education and Skills: Education 2030*, 3.

15.   For an explanation of how radical environmentalism is meant to
      globalize the world's governments, see Jasper, "The United Nations:
      On the Brink."

16. OECD, *Preparing Our Youth for an Inclusive and Sustainable World*, 2.

17. OECD, *Global Competency for an Inclusive World*.

18. Ibid., 2. Emphasis added.

19. Ibid.

20. Carcillo and Valfort, "LGBT Inclusivity: A Priority for the OECD."

21. See OECD, "LGBTI Inclusiveness."

22. See United Nations, "Sustainable Development Goal 4," https://sustainabledevelopment.un.org/sdg4.

23. Ibid.

24. Gomes, "How PISA Is Changing."

25. OECD, *Preparing Our Youth for an Inclusive and Sustainable World*, 2, 13.

26. Ibid.

27. Kankaras and Suarez-Alvarez, "OECD's New International Study."

28. Ibid.

29. OECD, *Social and Emotional Skills*, 5.

30. UNESCO, *UNESCO ICT Competency Framework for Teachers*.

31. TEDx Talks, "Reimagining Learning."

32. Massive data collection also allows those who wield the data to sell it. Data has been called "the new gold" and it is just that. Retailers, recruiters, and others pay big money to zero in on their target audiences and access children as consumers. See Adams and Judd, "Data Is the New Gold."

33. The original word here is "kindergarten." In Germany, kindergarten commonly begins at age three.

34. Schleicher, "Use Data to Build Better Schools."

35. UNESCO, Incheon Declaration and Framework for Action, 10.

36. Ibid., 49–50. Emphasis added.

37. Ibid., 7.

38. Ibid., 62.

39. Global Partnership for Education, "About GPE."

40. Ibid.

41. See infographic at Global Partnership for Education, "How to Improve Health and Learning," showing comprehensive sexuality education as an integral part of global education. A push for in-school health clinics is already underway in the United States. These clinics are often administered by Planned Parenthood or by entities that refer students to Planned Parenthood to receive sexual services, which can include

providing contraceptives and sexual counseling to minors and securing IUDs in the wombs of girls beginning in the sixth grade without parental consent. It may also eventually include abortion without parental consent. See Clallam County Republican Party, "School-Based Health Centers—a Bad Idea?" See also Butts, "PA School Mulls Planned Parenthood Clinic"; AccessMatters, "AccessMatters Knows Planned Parenthood Matters."

42. Mount, *The Subversive Family*, 35.
43. Lewis, *Full Surrogacy Now*, 118.
44. See https://www.globalpartnership.org/funding.
45. WHO Regional Office for Europe and BZgA, *Training Matters*.
46. Osher et al., *CASEL/NoVo Collaborating Districts Initiative Evaluation Executive Summary*.
47. See "Collaborative for Academic, Social, and Emotional Learning, CASEL," Education for Safety, Resilience and Social Cohesion; Kyllonen, "Social-Emotional and School Climate Assessment."
48. NoVo Foundation, "About Us."
49. Lewis said we must confront "the need for ever deeper revolutionary transformations of the home" in order to transform society (*Full Surrogacy Now*, 151).
50. CASEL, *Key Insights from the Collaborating Districts Initiative*.
51. CoSN, "About CoSN."
52. CoSN, "Rapid Technological Changes."
53. CoSN, "Driving K–12 Innovation Advisory Board."
54. Utah TCC, "Utah CoSN Chapter."
55. CoSN, "Innovating Rural School Districts."
56. Ibid.
57. Ibid.
58. In addition to CoSN's direct involvement in Utah schools—which will likely lead to the expansion of CSE—legislation calling for the adoption of CSE and an abandonment of abstinence-based sex education (which has helped Utah maintain some of the lowest STD rates in the nation) is consistently being pushed in the state legislature in the name of saving children from sexual disease. Similar efforts in other states are being advanced through state legislatures and school boards. See "SETDA Launches Updated Digital Instructional Materials Acquisition Policies for States (DMAPS) Portal" to see how State Educational Technology Directors Association (SETDA) helps schools in Utah and elsewhere choose curricula. For information on

Google data collection in schools see Malkin, "How to Protect Your Kids from Google Predators."

59. USBE Media, "March 19, 2020 Utah State Board of Education Board Meeting."

60. Huxley, *UNESCO: Its Purpose and Its Philosophy*, 30–34.

61. Pauvert, *A Methodological Guide to the Application of Various Categories of Education Personnel*.

62. UNESCO, "Cooperation Agreement between UNESCO and Microsoft Corporation," 3.

63. Schlafly, "Microsoft Founder Bill Gates Teams Up with UNESCO." Emphasis added.

64. Gates, "Bill Gates—National Conference of State Legislature."

65. Ravitch, "Mercedes Schneider Explains."

66. Ibid.

67. Bill & Melinda Gates Foundation, "How We Work."

68. For information on blockchain technology, the OECD, Microsoft, and the United Nations, see OECD, "OECD Global Blockhain Policy Forum Agenda"; Parker, "ID2020, Held at the United Nations, Features 'Lots and Lots of Blockchain'"; ID2020, "ID2020 Alliance"; Jenkins, "Is Blockchain the Future of Academic Credentials?"

69. Gwertzman, "U.S. Is Quitting UNESCO."

70. Ibid.

71. The United States said it would continue "to further the international cooperation in education, science and culture and communication that UNESCO was originally created to promote." This means the United States understood that "furthering educational cooperation in education" is possible without cowering under the stained umbrella of UNESCO.

72. Newman, "Creepy 'World Government Summit' Targets America."

73. Despite indications that they would cut ties with Common Core, the U.S. Department of Education under the Trump administration is cooperating directly with the OECD, perhaps unaware of the deep ties the OECD has to the global sexual education agenda. For a report on high-level meetings between U.S. education entities and the OECD, see OECD, "Using Educational Research and Innovation." See also Berry, "Trump Administration Proposes Merging Education and Labor."

74. OECD, "Recommendation of the Council on Artificial Intelligence."

75. Ibid.; National Telecommunications and Information Administration, "U.S. Joins with OECD in Adopting Global AI Policies."

76. Socialist International, "Progressive Politics for a Fairer World."
77. Wikipedia, s.v. "Irina Bokova"; Montesquieu Institute, "I.G. (Irina) Bokova." See also Bilefsky, "Bulgarian Who Is to Lead UNESCO."
78. Houeix, "Hollande's Protégé Azoulay Wins"; Wikipedia, s.v. "Audrey Azoulay."
79. Wikipedia, s.v. "Jose Angel Gurria." See Gurria's speech for the Socialist International global council meeting here: https://www.socialistinternational.org/councils/paris-2010/speech-by-angel-gurria-secretary-general-of-the-oecd/.
80. Socialist International, "About Us: Full List of Member Parties and Organisations."
81. Socialist International, "Councils: Paris Council."
82. "Ben Levin Defends Child Porn," *The Interim.*
83. Warmington, "Ex-Deputy Education Minister." Levin's language is so disturbing I have declined to include it here. The children's Canadian sexual education curriculum Levin claims responsibility for creating "introduces homosexuality and gender identity in Grade 3, [self-stimulation] in Grade 6, and non-vaginal sex in Grade 7. It advises Grade 7 children to carry a condom in case they engage in sexual activity, and Grade 8 children to think up a sexual plan. It teaches there are six genders rather than the two biological sexes of male and female. At no point does the sex-ed speak of marriage." See Laurence, "Ontario Conservatives Will 'Restore' Sex-Ed."
84. Paraphrased from JaKell Sullivan, with permission. In many countries and in many states around the world, CSE has already been eagerly adopted and is being delivered in "crosscutting" curriculum that reinforces sexual openness in virtually all academic subjects. The Guttmacher Institute reports that in the first half of 2019 alone, seventy-nine sex education bills were introduced in thirty-two U.S. states, most of which utilize a sexual rights framework. See Nash et al., "State and Federal Lawmakers Promote Sexual Consent."

Chapter Twenty: The Artificial Mother

1. Komisar, *Being There,* 4.
2. Peterson, *12 Rules for Life,* 134–35.
3. Ibid., 135.
4. Bornstein et al., "Emotional Relationships," 113–23.
5. Garcia and Weiss, *Making Whole-Child Education the Norm,* 5.
6. Ibid.

7.   Ibid.
8.   Landau,"Mothers' Talk Is Key."
9.   Bornstein et al., "Emotional Relationships."
10. Ward, "Defamilialisation." This article is a solid overview of the
     family-vs.-state question as related to the OECD.
11. "Gyeongju Action Plan," Education for Global Citizenship.
12. McDonald, "Harvard Study Shows the Dangers."
13. Ruse, "Your Children 'Soft Entry Points.'"
14. Newman, "UN LGBT Czar on Indoctrinating Children." The term
     "sexual diversity" refers not only to differences between men and
     women, but to gender confusion and a wide range of sexual behaviors.
     "Vulnerable populations" can include any group of people espousing
     behaviors those in charge wish to normalize.
15. UNESCO, "Target 4.2—Early Childhood."
16. Ibid.
17. UNESCO, "About Us"; UNESCO, "Funders."
18. Himmelstrand, "Swedish Daycare." This article is part of an excellent
     two-part discussion by Jonas Himmelstrand on Swedish daycare and
     its possible effects on children.
19. Ibid.
20. Weale, "'It's a Political Failure.'"
21. Ibid.
22. Interestingly, there have been almost no studies done on the possible
     effects of having 90 percent of Sweden's population reared in daycare
     facilities. Swedish writer Jonas Himmelstrand notes that "the Swedish
     government will go far to refute any causal claims regarding daycare
     and negative social data. This is understandable. If causality could be
     established it would be a near political disaster." Himmelstrand
     explains further, "Parents see well-planned daycare centres with
     abundant pedagogical materials and it is easy for them to feel they can
     never offer anything similar to their child. But what daycare offers is
     not what children need, especially not for small children under three or
     four years of age . . . Swedish children and youth clearly need more
     involvement from those responsible for them—the key persons being
     parents. But presenting this message is no longer easy for a generation
     of parents who have been led to believe daycare, school, and before-
     and-after-school activities will do a good share of the parenting, and
     furthermore, do it better than they can." See Himmelstrand, "Swedish
     Daycare Part II."

23. Baker et al., "Universal Childcare."
24. Ibid.
25. Charen, "Unwarranted." Access the original study at https://www. nber.org/papers/w18785.
26. McCormack, "The Real Cost of Institutionalised Child Care." See also National Institute of Child Health and Human Development, "Study of Early Child Care and Youth Development."
27. See Erica Komisar's landmark book, *Being There*, for a thorough treatment of how mothers influence the social and emotional development of their children.
28. Rosenthal, "President Vetoes Child Care Plan."
29. Ibid.

Chapter Twenty-One: Potent Weapon

1. Interestingly, the modern children's rights movement encourages relinquishment of the mother and father by the child.
2. Figes, *The Whisperers*, 20–31.
3. One example of this is mothers taking their children to "Drag Queen Story Hour," wherein men with names like "Lil Miss Hot Mess" engage in mockery of womanhood in the name of diversity, tolerance, good morals, being yourself, acceptance, and love. See Pike, "Parents Hail 'Drag Queen Story Time'"; "Drag Queen Story Hour," CBS News.
4. Skousen, *The Naked Communist*, 37. Russian communism was said to be "permeated by a spirit of militant atheism" (51).
5. In communist China, religion is fiercely suppressed by the state. An article in February 2019 reported that some students in China are required to sign agreements stating, "I will adhere to the correct political direction, advocate science, promote atheism, and oppose theism." Junying, "Students in China Are Forced to Sign Away Their Religious Commitments." See BitterWinter.org for ongoing information on religious persecution and related human rights offenses in China.
6. See Chapters Three and Four.
7. Lewis, *Full Surrogacy Now*, 158.
8. Hinckley, "First Presidency Message: These, Our Little Ones," 2–7.

Chapter Twenty-Two: In the Cellar

1. See "Comprehensive Sex Ed Is Now the Law" for information on the California CSE mandate that took effect in 2016.
2. "AMAZE Brings Sex Education Online to End Sexual Assault Epidemic." The child-friendly AMAZE cartoons give instruction on sexual orientation, transgenderism, self-stimulation, consent, puberty, contraception, etc.
3. AMAZE Org, "Gender Identity: Being Female, Male, Transgender or Genderfluid."
4. United Nations, Universal Declaration of Human Rights, Article 26.
5. The National Center on Sexual Exploitation (NCOSE) is a leader in combating indecency worldwide.
6. For all information and references related to Hungary in this chapter I am indebted to James Michener's book, *The Bridge at Andau*.
7. Michener, *The Bridge at Andau*, 74.
8. Ibid., 175–76.
9. Ibid., 176.
10. Ibid.
11. Ibid., 177.
12. Ibid.
13. Ibid., 167.
14. Ibid., 193.
15. Ibid.
16. Ibid., 188.
17. Ibid., 189.
18. Ibid., 191.
19. Ibid., 189.
20. Ibid., 191.
21. Ibid., 191–92.
22. Ibid., 192.
23. Ibid., 196.

Chapter Twenty-Three: Stand

1. See Sutherland, "How Strong Families Help Create Prosperous States"; Wilcox, "The Nuclear Family Is Still Indispensable."
2. Kimball, "Families Can Be Eternal," 4.

INDEX

A

abolishment of parental rights, 32,
123–24, 127, 149, 162, 184–85,
193
abortion
euphemism, xi, 45
forced, 46, 99, 151–53
in China, 38–44
rights, 144, 149, 151, 161–63,
172–73, 175–78, 189
risks and dangers, 150
socialism and feminism, 43, 45–46,
217–18
US policy, 184, 299
See also Planned Parenthood
adoption
belonging and responsibility, 2–3
for protection of the child, 63, 91,
97
versus surrogacy, 98, 101
Alberti, Leon Battista, 80
Allen, Jeffner, 32

American Psychiatric Association, 113,
290
Anonymous Us Project, 101
Aristotle, 7

B

Bachofen, Johann, 18–19
Banbury, Anthony, 166
Bane, Mary Jo, 62
Beauvoir de, Simone, 5, 110–112, 115,
224
Ben-Shalom, Miriam, 116–117
biological motherhood, 17
biological parents
ability to claim a child, 107, 119
children's sense of belonging, 2, 4,
32, 103, 122–23
in same-sex marriage, 92–93
safest place for children, 128–31
birth quotas, 39
Bourguet, Didier, 165–66
Bronfenbrenner, Urie, 61

C

capitalism, 18, 31–32, 191, 311
Centers for Disease Control, 128
Chi An, 37–47
child-bearing, 5
child's right to parents, 91–92, 106
China
  Mao, 16, 280–81
  population control and the family,
    37–47, 63, 98, 152–53
  religious persecution, 318
Civil Rights Act, 148
Code Blue Campaign, 164–66, 168,
  306
Commission on the Status of Women
  (CSW), 139, 143–44, 146, 171,
Common Core, 201–2, 315
communism,
  as socialist regime, 222, 228–33
  of families, 31
  See also socialism
Communist Manifesto, The (Marx
  and Engels), 14
comprehensive sexuality education
  (CSE), 171–77, 179–85
  in socialism, 198–99, 217–20
  monetary interest, 215
  sexual rights, 227
  the United Nations, 184–185, 187–90,
    203, 206
Confucius, 7, 11
Consortium for School Networking
  (CoSN), 200–201, 206, 314
Convention on the Privileges and
  Immunities of the United Nations,
  167
Convention on the Rights of the Child
  (CRC), 91, 160–61, 164, 182, 185
cross-sex hormones, 119, 177

D

Dalglish, Peter, 164
Deng Xiaoping, 37

Dialectic of Sex, The (Firestone), 25
donor-conceived people, 101–2, 289
Dreyfus, Mark, 126

E

Early Childhood Education and Care
  (ECEC), 211
Ecker, Nanette, 173
economic independence, 27
effective altruism, 72–74
empowering women
  abortion and sexual rights, 45, 143,
    151–52, 218
  as mother, 13, 71, 143, 145, 150
Engels, Friedrich, 206
  family and marriage, 58, 67–68,
    78, 122
  socialism and feminism, 13–21, 23,
    29, 50, 87
Equal Rights Amendment (ERA), 149,
  294
Equality Act, 148–49

F

familial love, 58, 72–73
family abolition, 14, 32
family-based living, 11, 23, 25, 37,
  139, 218
feminism
  as response to gender, 5–6, 21, 87,
    204, 217, 220
  in cooperation with socialism, xii,
    11, 21, 24–25, 106, 124–26,
    222
  See also Firestone, Shulamith
feminist theory, 5, 24
Firestone, Shulamith
  biological constraints, 5–6, 9, 55,
    145, 159, 181, 214, 220
  fathers, 78
  reproduction and abortion, 43, 50,
    98–99,

socialist goals, 25–31, 67, 87–88,
118, 122–24, 200
forced abortion, 40–42, 99
freeing the woman, 7, 11, 13, 15, 140
Full Surrogacy Now (Lewis), 30–31.
See also surrogacy

G

Gallo, Peter, 165, 167–68, 306
Gandhi, Indira, 153
Gandhi, Mahatma, 7, 11
Gates Foundation, 190, 202
gender dysphoria, 113–14, 121
gender ideology, 179, 184
transgender ideology, 113, 177
Global Education Monitoring Report
(GEM Report), 211–12
Global Partnership for Education
(GPE), 188, 198–99, 206, 313
Gordon, Linda, 6, 24
Gorman, Clem, 78
Greer, Germaine, 151–52
Guterres, Antonio, 168, 205

H

Hadjok family, 231–33
heteronormativity, 93, 220
Hitler, Adolf, 8, 11
human gestation, 50
human reproductive system, 82
Human Rights Council, 146–47

I

illegal pregnancy, 38
inequality, 5, 14, 23, 28, 55, 59–62,
67, 72, 139, 145,
International Labour Organization,
164
International Planned Parenthood Federation (IPPF)
China, 42

CSE, 180, 206, 184–85, 189–90,
206
sexual rights, 143, 151, 157–58,
161, 175–77
UN involvement, 171
*International Technical Guidance on
Sexuality Education*, 159, 171,
176–77, 183
It's All One curriculum, 174–76, 180

K

Kennedy, John F., 7
Kinsey, Alfred, 173
Komisar, Erica, 210, 318

L

LaFollette, Hugh, 62–63
Lenin, Vladimir, 8, 16, 210
Lewis, Sophie
biological constraints, 55, 223
feminism and socialism, 30–33,
87–88, 199–200, 294
LGBT movement, 109, 116, 221–22,
291
licensing of parents, 62–64

M

Mandela, Nelson, 7
Mao Zedong, 7, 11, 16, 37, 42–44,
281
marriage equality, 94, 101, 103, 106–7,
115, 124–26
Marx, Karl, 13–14, 16, 18, 23, 58,
206, 222, 228
masculinity, 83, 218
McCarthy, Margaret, 6
McLanahan, Sara, 130–31
Mexico City policy, 153, 184
Michaeli, Merav, 78, 122–25, 127–28,
141–42
Michener, James, 229

militant atheism, 23
Millett, Kate, 6
Mises, Ludwig von, 126
monogamous marriage, 16, 18–19, 30, 281
mother right, 18–21, 27, 45, 94, 115
motherhood
    importance, 10–11, 65, 100, 133
    education, 211
    socialism and feminism, 17, 23, 27, 31–32, 87–88, 216, 218–19

N

National Fatherhood Initiative, 78
National Incidence Survey, 129
New International Economic Order, 203
Newell, Peter, 163–64
Nixon, Richard, 213
Nucci, Ezio Di, 74
nuclear family, 24, 31, 33, 75

O

One Child Nation (film), 40
Organization for Economic Coopera-
    tion and Development (OECD), 190–94, 196–98, 201, 203–6, 211–12
ownership
    by the state, 40, 44
    of children, 2, 40,
    of private property, 13, 21
    of women, 18,

P

parent–child bond, 32
parenthood
    abdication of posterity, 119,
    as love, 69
    as right, 90–92, 97–98, 106–7
    biological, 130

fatherhood, 3
    freedom in and regulation of, 61–62, 64–65
    planned, 42–45, 47. See also Planned Parenthood
    commercialization, socialization, redefinition, and destruction, 11, 153, 88, 124
    responsibilities of, 215–16
Paul, Jean, 10
Peterson, Jordan, 64, 210
Pizan, Christine de, 24, 287
Planned Parenthood, 154, 174, 179
Programme for International Student
    Assessment (PISA), 192–93, 196–97, 212–13, 228
political autonomy, 27
population control, 38–39, 43, 151–53
Powell, Gary, 100–101
pregnancy
    as problem, xi, 9, 30–31, 175, 218
    illegal, 38
    private possessorship, 21, 26–27, 50, 98, 151, 224
    prevention of, 182–83
private property
    in socialism, 13, 23, 41, 59, 126, 206
    of women, 19, 25–26, 237
    See also pregnancy: private possessorship
puberty blockers, 119, 293

Q

Qian Xinzhong, 153

R

Read, Herbert, 7
Reagan, Ronald, 203
Ribar, David, 128
rights. See abolishment of parental
    rights; abortion: rights; child's right

to parents; mother right; parenthood: as right; sexual rights; United
Nations: rights; UNESCO: sexual
rights; WHO: sexual rights for
children
Rights, Respect, Responsibility curriculum (The 3Rs), 175, 179–80
right to parenthood. *See under*
parenthood
Roache, Rebecca, 74

S

same-sex marriage
and transgenderism, 120
as biologically inherent, 109
effect on biological parenthood and
family, 92–95, 106, 121–22,
124–27, 222
right to parenthood, 97, 99
sexual exclusivity, 104
sexual and reproductive health and
rights (SRHR), 143, 161, 177, 181
sexual chaos, 18, 121–22
sexual equalism, 103, 106, 125–26,
222
sexual equality, 92, 94, 215
sexual exclusivity, 3, 103–5
sexual freedom, 29, 89, 163, 217–18,
221
sexual radicalism, xii, 11, 21, 83, 204,
218, 220
sexual rights
advocacy, 173, 176–77, 221, 227
definition, 143–44
education, 177, 189, 205–6, 209,
218–19
for children, 29, 89, 157–61, 203
for women, 149, 154–55
monetary interest, 215
United Nations and the United
States, xi, 163–64, 171, 180,
182–85, 188, 193, 240

Sexuality Information and Education
Council of the United States
(SIECUS),
advocacy and education, 176,
180–81
founders, 173
sexually transmitted diseases (STD)
CSE, 171, 182–83
exclusivity and abstinence as pre-
ventive measures, 104, 154,
in children, 29
in women, 301n22
Singleton, Mary Lou, 117
slavery, 16
socialism
and feminism, xii, 11, 21, 24–26,
28, 31, 106, 124–26, 222
in China, 43, 47
Marx and Engels, 13–14, 18, 23
redistribution, 94
theory, 51, 217
UN, 191, 204, 220
socialist society, 15–16, 28, 43
socially productive work, 16–17, 141,
237
Stalin, Joseph, 16, 228, 230–31
Stanton, Elizabeth Cady, 24
state-ownership philosophy, 40–41.
See also private property
Sullins, Paul, 128
surrogacy, 31–33, 97, 99–101, 107,
115, 125, 219
Sustainable Development Goals
(SDGs), 146–47, 188–90, 204

T

testosterone, 113
transgenderism
born that way, 109–111
effect on women, marriage, and the
family, 114, 118–20, 149
gender activism, 146–47
therapy, 113–14

Truth, Sojourner, 24

U

UN Women, xi, 147, 171
UNAIDS, 159, 171
UNICEF, 157, 162–64, 166, 177, 185, 198, 206
Union of Soviet Socialist Republics (USSR), 16
United Nations (UN)
    children, 157, 160, 185; sexual abuse of, 163–167
    diplomatic immunity, 167–69
    education, 188, 195–96
    families, xi–xii, 87, 90
    rights, 92, 138, 149, 154
    socialism, feminism, and sexual radicalism, 11, 13, 139, 142–44, 153, 184, 203–5, 220
United Nations Educational, Scientific and Cultural Organization (UNESCO)
    CSE, 93, 171, 173–77, 183–84, 188–90, 195, 197–98, 201–202
    leadership, 205–6
    sexual rights, 157, 159, 163; 185
    withdrawal from, 203–4, 228
United Nations Population Fund (UNFPA)
    coercive population control, 153
    sexual rights for children and CSE, 159, 163, 171, 175, 177, 182
United States (US)
    CSE, 184, 200
    gender equality, 90, 148–49
    involvement with UN organizations, 190, 203–4
Universal Declaration of Human Rights, 3, 83, 90, 107, 146, 227
utilitarianism, 72–73
utopia, 13, 20, 57
utopian socialists, 24, 30, 57

W

Washington, George, 9
Wei Xin, 37–38, 40, 42, 44, 47
Wilcox, Bradford, 129,
Women's Liberation Front, 117
World Health Organization (WHO)
    parental consent, 163
    sexual rights for children, 159, 161, 171, 199, 206
    sex work, 182

Y

You, Your Life, Your Dreams curriculum, 175, 177, 180